They
Closed
Their
Schools

On the cover:

Robert Russa Moton High School
Farmville, Virginia

Future site of
The Robert R. Moton Museum:
A Center for the Study of
Civil Rights in Education

Cover design by Lamp-Post Publicity
Meherrin, Virginia

Photo by Jon Marken

Published By
Martha E. Forrester
Council of Women
Farmville, Virginia

They Closed Their Schools

PRINCE EDWARD COUNTY,
VIRGINIA, 1951–1964

Bob Smith

To my mother and father
for their
love, understanding, and encouragement

ACKNOWLEDGEMENTS

The republication of *They Closed Their Schools* was made possible through the generous support of:

American Friends Service Committee
Philadelphia, Pennsylvania

Anonymous (2)

Viola Osborne Baskerville
Vice Mayor, City of Richmond, Member, Board of Visitors of Longwood College
Richmond, Virginia

The Cobbs Family
Pamplin, Virginia

William and Martha Dorrill
President, Longwood College (1988-1996)
Farmville, Virginia

Willie J. Edwards
Orange, New Jersey

Marilyn Brown Hart
Springfield, Virginia

The Law Firm of Hill, Tucker, & Marsh
Richmond, Virginia

John Lancaster
California, Maryland

Ben Marshall
Farmville, Virginia

Norman "Carl" Neverson
President & CEO, E.M.I. Communications
Washington, DC

The *Virginian-Pilot* Newspaper
Norfolk, Virginia

Jacqueline Jardine Wall and Family
Farmville, Virginia

Lt. Gen. Samuel V. Wilson, U.S. Army (Ret.)
President, Hampden-Sydney College
Hampden-Sydney, Virginia

Their reflections on the importance of this work follow.

REFLECTIONS

When the American Friends Service Committee (AFSC) went to work in Prince Edward County, Virginia, in 1959, it responded to the black parents who said, "We want our children to have some education–they just can't sit here while the white children go to the academies." AFSC conducted an emergency placement program that placed young black students from Prince Edward County with families in six states and ten communities. This was the AFSC's human response. Our staff not only walked the roads of the South with parents and fostered their exercise of power; they also walked the corridors of power in Washington, D.C., and challenged power and policy there.

We are reminded of the 1950s and 1960s struggles against overt racism and segregation by today's rash of arson attacks against black churches in the South. Once again the AFSC and its partners challenge public leaders to help change the climate in which these acts of violence, scapegoating, racism, and hostility flourish.

Since the 1920s when the AFSC worked with striking Appalachian coal miners, we have remained deeply concerned about the centrality of economic barriers to achieving the vision of society we seek. We continue to work with poor people of all racial groups, and, as we did in the Poor Peoples March of 1968, we bring them together to seek economic change in the U.S. and around the world. Today we work with documented and undocumented immigrants and refugees who are swept up in the massive dislocation and movement of people and capital across national boundaries.

Our work in Prince Edward County was an important chapter in AFSC's 80-year commitment to establish freedom from social and economic injustice for all members of our global society. We continue to work in partnership with communities throughout the world as they struggle to dismantle systems of exploitation and oppression and to establish an open and non-exploitative society which recognizes the infinite worth of each human being. That is the principle on which the AFSC, established by members of the Religious Society of Friends (Quakers), is founded.

American Friends Service Committee

🐌

In 1963 Louisiana State University Press published a collection of the short stories of the Virginia writer Ellen Glasgow (1873-1945), edited by a young scholar named Richard K. Meeker. Meeker did the work for this edition while he was teaching in the English Department at Longwood College in Farmville, Virginia, a state-supported institution then devoted to the education of white women.

Richard Meeker was an exemplary teacher, according to a former student who recalls that he encouraged her to pursue a doctorate (and she did so successfully). A friend from the community describes stimulating intellectual discussions in which he participated. However, by the time the Glasgow volume appeared with Meeker's fine introductory essay, he had left Longwood for a position at the State University of New York at Buffalo.

Meeker left Longwood College not only for a perhaps more prestigious position, but also because of the effect of closing the Prince Edward County schools to avoid integration. A native of New Jersey, Meeker spoke out openly and wrote several thoughtful letters on the subject to the *Farmville Herald.*

If Richard Meeker had felt that Prince Edward County was a good place to raise and educate his children, Longwood College might have continued to benefit from his teaching, his scholarship, and the courage of his convictions for many years.

In memory of Richard K. Meeker (1925-1968)

🐌

When I remember Reverend L. Francis Griffin, I am reminded of no more encouraging fact than the unquestionable ability of a mortal being who elevated his life and the life of others by conscious endeavor.

Reverend L. Francis Griffin:
  • by example taught us that what lies behind us and what lies before

us are tiny matters compared to what lies within us.

- had a commitment to academic excellence based on an integrated public school system supporting his belief that things which matter most must never be at the mercy of things which matter least.
- gave advice to a sitting Attorney General of the United States and a future Supreme Court Justice, but remained a humble man who believed that there can be no friendship without confidence, and no confidence without integrity.
- committed the Golden Rule to life.
- believed that there were parts of human nature that cannot be reached by either legislation or public education, but require direct intervention from God.
- believed that as human beings, we cannot perfect ourselves because we see ourselves as human beings having spiritual experience, instead of spiritual beings having a human experience.
- struggled to balance his life as a man, husband, father, activist and spiritual leader. He considered the struggle worthwhile and fulfilling because it gave meaning to his life and enabled him to love, serve and try again, against what appeared to be impossible odds. He fought back with all the means available to him during his time and place.

Forgive me if my fragile humanity has caused me to give the impression that I have written Reverend L. Francis Griffin's life story. All I have tried to say is: I have been blessed to have worked with, to have sat at the feet of, been counseled by, and looked in the face of "Amazing Grace."

In memory of Rev. L. Francis Griffin (1917-1980)

If one could read the red soil of Prince Edward County, the earth would reveal much to those who would listen and learn. Often individuals are not made aware of their own connectedness to history unless there remains an effort to produce a permanent record of those significant events which have forever changed the times. The efforts of the Martha E. Forrester Council of Women to purchase the historic site of the Robert Russa Moton School in Farmville and to create a Center for the Study of Civil Rights in Education are commendable.

Not far from the town of Farmville lies the birthplace of my father. The year 1951 marked the protest of African-American children to inferior school conditions in Prince Edward County; the year also marked my birth. As a small child I remember well the Sunday visits to our grandparents' home and the frequent trips "into town." Many happy daylight hours spent secure with family were concluded with early evening return road trips in preparation for Monday morning attendance in Richmond's segregated but open public schools. It was not until years later that I realized my country cousins and playmates were either attending severely inferior schools or not attending schools at all because they were closed.

An African proverb states that we stand tall because we stand on the shoulders of those who went before us. Because of the courageous stand of those students in Prince Edward County in 1951, a chain of events was set in motion to challenge segregated public schools throughout Virginia and in the country. Because of the dedicated efforts of civil rights attorneys such as Oliver W. Hill and Spotswood Robinson, public education was desegregated. The impact resonated around the country.

As a graduate of the College of William and Mary, I am grateful to the efforts of many who helped desegregate public education. As a resident of and currently elected official representing the City of Richmond, I am proud to acknowledge Oliver W. Hill as one of our most distinguished citizens instrumental in desegregating Richmond's City Council as well as fighting for civil rights in education. As a member of the Board of Visitors of Longwood College, I am thankful for those forward thinking and acting faculty members who seized the opportunities created by those troubling times to forge a new meaning of education and educational access for all.

Viola Osborne Baskerville

🍂

Our sincere thanks to all the fine teachers of Robert R. Moton High School for your role in making our lives better.

The Cobbs Family
Alumni of Robert R. Moton High School:
    Grace Cobbs Payne
    Earl Spencer
    Ethel Cobbs Spencer
    Claude Cobbs
    Joan Johns Cobbs

William Cobbs
James Franklin
Patsy Cobbs Franklin
Alma Cobbs Stephens
Samuel Cobbs
A. Leon Cobbs
Freddie Cobbs

🐝

Dr. C. G. Gordon Moss came to Longwood College as a professor of history in 1944. In 1960 he was named chief academic officer. As recounted in *They Closed Their Schools*, Moss became increasingly involved in the struggle for integrated public education in Prince Edward County. In 1965 Clyde C. Clements, Jr., called Moss "more than anyone else . . . the voice of white liberalism during this trying period."

Gordon Moss was clearly a man of hope as well as conviction. In a 1961 article in the New York *Herald Tribune*, he spoke of meetings between Longwood faculty members and leaders of the black community: "The purpose of the group is to prepare Negroes for the gains they are eventually going to win."

There were questions about whether Moss in his position as dean of Longwood could espouse his individual opinions; but President Francis G. Lankford, Jr., supported his right to freedom of expression. When Moss stepped down in 1964, the student body presented a portrait of him to the College. Until recently the portrait hung outside the doors to the Academic Affairs office.

When asked his opinion of *They Closed Their Schools* in 1965, Dr. Moss answered: "During the course of Bob Smith's visits to Prince Edward County, I saw him frequently. . . . I concluded he was primarily interested in the discovery of fact rather than trying to prove a pre-conceived thesis. For an outsider, talking with people as circumstances made possible, it's as full and as factually accurate an account as possible."

Today, members of the Longwood community ranging from faculty members who served under him to students who have recently studied the history of civil rights in Prince Edward County acknowledge the legacy of leadership and of bravery left by C. G. Gordon Moss.

In memory of C. G. Gordon Moss (1899-1982)
William and Martha Dorrill

On that hot, humid and hazy infamous August day in 1959, akin to the "proverbial" thief . . . prejudice came into my life, the news found my home and my life was forever changed. Could it be real that my beloved Prince Edward County would deny me an equal opportunity to attend school in such a civilized society? At that moment in time, I began to wonder just where would the road turn for me.

With great apprehension, I journeyed to North Carolina's Kittrell High School in pursuit of my education. Little did I know that this would be the last time for bonding as a family under the same roof. I thank God for Eloise and Jack Brown, devoted and unswerving parents, and for the Almighty's mercies and blessings bestowed upon me.

Such a blessing was demonstrated by the American Friends Service Committee as they shepherded me from North Carolina to Yeadon, Pennsylvania, where Mr. and Mrs. Childs graciously opened their home to me. Subsequently, I graduated from Yeadon High School because of their unceasing support.

My road had many crossroads and one took me to Jerry C. Hart, my childhood sweetheart and late husband. We were blessed with three wonderful children, Adrienne, Jerry, Jr., and Veronica, and one grand-son, Jerry, III. As a military family for 23 years, we traveled extensively and were exposed to new cultures. My husband Jerry died, a victim of Agent Orange. Ironically, he chose to fight in Vietnam for the very freedoms that we had been denied.

They may have closed our schools, but not our hearts and minds. Compassion and love for all peoples was my strength.

Marilyn Brown Hart

&

The law firm of Hill, Tucker, & Marsh is proud to salute the heroic African-American children of Prince Edward County, Virginia. Their courage and commitment to the true principles of America's promise of freedom and justice for all inspired a generation of heroes and sparked a movement which changed the course of history.

Oliver W. Hill, Spottswood Robinson, Samuel W. Tucker, Henry L. Marsh and other members of the law firm regard their involvement in this struggle as a high point in their legal careers. The inspiration gained from their association with the black citizens of Prince Edward County during this epic battle helped to make Hill, Tucker, & Marsh an effective instrument for change during the civil rights revolution in America.

Just as the children of Prince Edward County are now contributing in valuable ways in the current struggle, the law firm of Hill, Tucker, & Marsh continues to participate in the effort to make our nation live up to its promise of equal justice and equal opportunity for all.

Hill, Tucker, & Marsh

&

The republication of *They Closed Their Schools* will make a significant contribution to understanding the true meaning of the American democracy experiment.

As president of the Prince Edward County Parent Teachers Association at the time of the student strike, I had the opportunity to work with parents who sought adequate schools for their children. There appeared at the time to be a degree of reluctance on the part of persons interviewed to speak openly and freely, possibly from fear of intimidation, or guilt. Some may have questioned the true motives of the interviewer. The passage of time (45 years after the student strike) should lessen these possibilities. The opportunity for research into the social action drama of the times is great. I urge diligent pursuit.

John G. Lancaster

&

As a 13-year-old boy, I too was one of the approximately 14,000 residents of Prince Edward County, Virginia, whose senses were irrevocably altered by the 1959 moratorium on public education. However, some 37 years later I have concluded that this NADIR of universal disgrace really was the great ENABLER which ushered in progress to those venues where malaise, stagnation, and obfuscation used to lie.

First, let us not forget the forces of "Massive Resistance" which led the efforts. Today, we recognize that they were the forces of ignorance, and I accept the belated apologies so offered.

Secondly, massive resistance exposed ignorance of the majority culture as never before seen in western civilization. Paradoxically, Thomas Jefferson understood and captured this moment with the following quotation: "I HOLD THAT A LITTLE REBELLION EVERY

NOW AND THEN IS A GOOD THING. IT IS AS NECESSARY FOR THE POLITICAL WORLD AS STORMS ARE FOR THE PHYSICAL WORLD. GOD FORBID THAT TWENTY YEARS SHOULD PASS WITHOUT A REBELLION."

Finally, if you could travel throughout America with this writer for brief periods you would have the opportunity to meet, touch, and to see hundreds of us who were forced to leave Prince Edward County in 1959 in our search for public education. We fled to the four corners of the earth with nothing but courage so bequeathed by our courageous parents and families. With nothing but courage we became great civil servants, military leaders, Ph.D.'s, medical doctors, entrepreneurs, heads of corporations, educators, and America's role models.

Norman "Carl" Neverson

While respecting the past, we devote our energies to the present in hopes of promoting greater understanding, harmony, and peace in the generations to come.

Jacqueline Jardine Wall and Family
    Jacqueline Jardine Wall
    Barrye Langhorne Wall
    Marjorie L. Wall Wolfe
    Geoffrey Hanes Wall
    Angus Alexander Wall

Near Farmville, "Pleasant Shade" sat on the western ridge overlooking Saylers Creek, south of the junction with the Appomattox River. Samuel Vaughan and Lucy Lockett went there to live in 1846, the year they were married. A thriving plantation of some several thousand acres, the extensive rolling fields and pastures of Pleasant Shade were fertile and productive, demanding of backbreaking hand labor. And, there were slaves, from whom descended in the immediate aftermath of the Civil War a small black boy named Robert.

Born in 1867, Robert was quick to learn and insatiably curious about the world around him. Continually seeking to be helpful, he early became a great favorite of the gentle Lucy Lockett, who made him the keeper of various house keys. Having accidentally learned that Robert's mother was giving him lessons in the evenings, Mrs. Vaughan began secretly helping to teach small Robert how to read and write.

Each weekday morning, the Vaughan daughters studied at Pleasant Shade under the tutelage of a French governess. As soon as the girls' lessons were finished, Lucy Lockett would get the crayons and slate and work with young Robert, helping him to form and manipulate letters and figures. One spring morning while she was so engaged, she suddenly became aware of a figure standing in the doorway, quietly watching. Before anything could be said, Samuel Vaughan turned on his heel and walked away. That night dinner was eaten in silence as Lucy Lockett awaited the outburst.

The silence dragged on after dinner. Samuel Vaughan was standing with one arm on the mantle, staring at the smoldering coals in the fireplace and swirling the wine in his glass. Unable to hold back any longer, Lucy came up behind him and put her arms around her husband's waist. "You saw of course what I was doing today, Sam," she said. "Please don't be hurt with me. I have to do it." Sam turned around with tears in his eyes: "God bless you, Lucy Lockett!"

The lessons continued.

In time, Robert Russa Moton went away to school. A graduate of Hampton Institute, he later succeeded Booker T. Washington as head of Tuskegee Institute. Moton went on to become one of America's great educators. His autobiography on his personal struggle to overcome racial prejudice in education became an inspiration to all thoughtful Americans.

Lt. Gen. Samuel V. Wilson, U.S. Army (Ret.)

"Nothing is so strong as gentleness,
nothing is so gentle as real strength."

Barbara Rose Johns Powell was part of the Robert R. Moton High School student movement for better school facilities. She emerged as the spokesperson and leader of the student body walk-out on April 23, 1951. Her contribution to the civil rights struggle in Prince Edward County resulted in Prince Edward County's inclusion in the 1954 Supreme Court decision, *Brown v. Board of Education*.

Out of her parents' concern for Barbara's safety, she was sent to live with her uncle and aunt, Rev. and Mrs. Vernon Johns in Montgomery, Alabama. She completed her senior year in Alabama and attended Spelman College in Atlanta, Georgia, later transferring to Antioch College in Ohio. She received her Master's degree in Library Science from Drexel University and had been a librarian in the Philadelphia School System for twenty-four years, at the time of her death.

While attending Spelman College, she met and married Rev. W. H. Rowland Powell. They were the parents of four daughters and one son. She was a loving mother, sister, and friend to all who knew her, for much of her greatness was her tremendous strength and unselfish love.

Never forgetting her roots in Prince Edward County, she initiated the building of a family home, since the original home had been destroyed by fire. It was her dream to have the entire family reunited back in Prince Edward County.

Barbara fought many battles in her life, the final one being cancer, to which took her life in September 1991.

In memory of Barbara Rose Johns Powell (1935-1991)

PREFACE

Preface (1996 Edition)

   With the publication of *They Closed Their Schools* in 1965, I felt
that I had completed my work in Prince Edward County. If I returned
again at all, I believed it would be as a visitor–more than a casual visitor,
surely, but one with intention only to drop in on a few people I admired
for their pluck in fighting the county's movement to close its public
schools. They had lost that fight initially, and many African-American
children in the county had lost up to four years of education, but in the
way things move on, the focus of attention in race relations had shifted to
the national level. I supposed that little more needed to be said about
Prince Edward County once schools were re-opened in September, 1964,
under Supreme Court order.
   I went about the business of being a newspaperman in Charlotte,
North Carolina, until 1968, when I joined MDC, a multi-racially-staffed
non-profit in Chapel Hill, beginning what proved to be an ongoing effort
with federal and foundation funding to improve education and training
for disadvantaged Americans of all races. I plunged into that work and
let the Prince Edward story recede in my mind.
   I did take an opportunity to visit Farmville one weekend in the
1970s. There I found the Reverend L. Francis Griffin, who had stayed
home, spurning opportunities to convert his leadership role in the local
African-American community into state-wide or national positions, in
very poor health. I remember walking with him across the parking lot to
his office in the First Baptist Church, pausing several times to allow him
to catch his breath. I visited with him and Dr. C. G. Gordon Moss, the
Longwood College professor who had worked with him to try to head off
the school closings, and was glad for the opportunity, for not long

afterwards, the Rev. Mr. Griffin died.

I had no intention of returning to Prince Edward County again until friends in Virginia began sending me articles early this year about efforts there to preserve the old Robert R. Moton High School. It was in this building, in 1951, that the African-American children had conducted their walk-out protest to conditions in the "tar paper shacks" that were being used to handle the student overflow. That action put Prince Edward into the National Association for the Advancement of Colored People's portfolio of cases headed up to the Supreme Court–not for failure to provide "separate but equal" opportunity for education, which is as far as the students could see, but to test the question of whether "separate" ever could be "equal." And that, of course, led to the *Brown v. Board of Education* school desegregation decree of the Supreme Court three years later.

I was delighted to learn that consideration was being given to making Moton a civil rights museum and more–a place where efforts toward greater racial amity and mutual understanding in the community and elsewhere would be served. I was astonished to learn that one of the instruments for pursuing these goals was the editorial page of the *Farmville Herald*, which back in my days in the county had been a bulwark of support for massive resistance to school desegregation. But, then, more than thirty years had passed. Much had changed everywhere. After looking at a file of newspaper stories, including a series published by *Newsday* that found Prince Edward County the only "success" for integration among the five *Brown* communities, I decided to spend a few days trying to learn what had really changed there. After one visit, I found myself coming back for a longer, second look.

• • •

The pleasant assignment of writing a new preface for a reprinting of *They Closed Their Schools* comes as I continue to seek an answer to my question of what actually has changed in Prince Edward. It also comes at a time when anything written about the efforts of the Martha E. Forrester Council of Women to purchase the Moton property from the county to create the museum would be out of date before it could be read. I will content myself here with the observation that the impetus for reprinting the book came from the people of Prince Edward County. I was flattered at first to think that a book I had written all those years ago–and which I had not read all the way through since that time–still had meaning in the community. People showed me battered copies, dog-eared from being handed around. One told me she had Xeroxed copies for friends. Again and again, I was asked if there was any chance further copies of this long-out-of-print book could be found. I had to tell them that I had recently gotten three copies in as many years' effort, at rare book prices, in order that my children each would have one.

Now, as a result of the efforts of the Council and Lacy Ward, Field Representative for U.S. Rep. L.F. Payne, the way has been cleared for reprinting. The University of North Carolina Press has released the book to me and I have agreed to turn it over to the Council with the under-standing that the profits from sales will go to the Robert R. Moton project.

In the meantime, I believe I have come to an understanding of why the book is so earnestly sought by many people in Prince Edward County. It has nothing to do with whatever good qualities the book may have. The book serves a purpose to many African-American and white members of the community. It is proof of what happened these thirty-plus years ago, but it is more than that. It is a kind of water-mark against which to measure change. It not only marks as history what once was real, but also invites the reader to look about and see how things are today. I do not mean that these Prince Edward people want to boast of progress during those years, although they might well have the right. They want to experience simultaneously the past and present because it helps them look with raised hopes, a bit more optimistically toward the always uncertain future.

As that thought came to me, I realized that this is the purpose, as well, of the transformation proposed for the old Robert R. Moton High School. To let that school be razed would be to lose that history. To dwell exclusively on that history–as, for instance, to demand that the school be left in its present condition to mark an injustice never to be forgotten–would be to live in the past. But to bring the school back to life again in a newer, finer aspect would be to memorialize that past as prologue to the present and harbinger of the future. To provide a place where people of all races from near or far are welcome to come and sit together to meditate on the history before them, or to mediate differences in a spirit of mutual concern–that would be something worth waking the ghosts of the Moton School to join in celebrating.

Could such a creation actually come into being? I don't know, but, standing by my car in the street looking at the old Moton High School recently, I noticed something. The school had been vacant for a good while and yet I could see no sign of vandalism. On closer inspection, I could not find a broken window. A fragment of conversation from the past popped out. I was talking with the Rev. Mr. Griffin during the worst of the hard times before the school closings. He had been under considerable pressure–bills to merchants in town suddenly all came due and his credit was no good. A small "bomb," quite crude and probably not the work of children, had been found. But through all that, he maintained that whatever else happened, he did not expect violence in Prince Edward County no matter how high feelings raged. He described how, walking down Main Street, he would still be greeted politely by people he knew were members of the Defenders of State Sovereignty and Individual Rights and would still return that greeting cordially. To a "degree," he told me, emphasizing the word *degree*, "this still comes down to an argument between gentlemen."

Isn't it possible, I found myself wondering all these years later, that once that argument was settled, a Prince Edward where such civility was practiced was better prepared than many other communities in the South or the nation to handle the thoroughgoing integration of its schools that clearly was in store for this community where the races lived, if not side by side, at least back to back?

• • •

In agreeing to contribute a new prologue to this old book, I confess that I had an ulterior motive. When I had finally gotten around to re-reading *They Closed Their Schools* I had left the experience with mixed emotions. I regretted again, as I had during the process of writing the book, having to rely on second-hand accounts of the dramatic events surrounding the "tar paper shacks" and the rebellion of the students of Moton High School back in 1951. I was limited by what people would tell me of those events and other things that had occurred before I began my regular weekend visits to the county over the five years it took to write this book. I had no opportunity to see all this, observe, draw my own conclusions.

But I could make my peace with these limitations, for they are the usual ones confronting anyone dealing with contemporary social history– there are always prior events the author must try to piece together, relying on others' willingness to be forthcoming. A more difficult problem, it seemed to me, was raised by the book's final chapter in which the author had stepped out of his role as story-teller to share with the reader his own thoughts about the meaning of the Prince Edward story.

As I read that chapter, I tried to put myself in the place of the young newspaperman who had written it. I had interviewed a number of young African-American youths who were not getting schooling. Some were working, some were biding their time, others were, in effect, being placed on-hold in centers around the county hastily set up and not in any way ready to deliver quality education. These children were being called by one observer "the crippled generation" and I had that image in my mind, despite heroic efforts by the Free Schools, set up for them in the last year (1963-64) of the public school closings.

The situation in which these young people found themselves made me see that entire struggle as one in which there had been no winners. In this final chapter–as I read it now–the author still seems to have been right in pointing out that not enough effort nationally was put immediately on helping these young people resume an education critical to their life chances. But he was wrong in failing to give full credit to the victory won in the eradication of segregation in the school system. For all the pain it inflicted, the battle in Prince Edward County those long years ago was one that had to be fought and won. And the victory was not an empty one as the author feared back then; to the contrary, it now seems rich with significance.

• • •

This having been said, what remains is to repeat the credits I gave in the 1965 preface to *They Closed Their Schools.* My intention then was to thank all those who gave unstintingly of their time to answer my questions as fully and honestly as they could–no matter their views. I have enlarged that list somewhat in re-reading the book and present it alphabetically: Lester Andrews, B. Calvin Bass, Robert Crawford, Mary Croner, L. Francis Griffin, Oliver Hill, the Rev. and Mrs. Vernon Johns, M. Boyd Jones, the Rev. James R. Kennedy, John Lancaster, Francis G. Lankford, Maurice Large, T.J. McIlwaine, Dr. N.B. Miller, George Morton, Gordon Moss, Mrs. Barbara Johns Powell, John Stokes, J. Barrye Wall, Sr., and James Samuel Williams.

My debt of gratitude to Mrs. Shelton Whitaker, who put me up those many weekends in a room in her Farmville home, remains great. Editors who had faith were David Keightley, Peter H. Davison, and Helen King. Ted Morrison of the Harvard English Department was a big help in the early going. *Southern School News* was invaluable throughout. Among friends in history or journalism who were helpful were Ben Bowers, Herbert Clarence Bradshaw, Adam Clymer, Robert Mason, Benjamin Muse, Phillip Lightfoot Scruggs, and William Tazewell.

I have not touched a word in the book proper, which follows this preface. It is all as it was written more than thirty years ago, with whatever faults or virtues, it had then. My hope is that this new edition will be helpful and that it will, in however small a way, speed along the process of giving the Robert R. Moton High School a second life built upon the dedication, determination, and sacrifice it fostered so well in its first.

R.C. Smith

Jamestown, North Carolina
July, 1996

CONTENTS

PART ONE

STRIKE

1. THE TAR PAPER
SHACKS

On a bright fall day in 1949, a thickset Negro climbed heavily off a Greyhound bus at the terminal in Farmville, Virginia, the county seat of Prince Edward County. Leslie Francis Griffin stepped out of the terminal onto Main Street, suitcase in hand, and told himself that very little had changed.

He was thirty-two years old, the son of a Baptist preacher, and himself a belated student for the ministry. He was returning to the county where much of his youth had been spent, where his father had carried on his ministry for twenty-two years, where his father's house and church stood. The girl he had married at Shaw University in Raleigh, North Carolina, where he was a student, had preceded him to Prince Edward County and was staying with his parents in Farmville. He had dropped out of school to come home to help his ailing father with some preaching. Later, perhaps, he would finish up at Shaw.

Farmville is a tobacco and lumber town (1950 population, 4,375) in an agricultural county sixty-five miles southwest of Richmond in the rural underbelly of Virginia known as Southside. In its geographical sense, the name Southside refers generally to that part of Virginia south of the James River with the exception of the easterly Tidewater region. But Southside is more than a simple geographical designation. Southside, Virginia, is part of the South's "Black Belt," so called because of the dark soil typical of many of its counties stretching southward from Virginia into the Carolinas, Georgia, Alabama, and Mississippi. The Southside counties have the high percentage of Negro population that the term "Black Belt" has come to convey. In Prince Edward, at the northern tier of the belt, only 55.4 per cent of the 15,398 population in 1950 was white.[1] The counties of Southside tend to think in a southerly direction, to relate politically to the old, agricultural South rather than to the industrializing behemoth that is the new, urban South.

Griffin's father's church stands on Main Street at Fourth in Farmville. As young Griffin stood in front of the bus station, holding his suitcase, he could see the church up Main, around a slight bend in the road. He walked in that direction, across High Street, in front of the post office. The church was of old, red brick, bulking out to the sidewalk: a Negro church, snugly fitted into the stream of downtown commerce, across Fourth Street from the theater where only whites were admitted. But this was an ordinary anachronism of Southern towns whose growth surrounded and sealed in their beginnings. The Farmville merchants who had lived above their stores in the town's rougher days had moved to cool, shady streets outside, leaving Negro residences, in some cases, between their businesses and their homes. As Griffin looked south on Main Street from his father's church he could see white and Negro businesses and residences in close proximity. It was only farther out on Main that the street became all Negro. If he crossed over to High Street and looked west up the one block to where Longwood College for Women stands, he would bridge that distance between the rut of small-town commerce and the cool plateau of oaks and grass that is typical of Southside towns, too. Up there, wealthy whites had their homes, but even there a narrow lane beside an expensive white home would lead to a row of poor Negro houses. In Southside communities there is no single, big Negro section: Negroes and whites live not side-by-side, but back-to-back.

Griffin put down his suitcase in the lobby of the church. The church door creaked; Griffin smiled, thinking how many times his father's hand had opened it and shut it. He went back out on Main Street and began walking north, toward the center of town. He had been in Farmville and the county to preach on weekends during the past year, but in spirit he had been away a long time. Now he was back. He was looking for signs of something, anything, new.

Main Street in Farmville has that jumbled quality of small Southern towns torn between the past and the present. Its mixed rhythms of old and new, country and town, fix and fluctuation, suggest a deeply regional being: groups of Negroes clad in the rough denim of farm hands smoke and lounge on a street corner in immemorial posture; across the street stands a bank, where an ancient gingerbread façade of red brick overhangs a modern front of rose marble; the dark bulk of the Prince Edward Hotel with its musty air of abandonment contrasts, across the street, with an open-air market offering vegetables out of rude crates on the sidewalk; closer by, the Farmville Baptist Church (white) stands incongruously beside an Army surplus store and still closer, seemingly trapped between worship and commerce, looms the county courthouse, set back from the street by a green.

Up and down the street on this fall afternoon were sights typical of Southside. The presence of two noisy groups of Negroes at the corner of Main and Second Streets suggested to the knowledgeable visitor one of the Southside counties. Griffin remembered how that corner would look on Saturday afternoons, with the Negro tenant farmers in from the fields, jangling coins in their pockets and sending up joyful spirals of smoke and sound.

The cheap, rough clothes these Negroes wear tell more than that their wearers work at the soil. Like the patches of shabbiness on some of the buildings, they suggest a low per-capita income. In 1950, the Prince Edward per capita was $847 [2]—well above some counties in Southside but well below the state average of $1,222, and little enough to make the consumption of farm produce where it is grown a vital fact of life.

The twin, dark buildings at either side of the railroad tracks on North Main tell a story of Southside. The building on the west is the Dunnington Tobacco Company, dealers in dark-fired tobacco since 1870. This is the county's staple. On the right is the Craddock-Terry Shoe Company, occupying a tobacco factory remodeled by anxious Farmville citizens during the Great Depression and granted free to the company by this citizens' committee upon payment of $750,000 in wages within seven years of operation.[3] This is typical of the best of Southside, the enduring struggle to snap the strictures of the old, poor tobacco economy. The effort goes far back in the history of the county and takes the form of lambent prophecies that the county would one day be rich in minerals. Coal explorations were begun as early as 1837; marl, copper, aluminum, gold, iron—all at one time offered promise, but the veins discovered fell tantalizingly short of having commercial value. Well into the twentieth century the county worked to realize the dreams of the New South. A textile mill failed in the first decade of the century; a kitchen cabinet factory, built in 1928, could not survive the Depression. The forests made saw-mills and box manufacturing profitable but tobacco remained the bulwark.[4] In 1950, 1,525 of the county's male work force of 3,946 were engaged in farming.[5]

Griffin passed the Prince Edward Hotel. It was older, even more forbidding. Generals Grant and Lee had stopped there, only hours apart, on their way to the historic meeting at Appomattox Courthouse but a few miles away. The history of wars—partic-ularly this war—preys on the consciousness of Southside.

War. Reconstruction. The Old South. The New South. It was 1949 and Griffin was not long returned from a different war, one that was regarded as an international triumph over bigotry. It was a time of liberalism. A new Negro was emerging on the streets of America, molded not in the old stereotype of humility but in the brave, new hopes of the day. Jackie Robinson. Richard Wright. Ralph Bunche. These were men who would do things in the world, change the face of American life. Yet as he stared at the Prince Edward Hotel in Farmville, Virginia, Griffin felt the past rise up to choke him. The building looked as though the eyes within it were turned not to the future but to the past. It func-tioned, in 1949, as a hotel; yet while Griffin could go inside and chat with the clerk, he could not get a room—they would look on such a request as a sign that the colored preacher's son had taken leave of his senses. With the thought, Griffin's features split into a grin. It would almost be worth it to see their faces. The Reverend Vernon Johns's angry voice sounded in his memory. He chuckled out loud in a rumbling sound that came from his broad chest: Mr. Johns might just try it.

The public countenance of segregation in Farmville was open and without guile. There was no segregation where men stood up; there was nothing but segregation where they sat down. Negroes entered stores and were waited upon; they entered res-taurants or approached drug store counters only to get food to take out. They did not enter the town's only moving picture theater at all.

Griffin walked along, full of himself, wondering at the immer-sion into Southside mores he was contemplating. "I looked at all the businesses, who was running them, who was working for them. There were very few changes. The clerks were old and doty and their ideas were old and doty. I looked around at the housing and found some improvement. I remember that I said that there were a few more houses in town, period. I attributed some of this to the good wages that were paid during the war and the nearness of Camp Pickett. I noticed also how a few Negroes had ventured out of the area to work in the Norfolk Navy Yard. I saw that some of the good ones were gone and I debated whether the county was worth saving or possible to save." [6]

Griffin retraced his footsteps on Main back to Fourth Street, where he turned east. As he walked friends stopped to greet him. White people as well as Negroes stopped to speak to him. His father was well liked in the town, and Griffin was accepted as a townsman. The greetings from the whites were not just for this reason though. Friendliness, openness, and cordiality also were part of the meaning of Southside.

And, then, nobody knew what Griffin was thinking: "I knew this county definitely needed some leadership. The church needed some leadership outside its four walls. The community definitely was in need of a pastor-teacher. . . . I cannot truthfully say that I envisaged what happened, but there were definite inclinations on my part to change the social patterns. . . . I knew it was definitely needed to change opinions about politics being something that religion had no concern in." [7]

South Street, east of Main, is slummy in appearance and almost entirely Negro. Virginia Street, the next street east, is Negro on the north and south extremes and white in between. The house where young Griffin grew up and from which his father prepared his ministry is a green frame structure with a roof that once was red but had turned a dingy gray, and the usual rickety front porch that looked as though it were designed to hold the two straw-backed chairs and one rocker that sat there. The address is 313 Virginia Street.

In April, 1927, when Leslie Francis Griffin was ten years old, his father accepted the pastorate of the First Baptist Church in Farmville, and the family moved to the house at 313 Virginia Street. Behind the move were financial difficulties in the elder Griffin's former church in Norfolk, which had burned down and had been rebuilt at some pain. Exhausted after the rebuilding, Charles Henry Dunstan Griffin was ready to move on.

Griffin remembers his father as a "saintly" man, but not a

preacher who was likely to try to change the pattern of segregation in a small Southern town. His father wanted the best for
young Leslie. He had met another preacher, a brilliant man
named Vernon Johns, who was regarded as a firebrand and
treated with high suspicion by both Negroes and whites in the
community. But Mr. Johns had a good library, and Mr. Griffin
had affection for this dynamic outcast. He put young Leslie in the
way of books, his books and his friend's books. Mrs. Johns remembers that "his father had great patience. He never doubted that
Leslie would become a minister, and he never doubted that he
would finish school. They prayed every night for that." [8]

There was a streak of the rebel in young Leslie that gave his
father cause for some anxiety. As a toddler, he had tried to crawl
across a trolley track in the Berkley section of Norfolk to get to a
Jewish store where the woman gave him candy. His urge to run
away from home was great. When he was still small he got as far
as an all-day trip around town in Norfolk and once, in his teens,
disappeared for days, hitchhiking to the West Coast.

He was enrolled in due course in Moton High School, the only
Negro high school in the county. Mrs. Johns, who taught him
music and literature, remembers him as an "unusual" pupil: "He
knew what the lesson was all about, he read it long before most
times. All I could do was to try to encourage him to read more.
See, he had read his father's books—history and psychology he
liked best—and my husband's books were at his disposal. Sometime he would be so bored in school that he would slip out and go
out to Boland's. His father oftentimes would have a feeling that
he was not in school and would go out and get him and bring him
back to school." [9]

Jesse Boland was a welder, with a kind of genius for mechanics.
He had an airplane, and he would fly passengers about for a fee
from a strip of land known as Young's Flat off North Bridge
Street. Young Griffin became his devoted follower and at one
point tried to build a plane of his own. It got off the ground,
plunged into a row of trees at the end of the lot, and broke into
pieces, laying open Griffin's leg.

Mrs. Johns thought young Griffin was a rare case who might do
something worthwhile in science if he settled down to it. She
wanted him to go on to Fisk University in the five-year program
offered there by the Ford Foundation, as her daughters were to

do. She remembers that there was little outlet in those days for the scientific curiosity of the young Negro in Farmville: "The high school [Moton] didn't have any laboratory in the days when he went to school. Chemistry was just a few simple experiments in the classroom." [10]

Griffin's mother remembers him as a "rude," mischievous boy who "wouldn't pick a fight but liked one," [11] sprouting up like a wild weed, independent, unpredictable. He was always into something. He worked for a while as an assistant to a doctor in Farmville and she thought for a while—or hoped—that he would be a doctor one day.

The lot next to the Griffin house was wide open, ringed round with bushes, but clear in the center and ideal for sandlot baseball. The family that lived on the other side of the lot from the Griffins was white. There were other white families on the block. Griffin remembers the way they played: "There was no feeling of color between the kids, and it didn't seem that there was much between the adults about the kids most times. We all played in this lot, boys and girls too . . . so there wasn't this fear of sex, we all just mingled freely." [12]

Griffin's particular chums were the two white boys who lived across the lot. Mrs. Griffin remembers that the boys were around the Griffin house a good deal, sometimes to stay for dinner. One day the boys let slip to Griffin that they wouldn't be able to see so much of him in the future. Their mother had told them something about being careful not to play too often with the Griffin boy or to become too fond of him, something that impressed them once and for all with differences between them that no amount of friendship could bridge. Young Griffin understood what the boys were saying, probably better than they did, and "it hurt like nothing before and very little since." [13]

The boys' mother was less subtle when she came to call on Mrs. Griffin. Years later Mrs. Griffin remembered the interview. "I told her that he wouldn't bother them any more." [14]

A few blocks south of Young's Flat, where Griffin found and lost the inspiration of the Wright Brothers, was a large barn, long since replaced by a neat house. In this barn, Uncle Rinkum performed for Griffin and the other Negro youngsters who were at his beck. He was an aged Negro, bent and shiny black, who came from nobody knew where and made his slow way nobody knew whither. He walked with a stick and he was bald except for a fringe of white hair around his crown. He looked a little like Uncle Remus, but his stories were different.

He recalled, "We thought he was as ancient as the hills and knew everything. He used to make up stories about a no-headed person who walked through those parts and lived in the trees. There were trees all around here and they caused me concern getting home at night. . . . He would tell awful tales about recollections of slavery. . . . He told about the Negro who cut a white man in the fields, cut him in two at the trunk with a scythe. . . . He talked about how mean some of the masters were and always attached importance to what they were. I mean if the master happened to be German he would be a pretty good fellow, but smart and shrewd. . . . Then he might be "po' white trash" and Uncle Rinkum would identify these as English. The Germans were all recent arrivals and the English all had been here for a long time, according to Uncle Rinkum. . . . The longer they had been here, the meaner they would be. . . ." [15]

Griffin's brother, C. E. Griffin, was twelve years older and acted as "supervisor" of the younger ones. He remembers that his brother in his teens was a great reader—"a slave to it, near about." [16] The younger Griffin dug into the libraries available to him at his own home and at the home of the Reverend Vernon Johns in Darlington Heights in the county. Reinhold Niebuhr was an early influence, thanks to Mr. Johns. Griffin read into Plato, discovered psychology. He had a good mind but little discipline or sense of purpose. He was reasonably popular in high school, a member of the football team, a good if uneven student.

Mr. Johns came to preach from time to time in Mr. Griffin's church. The elder Griffin liked the fiery preacher and thought he should be heard, even though they had little in common theologically and Mr. Johns often angered members of the Griffin congregation. He believed in preaching on the realities of life—on the kinds of sins that were tangible, on segregation, on the docility and ignorance of the Negro. Those who had come to church to escape these realities were suitably offended. Mr. Johns believed this to be so much to the good. He and Mr. Griffin argued amiably about the best way to skin this particular cat, and young Griffin listened and was impressed. He felt that "Johns was an advanced thinker. Nobody liked him. He could tell a person something and make him mad where somebody else could say the same thing and everything would be all right. . . . Yes, he would arouse resentment. A prophet is not without honor except in his own country—and Vernon was born in Prince Edward." [17]

But young Griffin had not made up his mind to be a prophet, with or without honor. He would read Karl Barth one day and join Jesse Boland for a little parachute jumping and aerial photography the next. Nobody knew where he would be the day after that.

The war was the catalytic agent in Griffin's life. He was twenty-four years old when the Japanese attacked Pearl Harbor. He had not finished high school, having gone to New York for nearly a year to work as a shipping clerk and to Charlotte, North Carolina, in 1939, to work as a department store handyman. He went into service shortly after Pearl Harbor, survived yellow jaundice and yellow fever in Louisiana, and shipped out, eventually joining the first Negro tank outfit (758th Tank Battalion). He served under General George Patton and General Mark Clark. He was in service for more than four years, and somewhere along the line he decided to become a minister.

His brother remembers that the two had a "good fellowship" during this period and that he could tell from his younger brother's letters that he was reaching a decision on his career. His mother realized that "something was working on him." Griffin, himself, describes the experience as simply one of making up his mind after a long time of indecision: "There was nothing mystical about it. I had no visions, dreamt no dreams, saw no sights, and I didn't walk across hell on a spider web." [18]

Out of uniform, he had to finish high school. He was still restless and he was not keen on returning to Moton, partly because he was so much older than the youths he would be going to school with in his home town. His father's sister lived in Rich Square, North Carolina, and her son was principal of a high school there. Young Griffin went to Rich Square, took the last year of high school, and enrolled at Shaw University in North Carolina with the intention of finishing up as quickly as possible. From the summer of 1946 straight through until September, 1949, including all summer schools, he studied at Shaw.

When he returned to Prince Edward County on weekends, during vacations, and after summer school sessions, it was to preach. He had discovered that he could hold the attention of a congregation, and he was enjoying the sense of identity that came with his decision. He preached for a short time in Lewiston, North Carolina. Most often, he preached at his father's church. Mr. Johns was around and he became an even greater influence on Griffin as time went on. The older man called Griffin a "disciple," and Griffin felt complimented.

Griffin was becoming a devotee of the social gospel. He had discovered Walter Rauschenbusch and he was discovering, along with other Negro preachers of his generation, that the social gospel provided an excellent basis for an attack on the evils they saw. If the social gospel was old hat elsewhere, it was not to the Negro preacher in the South, because the evils it was designed to attack were present. There was poverty—palpable, deadeningly persistent; there was exploitation of man by man; most of all, though, there was segregation, and the Negro preacher of this stripe felt that it was his duty to attack here by awakening the social consciousness of the rural Negro. Docility was his chief enemy. Griffin looked at religion with a practical eye. "I never was a pie in the sky preacher. . . . Christianity was never something far away to me, but something near at hand. I've always thought that the only way man would truly become civilized and live up to his full capacities was through the practice of Christianity here and now. . . . I thought religion ought to be lived up to, squared with economics, politics, all that. . . ." [19]

Politics was a favorite subject at Shaw in 1948. The Henry Wallace campaign had touched a spark to the liberalism that had emerged from the war, and for a brief period there was ferment on the left. Griffin threw himself into it wholeheartedly.

At Shaw he was accused by his professors of being a dilettante, of caring for knowledge only as knowledge and of failing to concentrate his energies in a proper course of study. The truth was that for all the joys of reading, the life of reflection and concentrated study was not for Griffin. He wanted action. He felt the need for a mission.

In his second year at Shaw, he was married to a classmate, and a son, Skippy, was born the next year. Necessities began to bear on Griffin. His wife had taught for a year at Pinehurst, North Carolina, after their marriage, but when Skippy was born she went to her parents' home in New Jersey. The shifts were motivated by economics; the Griffins had no money, and the young student minister soon joined his wife in New Jersey, preaching for several months there. When he had to return to Shaw, his wife went to Farmville to stay with his parents.

In the summer of 1949 he faced a crisis. Money was still a problem and now he had a wife and child at home to support. His father was not doing particularly well either financially or physically. Although he had another term to go to get his degree, he came back to Farmville in September determined to help with his father's ministry for a while to earn his way.

In October, his father died. Members of the elder Griffin's congregation availed themselves of the opportunity of asking his son to take over his pulpit. Griffin recalls, "I had had another offer, a couple of others, but I was sort of flattered when I was offered a job, a chance to preach here. I had in my mind a two or three year pastorate and then to move on. . . . This wasn't the section of the country I wanted and I was thinking of my children, trying to imagine a place with better schools. . . . Then, too, this thinking might have been part of my wanderlust. . . ." [20]

Schools were a subject of vital importance to the Negro community at this time. A long fight to reduce crowded conditions at Moton High School had resulted not in the construction of a new school or permanent additions but in three temporary buildings: long, low frame structures covered with black tar paper. The Negro community dubbed the buildings "the tar paper shacks" and seethed at reports from students of poor heating and the need to tramp through ugly weather from class to class.

Griffin borrowed cars, drove into the county, talked with his parishioners and others. He was trying to find an atmosphere in which reform might take root and flower. He had come to Farmville thinking of the desperate need for more voters in the Negro community. As a student at Shaw, he had joined the National Association for the Advancement of Colored People, and increased voter registration was one of the association's chief goals. But the NAACP was very much interested in schools too, and Griffin was interested in the slowly burning resentment he detected in certain parts of the county with the way the white leaders of Prince Edward had handled the Moton situation. "After mingling among the people I saw that there were some with progressive ideas who wanted leadership. I remember that the shacks were a hot issue. . . . My first impression was that they were chicken coops. This was what made me attend my first PTA meeting. . . ." [21]

The white people of Prince Edward did not call the new buildings "shacks." Those who troubled to notice them at all saw no symbolism of shame in them.

To begin with, the idea of higher education for the Negro was still new in Prince Edward County's South. Before 1930 no high school accreditation was available for Negroes in Prince Edward. Before 1939 such high school as there was amounted to extra grades in one elementary school.[22]

Part of the explanation cuts across racial lines. Public education was slow to take hold in the South. The idea of private education had achieved a foothold in the plantation South, and after the Civil War the thrust for public education had come from the hated Yankee. Forty years after the establishment of a public school system, private schools were still conducted in Prince Edward homes.[23]

The Negro schools built after the Civil War by the Freedman's Bureau were segregated schools. The South elected to keep them that way. The one area in the country that could least afford a single school system—the rural, tobacco-poor South—elected to build a dual school system.

The Negro's "place" in Southern society seemed to most Southerners to demand what was loosely held to be "vocational" training. This belief provided an excuse to neglect expensive Negro high school construction altogether. In rural counties like Prince Edward, on-the-farm training for Negroes obviously would do as well.

Dr. N. P. Miller, a dentist and one of the few Negro professional men in Farmville, remembers the Negro effort to get high school grades added to the Mary E. Branch Elementary School prior to 1939. "They [the school board] gave us quite a bit of runaround. We had to stay with them until they did something. They agreed to put on the tenth and eleventh grades. We raised nine hundred dollars for the teachers' salaries. We did that for two years. Finally they decided they were asking too much and would handle it themselves in the future." [24]

When Moton High School was built in 1939 it was separate, but it was hardly equal. After a fire in 1939, the white Farmville High School had been rebuilt in part with Public Works Administration funds and insurance. It had a gymnasium, cafeteria, locker rooms, infirmary, and an auditorium with fixed seats. Moton had none of these. More importantly, as it turned out,

Moton was built for a capacity of 180 children when 167 were ready to move in the first year.

Superintendent of Schools T. J. McIlwaine could recall that when he came to Prince Edward in 1918 two-thirds of the Negro school buildings were one-room schools. He would point out to visitors after Moton's construction that it was one of only twelve such Negro high schools in rural Virginia. Yet he was sorely disappointed by its insufficiencies. He says that he favored a larger building but was limited by "financial considerations." This meant simply that the forty-thousand-dollar building was the best the supervisors would authorize. Moton was built with Public Works Administration funds and a loan from the State Literary Fund, which in Virginia is established to help localities meet the costs of school construction. The South, once again, had defined "equal" in traditional terms.[25]

There were extenuating circumstances. W. I. Dixon, supervisor of building for the Virginia State Board of Education, points out that the Depression had depleted local coffers.[26] Segregation forbade taking the logical step of combining facilities to reduce the cost of new construction. The South's self-imposed chains tightened and gouged. The 1940's saw a tremendous increase in Negro high school enrollment; in Prince Edward it went from 219 in 1940 to 477 in 1950.[27] The awakening of desire by Negroes for education during the war and postwar years proved the fatal element in the formula. Poor Moton High School soon was hopelessly overcrowded.

By 1947 some 377 students were stuffed into a school originally designed to handle a maximum of 180. Principal M. Boyd Jones, who arrived at Moton that year, told of "going out and beating the bushes" for more students, so devoted was he to the article of faith that education for the Negro had become. Yet with each new student the crowding problem touched a fresh dramatic peak. He recalls, "Sure we were crowded. You know the auditorium? Well, we held two or three classes in the auditorium most of the time, one on the stage and two in the back. We even held some classes in a bus."[28]

Moton parents had formed a Parent-Teachers Association in the early 1940's to try to get some relief from the crowding. Their appearances before the school board were studies in frustration. John Lancaster, a native of Prince Edward who had returned to his home county to take the job of Negro county agricultural

agent that his father had held before him, became president of the
Moton PTA in 1944–45. "When we first started in, it was my
feeling that the proper approach had not been made so that the
officials would know what we needed. Our attempt was to develop this knowledge of our needs. . . . We had a committee to
look at the situation, State Teachers Association and also State
Department of Education, and we were told that they were aware
and that as soon as they could get money, our school would be
taken care of. . . ." [29]

The school board toyed with the idea of building an addition
to Moton. State Building Supervisor Dixon discouraged this,
pointing out that the facility would be makeshift no matter what
was done to it. Nevertheless, the school board got a $50,000 state
appropriation in May, 1947, to build an addition. The board of
supervisors refused to appropriate the local funds.

By this time Maurice Large, a young head of a construction firm,
had taken over as chairman of the school board. Large felt the
need for new facilities for the Negro high school students, but he
believed that only a carefully modulated political campaign in
the county could bring approval of a local bond issue. He was not
aware of the need for haste. His idea was to have a survey done of
the county's schools by a committee of the State Board of Education. This would underscore the problem, he thought, and give
the school board some ammunition for its bond campaign.

The survey was undertaken and completed in October, 1947.
It called for a considerable expenditure to bring both white
and Negro facilities up to par. It found Moton "inadequate" and
recommended that it be converted into an elementary school and
that Mary E. Branch elementary school nearby be converted into
a high school with full facilities for six hundred pupils. The sur-
veyors warned graphically that Negro enrollment was sure to
increase. Stopgap measures clearly would not do. As though fear-
ful that its findings would be swallowed up by county officialdom without penetrating to the consciousness of the average
citizen, the committee offered a suggestion: ". . . that the county
officials, the various groups within the county, and the county
people at large be given a full opportunity to study this report
and to share in planning the educational program needed in
Prince Edward County . . . the amount that people are willing
to pay for a school program bears a close relationship to the
extent of their desire for the program. . . ." [30]

Could Prince Edward County afford th...
educational plant? The committee presentea
the county ranked thirty-third among one hu
income per school child and forty-fourth in taxa
county was above the median in both respects, i.
third of the state in income per school child.

The school board had its ammunition. Plainly, a bon... ...sue
would be needed to finance improvements in both white and
Negro schools. Large had felt that it was necessary to tie the two
needs together: "A lot of people around here would have yelled
loud and long if we tried to float a bond issue just to build a
'nigger' school—that's what it would be regarded as. We had to
add a couple of white school plans to get it through. We knew
that." [31]

In March, 1948, the school board met with officials of the State
Board of Education. Large later testified in court, "It was definitely apparent to the board that we needed additional, adequate, permanent structures to house the load at R. R. Moton." [32]

Yet despite the emphasis on "permanent" structures and despite the state board of education's recommendations, Large and
McIlwaine appeared before the board of supervisors in June to
outline a plan for temporary buildings to relieve the congestion
at Moton. Later that month McIlwaine reported to the school
board that the supervisors were "very co-operative" and had instructed the school board to do whatever was necessary to relieve
the congestion but not to exceed an expense of twenty-five thousand dollars—barely enough to build the tar paper structures
that were being used as stopgaps elsewhere in the state. [33]

What had happened to cause the school board to make the
crucial decision to build temporary structures? Large later testified that the board realized that it was too late by June to con-
struct permanent facilities by the coming September when
additional space was absolutely necessary. [34] But the survey had
been lying around for six months by then. There had been none
of the county-wide discussion that had been recommended.
There was no public record of the school board's intentions to
build a new school.

Large insists that the school board was as determined as ever to
build a new Negro high school. He says that the climate for a
bond issue was not right and that the board was engaged in
missionary work in the community to try to improve that climate.

e s critics later said that the chairman and the board must have been dragging their feet. Large says he was afraid the bond issue would be defeated if the groundwork for it were not laid carefully.

The history of bond issues in Prince Edward gives some credence to the school board's fears. Senator Harry Flood Byrd had raised fiscal conservatism to the level of a godhead. Capital improvements should be financed on a pay-as-you-go basis, the Byrd credo said. The former governor and head of the state's monolithic Democratic Party did not favor bond issues in large amounts. Prince Edward people traditionally looked upon bond issues with suspicion. A county-wide school bond issue for two hundred thousand dollars was tabled in 1924. County historian Herbert Clarence Bradshaw wrote of the early years of the twentieth century: "During the past generation no more bitter political battles were fought in the county than those in the districts that voted on school bonds . . . . Opposition centered largely on the increased taxation which would be required." [35]

The obstacles that the school board saw before it in June, 1948, were formidable, then. It had to sell a big bond issue for public schools to people traditionally lukewarm to the idea of public education. It had to sell a big bond issue primarily for a Negro public school to people whose history had not conditioned them to regard Negro education as necessary or desirable.

So, while the board worked to line up its political support, the Negro high school students would have temporary buildings. These structures had a five-year statutory limit upon their use, but many of them built in the 1930's and early 1940's had outlived their legal limit.[36] Across the state the demand for Literary Fund loans exceeded the fund's ability to pay. Some communities were bravely plunging into heavy expenditure for education; others, like Prince Edward, were putting off the day. The Prince Edward School Board got permission to build three of the tarpaper buildings in 1948–49 and soon afterwards appointed a three-man committee to find a site for a new Moton High School.

This is how the tar paper shacks came to be built. Their meaning was imprisoned in this history. It had something to do with the South's ancestral disaffection for mass education, the scars left by the Civil War, real poverty, the penny-wise tightfistedness of the Byrd administration, and the unexpected demand of the

Negro of the 1940's for high school education. All these, in one manner or another, were villains of the piece.

Yet the chief villain is no less difficult to see for all of the help it had. The white high school that was built in the same period as Moton embodied the hope rather than just the well-founded expectation of increasing enrollment. Moton was built without the expectation, but, more importantly, without the hope. The bond issue that the school board handled so gingerly would have been troublesome enough if it had to do only with improvements to white schools. The fact that it dealt primarily with Negro school improvements made it a matter for profound contemplation all around. The real villain of the piece was segregation—or, rather, the cumulative set of attitudes of white toward Negro that make up segregation's cause and effect.

Years later someone close to the situation in the county for many years observed that there would have been no trouble if the shacks had been put up on the grounds of the white high school for use by white students. This may be true. But of course they would not have meant the same thing at all. They might have looked the same. They might have inspired the same complaints. They would not have stood as fresh evidence of an inferiority that the white man's history strained to impose on the Negro.

The shacks at Moton did not cure the overcrowding problem, although they helped. They did raise new and ugly questions that the county eventually would have to answer in pain. They stood as symbols—with a new and potent meaning that the law soon would invoke—of the failure of "separate" to be "equal" in the schools of the South.

The Reverend L. Francis Griffin regarded the tar paper shacks as the raw material from which he might fuse the Negro community into a political force. The shacks were deeply resented across the whole spectrum of Negro society; resentment such as this could be harnessed if it could be brought to a focus.

The preacher had no faith in negotiations with the school board. But he realized that he could exercise leadership only through the PTA committee that was appearing with increasing frequency before the board. John Lancaster, the Negro farm agent, was one of the young members of the PTA, as was M. Boyd Jones, the Moton principal. To a certain degree, these men believed that their only hope lay in negotiations of this kind. Mr. Griffin fell in with them, had himself named chairman of the committee, and waited for them to lose patience with the school board.

Mr. Griffin's goals were hardly revolutionary at this point. He had no plan to overturn the community structure. He had no plan to force the white leadership to build a new school. He hoped to create through the issue of the shacks a solid Negro organization made up of the more progressive Negro leaders. Whatever progress he could foresee across the full range of improving the lot of his race in the county depended upon his success in this effort. He had engaged himself as a social missionary. "It was my contention long before the NAACP announced its policy that segregation was a blight to be cut off by surgery. I preached this publicly and privately. I would tell it to groups on the street corner, in church, wherever I could, that someone ought to be talking in terms of change. Right on the post office steps, on South Main Street—I got some antagonism from whites, and I had trouble controlling my own feelings at times. But these feelings ran counter to other feelings that Christian love was the most important thing in the world. . . . You know, they called me the love preacher sometimes. . . . Yes, even in front of pool rooms I strongly attacked these Negroes for their lack of aspiration, dreams, their pronounced complacence. In many instances I reprimanded them for blaming whites for things that they had done nothing about themselves. I had people attending my church from sixty and seventy miles away, from Lynchburg and Richmond, out of curiosity. Church attendance really went up. . . ." [37]

In this effort, as in his efforts on the PTA Committee, Mr. Griffin had to discredit the old, segregation-oriented leadership represented by Willie Redd, a well-to-do Negro contractor who had risen within the system of segregation and who thought that his race's best advantage lay in progress within the old, established bounds. Redd was the Negro leader *Herald* Editor J. Barrye Wall would consult when he wished to learn of the feelings of the Negro community on one subject or another. Redd's resignation from the PTA committee and Griffin's elevation to the chairmanship actually symbolized a revolution of leadership within this community, but the white leadership was not aware of this. Wall would continue to consult Redd and would continue to believe that Redd spoke for the dominant element in the Negro community.

The instrument of Griffin's power was to be the National Association for the Advancement of Colored People. He organized a chapter with slightly more than the necessary fifty members and became county co-ordinator. This threw out lines of communication to Richmond, where the state NAACP offices were located, and to headquarters in New York.

But, for the time being, his efforts would have to be entirely on a local level. He won a victory when the idea of improving Moton High School on its present location was turned down by the Negro community despite Redd's support of it. (The school board never took the idea seriously, and the State Board of Education eventually ruled that the improvement contemplated would not conform with state regulations; but the discussion did serve to draw the lines of leadership sharply in the Negro community.)

In the spring of 1950 the Moton PTA committee asked the school board if it could be of assistance in securing a site for the new school.[38] The school board's three-man committee had run into one roadblock after another—there was plenty of available land in the county but, apparently, none suitable for a Negro high school. Large later testified that the board had received an "outrageous" offer for a tract it was trying to purchase across Ely Street west of the present Moton. Large recalled later: "These people were worried about Negro occupation. They probably would have preferred a school if there had to be Negro occupation of the property but they were against any Negro occupation." [39]

The school board accepted the Moton PTA's offer of help in finding a site.[40] It was not long before Willie Redd tipped Maurice Large that some property belonging to F. H. Hanbury, Sr., owner-operator of the Buffalo Shook Company, makers of boxes and shook (staves and headings for barrels or casks), might be available.[41] While Redd preferred to see the high school built in town, he was anxious to see the matter settled amicably. Mr. Griffin and John Lancaster, with Redd acting as go-between, talked to Hanbury, one of the county's biggest employers, and were told that if the school board would come to him, he could work it out. Mr. Griffin and his group hurried to the school board with the news.

Mr. Griffin remembers the reaction. "The board seemed surprised that the committee would be interested in land that far out. We told them we didn't care if it was half in Prince Edward and half in Cumberland County just as long as it was a good school." [42]

These sixty-three acres were three miles south of Farmville, on Route 15, in a location easily accessible to town. The board recognized that it would have difficulty finding anything else as good. The land could be purchased for eight thousand dollars.

None of the principals clearly recalls the dates, but the consensus is that the discussions on sale of the land took place in the summer, probably before August, 1950. Yet it was not until November that the school board minutes reflect that Large was directed to get in touch with Hanbury to see if the purchase could be made.

In court later, Large attempted to explain the time lag: "It was a rather involved process there. I had a good deal of difficulty in getting hold of the owner of that property. He had business interests out of town, and I have some business interests that occupy a reasonable amount of my time . . . a matter of some two or three months, possibly, was taken up endeavoring to negotiate the price that my Negro friend told me the property could be bought for." [43]

The lapse of time proved important. Each passing month implanted deeper the impression in influential segments of the Negro community that the school board was stalling or did not care. Sixteen months had passed since its site committee had been told to go to work. Independent men on the Moton PTA, like farmers George Morton and Otis Scott,[44] were beginning to share the convictions of Mr. Griffin and John Lancaster. Parents of the Moton students themselves felt the string of frustration draw tighter with each negative report the PTA committee returned. The reports themselves were filled with Mr. Griffin's lively skepticism: "I didn't believe them [the school board] that Hanbury was that hard to catch up with, and I asked them did he have wings. I said I could catch up with Public Enemy No. One in the time it was taking them. . . ." [45]

Large was a busy man and so was Hanbury. But the connection would not have been so hard to make if the board had correctly read the persistence with which Mr. Griffin's committee returned month after month to the old question of the land. It would not have been so hard to make if the school board knew that with the coming of winter the bitter complaints about the bad heating and leaky roofs of the shacks would redouble. But the school board was entirely isolated from the sentiment of the Negro community.

And the Negro community was more or less isolated from the thinking of the school board. Large contends that during this period Griffin's PTA committee failed to give accurate reports of what went on to their Negro families. He bases this judgment on talks he had with Negroes who attended the PTA meetings and heard committee reports.[46] Mr. Griffin denies holding back any information passed on by the school board.

There was plenty of room for misunderstanding. The *Farmville Herald* did not cover the school board meetings. Consequently, the only people, black or white, who knew anything about the meetings of the PTA and the school board were the members of those bodies and those they chose to confide in. Editor Wall says that he had very little knowledge of what was going on in the school board meetings: "I thought the school board was handling things all right. I didn't know they [the Moton PTA] were showing up there every month . . . . I feel now that not reporting the school board meetings was a sin of omission. I wasn't aware or didn't recognize what was happening. Nobody else in the community was either. . . ."[47]

If the *Herald's* reporting was lax, why didn't the school board then see to it that the public was informed of the important discussions with the Negro PTA group? Large concedes that working behind the scenes may have been an error. But he also argues that the publicity might have unleashed a controversy, and this the board feared more than anything else. If the bond issue were to be a success, the board felt, an open fight with all the ugly by-products of debate over sensitive economic and racial issues had to be avoided. Large said, "Every time you'd take a school budget to the board these same people would be there saying whatever you do, don't raise taxes. We could see the idea of a bond issue being killed around these country crossroads. We thought if we played it right we'd get 60, maybe 65 per cent of the county people for a bond issue package."[48]

So Large worked with the opinion leaders in the county. Whatever is to be said for their opinion-making abilities, they were not all of the people of Prince Edward County. The real test never was made. The board never went to the people of Prince Edward with a statement of its needs.

For one thing, the school board did not understand that it was confronted by a deepening crisis. It did not believe that the Negro community would follow leadership like that of Mr. Griffin. The board was cut off from the Negro community by the tradition that said that the Negro must come to the white man in respectful request; the white man did not go to the Negro, certainly not for information or help. The board was cut off from the Negro community by the same villain—segregation. The only information that could penetrate the South's color curtain was that carried by the old, complaisant Negro leaders who, themselves, were more surely each day out of touch with what was going on about them. Drugged by the habits of the separated society, the board accepted this misinformation cheerfully and so did not understand that time was running out.

There is another reason why the school board did not take to the community at large an appeal for support of a bond issue. There was no political tradition that called for this kind of action. The concept of town hall debate, of full participation from the grass roots of the affairs of society, is not native to Virginia. In Virginia, the tradition of government by the elite few and the fact of one-party, one-faction domination served as a further barrier. The organization headed by Senator Byrd—far from depending upon broad popular support—used such conscious devices as the poll tax to limit the electorate. Some of the staunchest supporters of Senator Byrd lived in the Southside, in Prince Edward. They were leaders of their communities. They had never contracted an affection for referenda.

So the school board took its time, looking toward the bond issue that it hoped would come up in June. Architect's sketches of the proposed new school were made and shown to the Moton PTA committee. Large cites them as evidence that the board was proceeding in good faith and that the PTA committee should have known that they were.[49]

But the board and the PTA committee were interpreting everything differently. The record proved to the board's own satisfaction that progress was being made, that land would soon be available, that plans were in process, that a scheme to get the money was hatching. The record meant the opposite to the Moton group: it proved that the committee itself had had to find the land, that the board was making no progress towards buying the land, and that only the vaguest kind of talk dealt with the problem of paying for the new school.

In December, 1950, the four-year building program of the county was submitted to the State Board of Education in Richmond. This tied down the county's share of a school construction fund set up by Governor John Battle, an amount that later turned out to be $274,214.77. The program called for construction of a Negro high school to cost $800,000. With the white school improvements included, the total bill would be $1,125,000. A local bond issue would have to cover the difference between the Battle Fund money and the total bill—around three-quarters of a million dollars.[50]

Not a word of this information got into the *Farmville Herald* or the state papers at the time. The Moton PTA, at its habitual post for the board's December meeting, was shown a plot of the Hanbury land, told that the school board hoped to buy it if a suitable price could be obtained, and informed that a bond issue would be necessary.[51]

In February, Large told the school board that the board of supervisors had given approval for the purchase of the land. Large and McIlwaine were to negotiate for it. The Moton PTA committee was told of this decision and further informed that as soon as the sale was consummated, there would be word in the *Herald*.[52]

The tone of these minutes suggests that the Moton PTA was being told that there was no point in its continuing to appear at the monthly board meetings. Mr. Griffin recalls that the committee was told at one of the meetings early in 1951 not to bother to return. Perhaps this was that meeting. It may be, too, that the night that the PTA committee reported to the PTA at large on this meeting, a pretty, fifteen-year-old Moton High School junior named Barbara Johns was in the audience. A few Moton students had begun to show up in the PTA meetings.

No record exists of a board meeting in March, 1951.

The minutes of the meeting of April 12, 1951, do not indicate whether the PTA committee returned. They do tell of the first formal steps to secure the Hanbury property. The process was to be an uncontested condemnation in order to secure a tax advantage for the property owner. If the Moton PTA committee was present, it was for the last time.[53]

For in April, the matter of what should be done about Moton High School passed out of the hands of the school board and the Moton PTA. Another element in the Negro community—one that proved crucial—had escaped the attention of the school board. In all likelihood the very suggestion that it should have received the school board's attention would have been greeted with blank stares. The last place that white leaders in the South of 1951 would have looked for symptoms of revolt was a Negro school. The last individuals the school board would have thought to consult on the problems of Moton High School were the Moton High School students themselves.

2. A LITTLE CHILD
SHALL LEAD THEM

Barbara Rose Johns had roots deep in Prince Edward County. Her grandparents and parents all had been born there. Her father, a solid, silent man, owned land in the Darlington Heights section. Her uncle, the Reverend Vernon Johns, preached there when he was not off preaching somewhere else, denouncing the country Negroes who filled the churches where he spoke for their impenetrable docility, for not caring enough.

Barbara was born in New York City. Her mother and father had hoped to get away from the farm and the slow, rural existence with its drab promise for the future. They lived for a time with relatives of her father, Robert Johns, in a rooming house on 129th Street. When Barbara was fourteen months old, the family moved back to the county and then, in 1942, to Washington, where her mother, Violet Johns, had found work with the government. Robert Johns entered the army that year, and the next year Barbara was moved back to the county to live with her grandparents. She was enrolled in Public School 14, a one-room school set in a patch of pine.

Barbara feels that she was protected from the realities of life during this time. She remembers no personal experience of color in her early years, but at night she and occasionally one of the more venturesome of her three younger brothers and one younger sister would slip out of bed to the door of the room where the family was gathered around talking: "You could hear stories about slavery and about the way Negroes were living in the old days. I don't know about whether any of this was real experience for them or what, and I know none of them actually had been slaves of course. . . . But I remember stories. . . . There was one story about a young white woman with this particular horse that she wanted groomed just right. She would come out and wipe a clean white cloth across the horse's body to see if it got any dirt. If it did the slave got whipped. . . . I remember that the story ended, and I know it sounds mean, but I always felt glad somehow. . . . Anyway the way it ended the horse threw her and she died. . . ." [1]

Barbara's maternal grandmother, Mrs. Mary Croner, was an alert person who had been born and brought up in the Darlington Heights section of the county but who had strong ideas about the need for leadership to raise her people. She remembered stories having been read to her of Negroes lynched and dragged through the street. [2]

There were others who felt this way, and they were frequent visitors at the Croner home. There was Sally Johns, Barbara's paternal grandmother (whom her mother says she resembles in character) and Uncle Vernon, who was managing to make himself disliked by whites and Negroes alike in the county. Barbara clung to him with a fierce loyalty: "My uncle was always outspoken and I used to admire the way he didn't care who you were if he thought that something was right. It used to be an admirable thing to me the way he would handle white men who would have an argument with him. . . ." [3]

In 1945 Barbara's father got out of the army and her mother left her job in Washington to return to the county. Violet Johns had an opportunity to see more of her ten-year-old daughter. She remembers that "Barbara was sort of strange, sort of—deep. I don't know. Anyway she would play for a while and then she would stop just as abruptly. I guess you could say that she was selfish. . . . She liked to be by herself quite a bit and she thought that a lot of the things other kids were interested in were silly. . . ." [4]

Before he had gone into the army, Robert Johns had operated a general store owned by Vernon Johns in a section of Darlington Heights, in which Negro farmers predominated. When he came out, Robert took over the store entirely. Despite the nature of the immediate neighborhood, the clientele was thoroughly mixed. White farmers were regular customers, white salesmen were regular visitors. Mrs. Johns remembers having difficulty adjusting back from the manners of Washington to rural Virginia: "People used to come in and I used to get so angry that they would . . .

call you by your first name. 'Violet, how about this'—and that kind of thing. I would tell them I thought only my personal friends called me by my first name. We used to have a verbal fight almost every day with some salesman or another." [5]

She remembers when Barbara was quite small that a white boy came into the store and asked for "Uncle Robert" and that she had to explain to her daughter that her father was not really the little boy's uncle.

When Barbara was twelve and thirteen she worked in the store, waiting on customers, when school was out. Of the job, she recalls, "I used to feel proud that I was able to give this service rather than go to them for service. . . . My father was on good terms with all the white around. . . . They would come, some of them, and sit around and play cards. . . . Well they were all poor dirt farmers, you know, and it didn't matter much to them . . . one white farmer's wife used to come over and talk and sit. . . . I remember she had a daughter and I used to think she was such a beautiful girl. She went to Farmville and got a job in the five and ten and I came in one day and she just turned away. . . . All the times we had talked and just this little thing turned her head. . . ." [6]

Barbara seethed, but smothered her flame. If she erupted at all, it was privately, in something she wrote down, or in brief, savage outbursts of anger. Mostly, she internalized her revenge. Years later, she wrote: "I remember as a youngster getting a special surge of pride out of discovering that the superior white man wasn't too superior after all. This came from visiting the Rose's and Newberry's five- and ten-cent stores in Farmville and finding out that the salesgirls couldn't count worth a darn. Example: I remember getting several (say five) 10-cent items and one 19-cent item. Instead of figuring 69 cents right off the bat, she got pencil and pad and wrote a list of five 10- and one 19-cent items and then added it up to be 79 cents. I asked her to recheck and she came up with 59 cents. Instead of taking advantage of her ignorance I got a greater kick from taking each item and counting them correctly out for her and seeing her face turn a crimson red and muttering 'Oh, yes, that's right.'" [7]

Barbara played with her Uncle Vernon's daughters, admirable girls who studied music and used the resources of their father's library and of his mind to move far ahead of their classmates. Barbara and the girls wrote plays. Once they sold tickets to one of their plays and raised enough money to have electric lights installed in the school. Writing thrilled Barbara, and she was to work at it from time to time in later years, with no commercial success but with the feeling that she could find satisfaction from the effort. She went to school movies, fifteen-cent pictures like "Sentimental Journey." An Italian boy with Negro blood who could pass and sit with the whites in the Farmville theater returned to the community of farms to regale the others with vivid re-enactments of the films.

Barbara read incessantly. Her mother remembers occasions when she searched the grounds and the house proper for her daughter only to find her, at last, perched in the attic with a book. She read Booker T. Washington's "Up From Slavery" and remembered Washington's gentleness and the way in which he refused to picture the white man as cruel but instead showed how white and Negro depended upon each other. She read *Little Women* and *Little Men* and, not much later, Richard Wright's *Native Son*. She even tackled H. G. Well's *Outline of History* from her Uncle Vernon's library. Barbara read, and her Grandmother Croner was impressed: "She was quiet, serious, Barbara was . . . didn't seem to want to get out much . . . seemed she had to do a lot of thinking and studying. She read good books, didn't fool with any of these funny books. . . . Then, too, there were people who influenced her. Vernon Johns was often in the home and you know she didn't get nothing but encouragement from him to do better. . . ." [8]

Mrs. Croner says this last and laughs the deep, chuckling, affectionate laugh that his friends have for Vernon Johns, a laugh that tells you that they consider him impossibly, marvelously, roguishly right.

Mrs. Vernon Johns saw a good deal of Barbara and liked her: "Barbara always had a very logical mind and she was frank. The Johnses are all known for that. She used to organize her mother's home and keep the children together." [9]

Her mother, too, saw Barbara's frankness as another link between her daughter and the Johns side of the family. She could not get Barbara to attend church regularly and still remembers her daughter's explanation that she did not understand what the preacher was getting at and could see no reason for listening under those circumstances. Her daughter "had a temper and she was sort of . . . stubborn, and anything she believed in she was determined to continue to believe in and if you wanted to change her mind you had to give a lot of reasons . . . . She was very outspoken, a little like her Uncle Vernon in that respect." [10]

Barbara considers that her life began to change when she entered R. R. Moton High School. Her classmates remember her during her freshman and sophomore years as a quiet girl, intelligent, and active in school affairs. Barbara joined the drama guild, the New Homemakers of America, the high school chorus, and she was elected to the student council. She traveled a good deal as a result of this office. She began to think that Moton High School was a blight on the county, on all the Negroes in the county, on her. [11]

She saw Huntington High School in Newport News, Solomon Russell High School in Lawrenceville, the Ralph E. Bunche High School in King George. She saw the Farmville High School closer to home, and in the forbidden distance from which she saw it glamour was attached. It was like the banana split she had seen in the window of the Southside Drug Store and had wanted to sit at a counter and eat. When she finally realized this ambition—not in Farmville, but in New York—the results were disappointing. Like the banana split, Farmville High School would have been a disappointment inside. But Barbara could not go inside.

The worst thing about Moton was the palliative the school board had found for the overcrowding, the tar paper shacks. Each of the shacks had a single wood stove for heat, and the students who sat close to the stove stripped off their sweaters while those who sat farther away wrapped up in overcoats. The teachers had to pause in their lessons to stoke the fire. The shacks leaked in some places, and colds were the usual thing in the winter.

These circumstances bothered Barbara perhaps more than any of her classmates. She was troubled by the reports of the boys who worked after school around the Farmville High School and who spoke of the excellent equipment in the shops. She was troubled by the fact that the students at Moton had to leave for school an hour early in order to be there on time because the buses used to haul the Negro students were so few and so dilapidated. They were largely hand-me-down buses, abandoned by the white school system when new ones were obtained there; this troubled Barbara most of all, that the school and all about it seemed makeshift, hand-me-down, second-rate . . . . [12]

The students talked about these conditions over lunch. They

talked but they did nothing, for most of them could conceive of nothing to do. Barbara realized that they would never act. She and they heard reports from their parents or other sources that the negotiations with the school board were not proving fruitful. Time hung heavily.

Barbara liked the school principal, M. Boyd Jones. She found him straightforward, not the kind of principal who would tell the students that all was well in the world. Jones taught fair play, she remembers, and she considers that he had a considerable influence over the course that events took, if only because his teaching made it all seem inevitable.

But it was not easy to talk to one's principal about the things that made anger well up. Jones was seeing a good deal of one of his teachers, a Miss Inez Davenport, whom he married shortly afterwards. Barbara went to Miss Davenport: "I told her how sick and tired I was of the inadequate buildings and facilities and how I wished to hell (I know I wasn't this profane in speaking to her but that's how I felt) something could be done about it. After hearing me out she asked simply, 'Why don't you do something about it?' I recall smiling at her, dropping the subject, and going about my other activities. But I didn't forget that statement, for it stuck with me for several days and out of it was conceived the idea of the strike." [13]

One of the first students Barbara Johns thought of was John Stokes. Any planning would have to include him, and he and his sister, Carrie, would have to be in favor of the plan.

The Stokes family in Prince Edward County was unusual. One measure of this fact was that the *Farmville Herald* had carried a full-length feature on John when he was elected state president of the New Farmers of America (the Negro 4-H). [14] It was rare that the *Herald* carried stories about Negro achievements of longer than brief "colored news" length. In the story John was described as the son of Luther Stokes, a farmer, and head of an "outstanding" county family. One older sister, Lieutenant Martha Stokes, a graduate of St. Philip's Hospital in Richmond, was with the United States Marine Corps at Fort Dix, New Jersey. Three older brothers had served as noncommissioned officers in the army during World War II, and were now, respectively, an instructor of agriculture, dispatcher for a transit company in Washington, D. C., and student at Livingstone College in Salisbury, North

Carolina. John's younger sister, Carrie, was president of the student council at Moton.

John Stokes, himself, had a record any high school student might have envied. He was vice-president of the student council, business manager of the "Motonian," a top student, a track star, and orator for the New Farmers of America. Like Barbara Johns, he used his opportunities as a student leader to travel. Twice he went to Atlanta and made frequent shorter trips around Virginia. He thinks that getting out of the county and listening to his older brothers and sisters talk about life in the north and in other countries contributed to his dissatisfaction with conditions at Moton: "I believe my brothers and sisters had influenced me more than anyone else. They had taught me the importance of being a good student so that I would not be hampered by my color, and the importance of not believing that I was inferior. . . ." [15]

The Stokes family was "outstanding" in ways that the *Herald* did not know. The home was one in which could be found the latest books, magazines, and newspapers that ranged far beyond the confines of Virginia. The Stokeses were thoughtful people to whom many of the farmers in their section of the country came for advice. They were genuine opinion leaders for the county's Negro population.

The feature story about John Stokes appeared in the *Herald* of September 15, 1950. Dates of student meetings that ensued were never recorded, but it was not more than two months later that John Stokes was taking part in a student conspiracy directed at the authority of school officials of the county.

John Stokes remembers that Barbara Johns privately collared about five of Moton's student leaders—among them John and his sister, Carrie—and asked them to meet her in the bleachers around the athletic field one afternoon late in the fall. The students knew what the meeting would be about, although Barbara's plan was a mystery to them. The meeting was sure to be about conditions at the high school. John Stokes was prepared to agree that something had to be done: "The buildings, the shacks themselves, well to tell you frankly I used to catch colds in them. They were drafty and they were cold. If you sat around the stove you were too warm and if you sat away from it you were too cold. It was no way to be taught, and we considered that we were not getting the best education that way. . . . And we used to be embarrassed. People would stop by the highway and ask what those buildings were. We would say they were part of the school. They would say: 'School! Looks like a poultry farm!' " [16]

John knew from his travels that the situation of Negro high school students elsewhere in Virginia was superior to that of the Moton students. He was not hard for Barbara to persuade. He found that "she opened our eyes to a lot of things. I guess it was her environment that made her such a person. You know she was quiet, very slow spoken. She talked to us just that way that day. But I guess maybe her uncle had quite an influence on her." [17]

Barbara spoke to the students about the efforts their parents were making through the Moton PTA to get improvements in the school, and she contrasted Moton with other, more modern, Negro high schools in the state. She asked them why they thought their parents could make no progress with the school board in looking toward a new school. She asked the student leaders to watch the results of the next PTA–school-board meeting to see what progress was made. John Stokes recalls: "Then she said our parents ask us to follow them but in some instances—and I remember her saying this very vividly—a little child shall lead them. She said we could make a move that would broadcast Prince Edward County all over the world." [18]

The meeting ended with Barbara asking the student leaders each to bring one more reliable student to a meeting that would follow soon. This second meeting, John Stokes recalls, was held indoors at the school during the winter of 1950. About ten student leaders were on hand. Barbara told the students that their parents were not taking a stand. She talked about action. She suggested that the students assembled there make plans to take the entire school out on strike in the spring. They would make and carry placards just like any other strikers. They would not come back until the school board promised a new school. Stokes recalls that those in attendance agreed wholeheartedly to the plan.[19]

On Barbara's advice the students present agreed to keep the plan to themselves. The atmosphere of conspiracy was thought to be necessary as much for the protection of Moton authorities as for the plan itself. Barbara emphasizes that the students did not want Principal Jones, who was generally admired, to be hurt by what they did.

A third meeting of the student leaders—now grown to between

fifteen and twenty in number—was held after Barbara and John had attended a Moton PTA meeting, possibly the one in April, 1951. Reasonably complete machinery was organized to set the rebellion in motion. It was not decided what the students would do once the entire school was out on strike. Stokes remembers that one plan was for the students to carry placards to advertise their plight and, if this did not bring action, to walk over to the white school, take seats, and stay until removed. Stokes later labeled this idea as "crazy" and it is one that never was tried. The placards, however, were made.[20]

There was doubt about method but none about goals. The students wanted a new school. Barbara, John, and other student leaders were agreed on this point. The NAACP had by this time filed its first desegregation suit, in Clarendon County, South Carolina, but it is doubtful if the Moton students were even conscious of this. On Sunday, April 22, delegates of the Fourth District NAACP conference met in Sussex County, to hear the respected Virginia NAACP lawyer Spottswood Robinson speak. Robinson talked about Clarendon County: "Before the end of 1951 we hope to see a judicial declaration of the invalidity of racial segregation in at least one Southern school system . . . this nullification may come from the Supreme Court of the United States. . . . The NAACP has undertaken its non-segregation policy after realizing that previous experiences had proven that there can exist no equality in a segregated school system." [21]

The Moton students did not know about Robinson's speech, but on the other hand, he did not know about them. While Farmville High School seniors were being given a guided tour of Washington, D. C., a small group of Moton conspirators were spreading the word of the plan for Monday to a picked group of juniors and seniors who were considered reliable enough to be told in advance. There would be enough of them, of the right sort, to carry the entire student body out of the school.

3. THE EYES OF THE
WORLD ARE ON US

Shortly before 11 A.M. on April 23, 1951, the telephone rang in the office of Principal M. Boyd Jones, of Moton High School. The caller informed Jones in a muffled voice that two Moton students were at the Greyhound bus terminal and that they would be in trouble with the police if Jones didn't hurry over there. Before the principal could ask any questions, his caller hung up.[1]

The principal got in his car and drove to the bus station, thinking that he had a rescue mission on his hands. He had warned the students time and again not to expect sympathy from him if they stayed out of school and got in trouble with the law. He was prepared to enforce discipline in this case.

Jones drove around the block twice without seeing any Moton students. Two policemen were parked in the block, and he asked them if they had seen any high school students hanging around the bus station. They had not. Neither had they heard any report that students were supposed to be at the bus station. Puzzled, Principal Jones parked the car and went inside the station to see for himself. No students were there, and the ticket agent had seen none that day. The principal looked around a few moments more and then got back in his car and turned up Main Street toward Moton.

Meanwhile, the Moton student body had been undergoing a strange experience. As soon as the principal had left the school, a listening student had signaled the auditorium, which was used as a study room. Barbara Johns, in the auditorium, handed slips she had written out to four other students and dispatched them to the classrooms: "Our principal often sent to all classrooms notices requesting the presence of all teachers and pupils in assembly at

11 o'clock. He signed the notices only with the signature 'J.' I too wrote a notice requesting attendance in assembly and signed the signature 'J.' " [2]

Moton High School is built in wings leading off from the auditorium. To get from classroom to classroom, from the library to a classroom, or from the principal's office to anywhere else in the building, it is necessary to pass through the auditorium. This type of construction was popular because it was inexpensive, with the auditorium actually being used for corridors. As the students and teachers began swarming into the room, arranging the folding metal chairs with a great scraping, Barbara Johns and several other student leaders disappeared behind the thick, green curtains on the stage. With them, by this time, was the student whose bogus telephone call had called Principal Jones away from the school.

When the approximately 450 students had been seated a few minutes after 11 A.M., the stage curtains parted to reveal the student committee. A ripple of surprise ran through the assembly. Barbara was at the rostrum, and Principal Jones, who had supposedly called the meeting, was nowhere to be seen.

Barbara announced that the meeting was for the students only and that they would be obliged if the teachers would leave. At this, the confusion heightened. One of the teachers protested, and Barbara singled him out by name and asked him to leave. Another student remembers one teacher's being booed off the stage. Barbara remembers that a teacher who did remain through part of the meeting was removed bodily from the auditorium for protesting. But most of the teachers did leave voluntarily.[3]

Barbara began delivering what John Stokes called "her soliloquy." [4] She wrote later in recollection: "I do not remember exactly what I said that day, but I do know that I related with heated emphasis the facts they knew to be the truth—such as the leaking roofs, having to keep our coats on all day in winter for warmth. Having to have the gymnasium classes in the auditorium, inadequate lunchroom facilities and food, etc. My sister says that I reminded her of a politician standing on a platform denouncing the sins of his opponent and promoting his own ideas with such intensity that you automatically believed and followed instructions. I don't know about this—but I do know we mapped out for those students . . . our wish that they would not accept the conditions of our school and that they would do something about it." [5]

Mrs. Croner recalls asking Barbara's thirteen-year-old sister, Jo-anne, what Barbara had said at the meeting: "Joanne said she took off her shoe and hit it on a bench and said I want you all out of here. Joanne said she was afraid Barbara was going to hit some-one on the head with that shoe." [6]

John Stokes remembers that Barbara called upon the students to stay out of school as long as was necessary to bring about a change in conditions: "She informed them that things would never be better until we had integration. . . . She said we would not come back until we got better schools, but she didn't stop there. She went on to say that they wouldn't be better until we went back to school with others of other races." [7]

Whatever she said, Barbara got the auditorium audience of high school students solidly behind her. Some questions were asked, but only one that the committee members remember as "unfriendly" to the plan, and that that one came from a youth whose parents were considered in a poor position to incur the anger of the white community. James Samuel Williams, a big, enthusiastic lad who had been in on early student meetings, did ask other questions and managed to leave with some of the com-mittee the impression that he was opposed to the plan.

Williams' explanation is that he arrived at the meeting late— "I knew about the plans, that we were to strike, but it took me by surprise that it was to be that day. I didn't know about that." [8]

Williams' mother, a teacher in Cumberland County, was op-posed to the plan, most of his classmates agree. Williams had told her about what was going to happen, and his reaction may have been keyed to hers. John Stokes had not told his parents what was up, and he was surprised to see his mother and another woman in the auditorium after the meeting had gotten under way. Mrs. Stokes explained later, "I was in Farmville at the time with Mrs. Daisy Anderson. . . . We were at a house on Main Street not more than a block or so from the school. . . . A little boy came running up and said there was a riot going on at the school. I went to the car and told my husband about this and then I went down to the school. . . . I didn't know what to think when I found them all meeting inside. I stood there a while scared to death. I left because there wasn't anything to do. . . ." [9]

During the height of the confusion of the question and answer period, Principal Jones arrived back at school. The plan to keep him away from the school until the auditorium meeting was over had failed by twenty minutes or more. John Stokes recalls what happened: "He rushed into the auditorium in a kind of hysterical state. At that time he pleaded with the students to go back to school. He said this would not solve our problems. He believed that progress was being made with the school board. Barbara asked him to go back to his office, and he finally did. The students did not boo him. They had a lot of respect for him." [10]

Stokes says that Barbara got complete control of the meeting after this. The students were with her. Stokes does not believe that this means that they had any special goal other than the elimination of the offensive features of the present Moton school. He doubts that any of the student leaders, Barbara included, thought of integration as anything more than a distant, perhaps unattainable, goal. [11] He believed that "seemingly Barbara was building this thing up. She brought out the idea of integration by stages. It was her belief that if the students stayed on strike long enough, the NAACP would come to their rescue." [12]

Patiently Barbara outlined the plan. She told the students that the jail was not big enough to hold them all and that, as long as they stayed together, none would be punished. They were to carry the placards that had been made for the occasion or go inside the classrooms and sit without opening their books. This was to continue until further notice. The students were to stay on the school grounds, away from downtown, so that they would not get into trouble with police. If they were asked why they were not in school, they were to say that they were not in school because of unequal facilities. The student committee would get in touch with the school superintendent and present the students' demands. [13] Stokes recalls that Barbara expressed her doubts to the students that the meeting with McIlwaine would prove fruitful and said that in the event that it did not a court suit might have to be filed. [14]

Barbara says that she did not have anything like a desegregation suit in mind. It was later, she remembers, in a meeting of the student committee in the library, that the idea of getting in touch with the NAACP came up: "It never entered my mind at that time that this would turn out to be a school desegregation suit. We didn't know of such things. We were thinking that the school would be improved, or at best, that we would get a new school." [15]

The students began by passing up their lunch hour, a gesture of determination that Barbara found significant and encouraging. The sequence of events of the day becomes blurred in the minds of the participants after this. But there were at least two telephone calls. One was to Mr. Griffin, who was summoned to the school and found student leaders behind locked doors: "They wanted to ask me one question, just one question. There was one boy who dissented, he went against the idea. All he said was that they should get the consent of their parents, and the others disagreed. They wanted me to advise them on this, and I advised them to take a vote among themselves. They did and all but this one boy voted against telling their parents first. . . . I don't know why the students called me, maybe because of what I had been preaching." [16]

Whatever reason for calling the preacher, the students found him entirely sympathetic to their cause. The charge was to be heard later that Griffin was a conscious agent in developing the plot that led to the strike. He denies this but concedes that he helped the students in every way possible once it had occurred. Principal Jones, too, is accused of having foreknowledge of the strike. He, too, denies the accusation but admits that, once he returned to the school and found the students in charge and many of the teachers in sympathy with them, he made up his mind not to interfere. At the same time, he was determined to try to fulfill his legal obligations to the school board. [17]

Jones notified Superintendent McIlwaine of what had happened. McIlwaine recalls Jones's mentioning a "rebellion" at the school that had got out of hand. [18] Gradually, the white and Negro communities began to learn that something unusual had happened at Moton.

The Moton students were enjoying themselves. Stokes recalls that many of them regarded the entire business lightly, as a good time, some excitement. Others busied themselves carrying the placards that had been made in shop earlier, and in making others. The placards proclaimed "We Want a New School or None At All," "We Are Tired of Tar Paper Shacks—We Want a New School," and "Down with the Tar Paper Shacks." [19]

The student committee failed to get an appointment with Superintendent McIlwaine that day. Several of the boys trooped over to School Board Chairman Large's office in the Farmville Manufacturing Company Building. Large met them and talked with them: "I told them I was not disposed to discuss it until they went back to school. I told them that nobody could promise them exactly when they would get a school because we had to promote a bond issue. I said 'My advice to you is to go back to school, nobody will talk to you about it until you do.'" [20]

Stokes recalls that a committee of three visited McIlwaine early the next day and was told that students could not use the school buses unless they planned to attend classes. A meeting between McIlwaine and the full student committee was to take place that afternoon. [21]

It is generally agreed that this meeting was inconclusive, that McIlwaine refused to talk terms until the students returned to classes, and that the committee refused to discuss going back to classes without assurances that their new school would be built. Stokes recalls that McIlwaine spoke of school conditions as greatly improved since his youth and Barbara answered "that it was a modern world, and we would appreciate growing with it." [22] Stokes also remembers that McIlwaine pointed out that the teachers at the school would lose their jobs if the students did not return.

Possibly the way in which the meeting was held meant more than anything that was said in it. The meeting was held in the courthouse, on Main Street, in Farmville. More than anything that was said, Barbara remembers the sensation of going to the meeting. She writes: "Our trek from the school to the courthouse did not go unnoticed, for the white people of the town swarmed out of their business establishments to watch and whisper. For this I give them credit—there was no jeering or unseemly conduct on their part. And as for us—you should have seen us, in our youthful wisdom pretending to be quite dignified and oblivious of all stares, for we did not want to appear immature, unruly and unintelligent. We found in Mr. Thomas J. McIlwaine a timid and evasive person who refused to be pinpointed by any question and who failed to look us directly in the face throughout the whole session. This . . . gave us courage however, and we bombarded him with zillions of questions about what his intentions were regarding our school situation. He first tried reasoning (his version), then he threatened us with expulsion, etc., but we refused to give in." [23]

McIlwaine is a slender wisp of a man with a nervous habit of looking away from strangers as he speaks to them. He had reason to be particularly nervous that day, for he was torn between his convictions and the necessities. He was a faithful servant of the public school system. He had worked for improvements in the Prince Edward and Cumberland systems for almost thirty-five years. A missionary's son, born in Japan but educated at Hampden-Sydney in the county and a life-long public servant in the county, he was well aware of the needs at Moton High School. Some part of his sympathies had to be behind any protest against the status quo in the education of the Negro. Yet his job required that he deal with the strike firmly.

And he was not sympathetic with the strike. He did not believe that it was an impulse emanating from the students at all, but a planned agitation. He placed the blame for this on Principal M. Boyd Jones: "I felt that the whole thing was rigged. The year before Jones had very nearly gotten fired for criticizing the school board in my presence. We had him in with Maurice Large, and he apologized on this occasion. He was always complaining. It was clear to me that he was behind this strike." [24]

The appearance and behavior of the student committee merely convinced McIlwaine that he was right. The questions they asked were, to him, those that "someone obviously told them to ask." He remembers: "They came into my office. . . . There were twelve or fifteen of them, too many to fit in here (that was why we went upstairs to the courtroom). . . . I was disgusted because I felt it was obviously a put-up job. . . . There wasn't any question of Jones's being able to control them. . . . They asked me why they couldn't go to Farmville High School and I said that it was just a matter of Virginia statute law. . . . I told them I couldn't tell them the consequences of what they were going to do." [25]

McIlwaine told them also that a new Moton High School would be built but that he could not give them a date.

The meeting was certain to be a failure from the start. Barbara had warned the student committee not to be moved by such blandishments as promises of a new school in the indefinite future.[26] Yet this was all that McIlwaine could promise, short of committing the community to approve a bond issue and setting the date himself. The students stamped out, their resolve hardening.

They had some reason to feel the blood of defiance by this time. They were not alone. The National Association for the Advancement of Colored People had been notified and had promised to look in. Whatever else might happen, the strike would not be stamped out contemptuously as the plaything of children.

There is some confusion about how first contact with the NAACP was made. Student leaders agree that a letter was written. Barbara writes that this decision was made in a meeting of the student leaders in the school library after the auditorium meeting about the strike Monday: "We had heard of lawyer Spottswood Robinson, of Richmond, Virginia, and decided to ask for his advice. Let me say at this point that we did not foresee the end results of our demonstrations such as the intervention of the NAACP, integration, etc. We only knew that we wanted better school conditions than we had. Carrie Stokes drafted and wrote the letter to Lawyer Robinson, and she and I signed it and mailed it." [27]

The letter was probably written on Monday as Barbara remembers. This part of the story does jibe with the version told in court later by Oliver Hill, then associated with Spottswood Robinson in Richmond. Hill testified: "On a Monday afternoon, I got a telephone call that some students in Farmville stated that they had gone out on a strike and they wanted me to come down there immediately. We were in a conference on a case that had gone to the Court of Appeals involving the situation at Pulaski County. We had to go back to Pulaski on that day. I told them I couldn't come down there. Over the phone, I suggested that they go on to school. But I said, 'If you are not going back to school, write me a letter and I will let you know when I can get down there.' I got a letter from them the next day. We got in touch with them, told them we would be in Farmville that Wednesday on our way to Pulaski." [28]

But what about the telephone call? Hill says that he is sure that it was from a student, a girl. He had thought it was from Barbara Johns. Barbara does not recall that any telephone call was made and is sure that she did not make one. There is no doubt that Hill is correct in his dates—that the call did originate on strike Monday—for it is charged to Moton High School on the school board's records for that date.

Hill testified that he told the student who telephoned to go back to school. In an interview later, Hill added some comment: "The child wanted me to come up there right away. . . . We had gotten the call in the library of our office where we were working on the Pulaski case. . . . I told the child I couldn't possibly do that. . . . I didn't consider the situation serious at that time." [29]

On Wednesday, Hill, Robinson, Dean Thomas H. Henderson of Virginia Union, and a teacher at Union started out for Pulaski County via Prince Edward County. As they drove, they listened to news of the strike on the car radio. Hill testified later, "We were talking about these children being out on strike and we were fully of the opinion that we were going to advise them to go on back to school because at that time the Clarendon County case had already been filed. . . ." [30]

Oliver Hill was no stranger to Prince Edward County. He testified in court that he had been to the county several times since the end of World War II to look into conditions at Moton. He said that he knew the Moton students were up against a "most deplorable situation." [31]

He recalls contacts in the county going back further than that: "Back in 1940–41 I worked on a citizens' committee on teachers' salaries. We had to work through a committee because the teachers wouldn't stand up for themselves. It was too easy for them to be fired. Once we got the salaries equalized, we attacked the problem of facilities. . . . I had to do the speaking then. As a result, when I came out of the army, the citizens called on me. We went before the school board a couple of times. This was in 1946–47. They told us they had no money to build schools. I had seen the overcrowded conditions at the Moton High School. I remember . . . those temporary buildings, with the drums for stoves; they couldn't help getting overheated, and they were a fire hazard all right." [32]

Hill was prepared for the situation in Prince Edward County that had caused the Moton insurrection. How, then, could he say that he and Robinson intended to ask the students to return to school?

One reason was that they did not know what kind of leadership was present in the Negro community. The strike itself sounded from afar like an angry and momentary reaction to an old problem rather than a serious turning of intention in a new direction. Hill's recollection of county leadership was that of the old guard: "In very few of the counties would you find people you would regard as militant. Most of them were long-suffering, just wanted to get some relief. . . . It was when the younger group came along that this all changed." [33]

Would the Moton students and, most important, their parents, be interested in fighting a long, fatiguing duel in the courts, not for a new Negro school but for integration?

Hill doubted that the answer to this question would be positive. Yet this definitely was the question to be asked in April, 1951. For the advent of the Prince Edward case almost coincided with a change in policy at the heart of the NAACP's legal strategy. For years, this strategy had consisted of striking hard blows for equalization of education facilities, partly to make the South pay dearly for segregation and partly to find out what the courts would say. NAACP leadership in the state made Virginia a testing ground for these equalization suits. Hill, who was later to become an official in the Federal Housing Agency in the Kennedy Administration, was a highly competent attorney and a man of strong will. Spottswood Robinson, his law partner and another native Virginian, was regarded as one of the ablest men before the Virginia bar. Robinson, himself destined for the deanship of the Howard Law School and later a seat on the federal appellate bench, remembers the line of argument the equalization cases necessitated: "Prior to June, 1950, in appearances before a court or a school board, I would never admit the validity of state-enforced segregation, and I would never argue that segregation per se was unconstitutional. . . . I can remember this much about the period. It put a lawyer in the position where he can't concede it but he wouldn't argue it. . . ." [34]

Disillusionment with the results of the equalization suits in Virginia set in early in spite of the successful prosecution of four of them between 1947 and 1950. Hill remembers that "a lot of us didn't know much in the beginning. In the early days I felt that as soon as we got equal buildings we would be all right. But about that time [1948] a survey was made by a prominent group in Washington, D. C., where they actually had two school systems and where if there could be equality with segregation it would show up. The survey showed that inequalities were gross. . . . Later we tried a number of equalization suits around different places. It was quite obvious that we were going around in circles and not accomplishing anything. . . . We were learning that we might get a new building but we still ended up with inferior facilities." [35]

By 1950 the NAACP's unhappiness was taking the form of more vigorous attacks on the old concept of "equal." In May, 1950, Robinson shook the school board of Cumberland County, Virginia, next door to Prince Edward, with an approach to "equality" in education that seemed to reach across the lines of segregation. In a stormy meeting in the Cumberland County courthouse, an irate board member threatened to "shoot the first" Negro child who tried to enroll in a white school.[36]

That same month the NAACP filed suit in Clarendon County, South Carolina, for educational facilities "equal in all respects" to those afforded white elementary school students. Could there be equality "in all respects" short of desegregation?

In June the Supreme Court went a long way towards answering that question in the negative. In a key case, the court held that Heman Sweatt, a Negro applicant for law school at the University of Texas, was justified in refusing to attend a segregated "law school" set up by the university for him alone. Chief Justice Frederick M. Vinson wrote: "In terms of the number of the faculty, variety of courses and opportunity for specialization, size of the student body, scope of the library, availability of law review, and similar activities, the University of Texas Law School is superior. What is more important, the University of Texas Law School possesses to a far greater degree those qualities which are incapable of objective measurement but which make for greatness in a law school. Such qualities, to name but a few, include reputation of the faculty, experience of the administration, position and influence of the alumni, standing in the community, tradition, and prestige." [37]

What Negro graduate school that the South might build would be equal to the old, established, segregated white university in "reputation of the faculty" or "standing in the community?" The answer was plain. The *New York Times* observed that "By the Supreme Court's yardstick there is not a single state-owned Negro school in the South that can measure up to similar white schools." [38]

The challenge was not just to graduate schools or to higher education, but to segregated public education itself. The NAACP did not dawdle. Before the end of the month a conference of NAACP attorneys in New York drafted a resolution calling for a shift of emphasis. Henceforth there would be suits for desegregation in education rather than equalization. The resolution was ap-

proved by presidents of state conferences at the association's
forty-first annual convention in Boston that month and by the
national board of directors in October.[39] By that time the Clarendon County case was being recognized as one for desegregation
of public schools.

Virginia's vigorous NAACP leaders wanted to send a public
school desegregation case up to the Supreme Court from their
state. But in April, 1951, it seemed to them that the case in
Pulaski, originally a suit for equalization, would fill the bill nicely.
Robinson and Hill were preoccupied with their thoughts of the
Pulaski case, which was destined to fall apart with the death of
the plaintiff. W. Lester Banks, executive secretary of the State
NAACP chapter, speaks of the Prince Edward case as something
that an "act of providence" [40] threw into their laps. On the morning of Wednesday, April 25, 1951, as Robinson, Hill, and Dr. Henderson drove to Pulaski via Prince Edward, they were oblivious
of the turn destiny would force them to make. Robinson remembers the trip: "We rode to Pulaski in Tom's [Dr. Henderson's]
car and we didn't think enough of the Farmville business even to
mention it to him until shortly before we got to Farmville. I don't
think Dr. Henderson even got out of the car. . . . I remember
that we had telephoned and finally reached one of the children
and advised them in this way to be sure to bring their parents.
. . . I had a horror of talking to a group of these kids with no
adults around. . . ." [41]

The attorneys arrived in Farmville between 9 A.M. and 10 A.M.
and went to the basement of the First Baptist Church, where Mr.
Griffin had arranged for space.

The church basement is a dark, dank place on sunless days. A
portrait of the founder hangs on the gray plaster wall at the
back of the room. There is a battered and ancient piano on a
platform raised above the concrete floor. An American flag hangs
over the podium. A potbellied stove obtrudes on the floor space,
which is sufficient to seat about two hundred. On this morning
the cheerless basement was nearly filled with students and some
parents.

Robinson recalls something of what transpired: "I asked one
of them [a student] what he would do if they didn't get a new
school, and he said they would just stay out of school. I pointed
out to them that there were attendance laws. That was when one
of them, I can't remember now which one, said that the jail was

not big enough for all of us. . . . It was apparent to us that they were not listening to anybody at this point. I think that the parents were taken aback too. I remember that they didn't seem to have any specific objective. We told them to think it over. . . . By April 1, 1951, my thinking on the cases was very clear, and we said plainly that we would be interested in nothing short of a desegregation suit. . . . What made us go ahead was the feeling that someone would have to show them something before they would go back to school." [42]

The two attorneys said that they could not be present at the mass meeting set for the following night because they were bound for Pulaski and would be there at the time of the meeting. But they were impressed with what they had seen. The students had not winced when they were told that the NAACP would enter the case only if they were interested in suing for desegregation. The big question was how the parents would react. Hill sums it up: "They [the students] handled themselves so well and their morale was so high that we didn't have the heart to say no. We said if their parents would support them we would back them up." [43]

John Stokes remembers that Hill and Robinson said the support of 95 per cent of the parents would be necessary, for the fight would be a long, hard one. [44] With some pride, Stokes guessed that his parents would support the strikers. But what of the others? How would an older generation of Prince Edward Negroes react to the brash plans of youth?

This is George Morton, farmer: tall and straight with powerful arms and the cracked, lumpy hands of a man who grapples with the outdoors. His farm—it is only a mile and a half from the farm he remembers from his youth—is in a heavily Negro farming community of Prince Edward County, southwest of Farmville, off Route 15 behind Hampden-Sydney College. He remembers: "No, we didn't have no year's school, more three months' school, more like three months. You'd go until you felt like you got enough learning and then you'd quit. Some of them, they was twenty years old and still in school. I stayed in school 'till I was sixteen, then I quit because this friend of mine wanted me to go to work on the railroad with him.

"We was living on a farm not far from here, back off the main road, and the school was about a mile, maybe a mile and a half

from there back down from Triumph Church, Baptist church.
. . . The farm was a pretty big one. Farms those days pretty big.
Sharecroppers sometimes had two families, three families on a
farm. . . . There was nine of us children, and I was the middle
one—four sisters and four brothers, and I was the middle one.

"Well, there was first reading, second reading, third reading,
fourth, fifth reading, then history. . . . School didn't hardly
start 'till November after harvest. I reckon it was about a mile
and a half's walk. Bad weather? Oh you would go to school then,
that's when you would go 'cause there was less to do on the farm.

"Inside, well there was a chair for the teacher, benches for the
children. There was a kerosene lamp if you needed light. . . .
The students would come in of an evening late and put wood in
the stove for the morning, just an iron stove, potbellied I guess
you'd call it. . . . It was a frame building. One-room school.
Sometimes had two classes going at once. . . . I don't recollect
the school was called anything, could have been Triumph
School. . . . We'd get there nine in the morning, turned loose
about four in the afternoon. . . . Sure, carry lunches, maybe in a
pail, big pail with enough food for five or six children: oh, sweet
potatoes, sometimes baked sweet potatoes, biscuit, yeah, called
it hoecake, beans, boiled meat sometimes. . . . The teachers were
getting around eighteen dollars a month best I remember. You
could make more money farming than teaching. . . . Teacher,
when he took a notion, he's send out for a dogwood switch, send
one of the children out after it. . . . There was a blackboard, oh
yeah. It was a wooden blackboard painted black. Hung from
ropes against the wall and we used crayons on it, easy to wipe
off. We had slate and slate pencil. . . . No, I don't remember no
library or dictionary. There was a map on the wall, think it was a
map of—United States map, I think.

"Well, we'd wear what they call brogan shoes to school, actually no more than a low quarter shoe, had to last all winter. . . .
Dance 'em out, run 'em out, but that's all for the winter. Overalls,
we wore, called 'em 'mammy-made' overalls. . . . Some Madison
people lived back from the school and we'd have to go back there,
maybe half a mile, to get water. . . . Had an outdoor john. . . .

"At the end of the year we'd have speeches and dialogues.
Called 'em dialogues, children would stand up and read various
parts. There'd be a dinner on the grounds when the school closed,
and the parents would bring the food. In this dialogue I was a

doctor, and the woman had a sick child and the baby had eaten this cake. I'd take the cake and I'd take a bite. Then I'd take another. Third time I'd take the cake and I'd taken down and slipped the cake into my pocket. 'Doctor, where's the cake?' she'd say. 'Oh I just did it for the baby's sake,' I'd say.

"No, I don't remember any diplomas or the like. Guess it was because everybody went as far as they wanted to go. Sometimes until they were twenty or so. I remember I'd done got up into history when I quit. . . . Quit to go to work on the railroad." [45]

George Morton is not a sharecropper, as was his father before him. He has owned the land he works for forty-five years. The land and the frame house in which he and his wife live have long ago been paid for, and now what is earned from tobacco and corn is clear. It is not much in terms of money, but it is clear. This is important to George Morton at sixty-four years of age. This fact and the memories of the crackerbox, one-room school behind Triumph Church are necessary to an understanding of how George and Emma Morton reacted the night of April 23, 1951.

Emma Morton's life and the lives of her children follow a familiar pattern of the rural, Southern Negro. She was born in Prince Edward County on a farm not far from that of her husband's family. In sixty-five years she has left the county only to visit. But her five children spread out from Virginia. One daughter, Grace, went to New York to get work, and she wrote back about the integrated schools and the different way of life. She stayed in New York, but with the fading of the first glow of release from the tight pattern of segregation, the laudatory letters ceased. Her daughter came back to Prince Edward to go to school. Like Barbara Johns, another daughter of the Southern Negro out-migration, Grace's daughter, Joy Morton Cabarrus, returned to the rural county in which her mother, but not she, was born.[46] Her coming back was less a social than an economic comment: the Negro female, who could rise to secretarial or teaching ranks and command good salaries in the North, remained there while as many dependents as possible were returned to the South, to live cheaply with relatives.

Joy Morton was enrolled in Moton. She was not one of the leaders of the strike. She found out what was going on along with most of the other students on the morning of April 23. Her grandparents found out about it along with the majority of parents on the afternoon of April 23. Mrs. Morton remembers her own reaction: "At first I didn't know what to think. Then when I heard a suit might be filed I didn't think that was right. But after they explained to us why they did it, I did think it was right. The children got so far ahead of the parents, they didn't have anything to say to us. . . ." [47]

It was this phenomenon—the surprise and pride and even chagrin in the adult ranks at the action of the children—that Griffin had to deal with. The community leaders he could count on had to be encouraged; the uncertain supporters like Mrs. Morton had to be rallied; the doubtful ones had to be swayed.

Griffin had reacted to the strike with a joyful reflex of action. Some of the other Negro leaders in the community found the action of the students difficult to assess. John Lancaster, for one, remembers being doubtful: "I was definitely behind the students but it was such a shock to me . . . . It was hard for me to realize that this community was as aroused as it was. . . . It had been my feeling that a two-year campaign to get voters registered was the next thing we should do. . . ." [48]

Mr. Griffin says that he would have agreed with the need for a gradual campaign before the strike. But, after avowing that he knew nothing of the student's plans until the strike had begun, he goes on to call the strike the best thing that could have happened to the Negro community. On the afternoon of the strike, he borrowed a car and set out into the county to talk to his congregation and any other Negroes who would listen. He was still at it that night. At last he had found some positive use for his reputation as a preacher: "Everybody was up with their kids. Parents were being asked to sign petitions for support. I went into some homes as late as twelve, or one, or two o'clock in the morning and people were still up. . . . From then on, I covered some miles. I stayed in the dust and the pines with other folks' cars. . . ." [49]

Prince Edward, like most rural Southern counties, has many Negro communities. Pockets of Negro habitation are scattered around town in willy-nilly integration. Along the dirt roads that lead off main highways to Rice, Prospect, Green Bay, and other of the communities of the county, different patterns occur. In most instances Negro farms end abruptly with the appearance of the first white farmhouse. Unless he sees the farm operators, the visitor may not be able to tell when this happens, but there will be no more Negro farms after this first white one. Yet in many of these districts, Negro and white farm owners live across the high-way from each other, and in all of them the deeply interlaced relationships of renter, tenant, and owner frustrate any real seg-regation.

The communities are similar but not alike. The Darlington Heights and Prospect areas, for instance, could be counted on by Mr. Griffin for heavy support for the strike. The Green Bay area, on the other hand, would be on the weak side. Community leadership was part of the answer, but it is also true that some areas of the county have a higher proportion of Negro tenant farmers—heavily dependent upon whites—than do others.

From the best of the county Negro leadership would come the strongest support for the strike. The Negroes in town worked at the sawmill or elsewhere directly in the white man's employ, where they were vulnerable to economic intimidation. But the Negroes who owned their own land, the George Mortons with a pride of ownership as expansive as their means were limited— these were the backbone of Negro Prince Edward.

They existed in considerable number. The history of the Negro in Prince Edward is as old as that of the white man, and many Prince Edward Negroes come from families with antecedents far back in the history of the county. Negroes were settled in Prince Edward with the early claims in the mid-seventeenth century. The Negroes (almost seventeen to one of them slaves) became numerically predominant in the county in the early nineteenth century and remained so until the Civil War and emancipation.[50] In the mid-nineteenth century, the county had the largest popu-lation of free Negroes in the state. In recent years it has been generally true that just over half of the county is white and just over half the school population is Negro. The farm census of 1950 showed that there were nearly as many Negro farm operators (600) as white (740). Not 2 out of 10 farmers in the county were tenants.[51]

So the Negro farmer of Prince Edward tended to be reason-ably independent. He owned his property, was in the process of buying it, or could rely on family to the extent that this livelihood did not depend on the approbation of the white community. He did not vote in great numbers, in spite of the lack of concerted effort to prevent him, but he was not a hireling to an alien system.

These were men like P. H. Shepperson, of Green Bay, a "short coat" preacher—a man who, in the words of an old deacon of his community, has no license but plenty of " 'victions." Mrs. Shepperson recalled much later how her husband reacted when their three children came home from Moton that day. Lester, the eldest, broke the news. She relates that "that same evening he came home and he told his daddy, 'Daddy, we've done something today and I don't know whether you approve of it or not.' We naturally thought it was mischief of some kind, and his daddy said, 'What did you do?' and Lester said, 'We struck today, Daddy,' and his daddy said, 'What do you mean struck?' and Lester said, 'We struck for a better school.' 'Who told you to?' 'Nobody, we don't know whether we done the right thing or not.' His daddy said, 'I think it's the right thing,' and he said, 'Well we feel better about it, Daddy, and we're not going back. Daddy, we think some of the parents are going to make the children go back.' 'Well, I'm not going to make you go back. . . .' " [52]

Barbara Johns wrote much later in a general way about the reaction of the parents: "I think indeed this account would not be complete if I failed to mention the pride I had in the parents (and others) who supported us. They were at first bewildered by it all—but they attended the meetings in full strength. . . . They stood behind us—timidly at first but firmly. I would like to say at this point that if you are wondering how my parents reacted to my part in these events, they did so without noticeable pride or knowledge of any existing change. My mother worked away at the time, and my father says he is never surprised at anything I do." [53]

Mrs. Johns had returned to her government job in Washington. Barbara wrote her of the plan to strike, and before she could answer with her approval, the strike had begun. The reaction of other student leaders' parents was various. John Stokes's parents supported the strike idea actively and enthusiastically. James Samuel Williams' mother was opposed. The majority lay between. In the struggle for supremacy, the balance may have been tipped by the pride the parents had for the responsible, thoughtful way in which the students had staged their protest.

Barbara went first to her Grandmother Croner with the news. Mrs. Croner remembers: "She came up to the house that evening. When she came in, she said, 'Grandma, I walked out of school this morning and carried 450 students with me.' Took my breath

away. I said, 'You reckon you done the right thing?' 'I believe so,'
she say. She say, 'Stick with us.' She say, 'Put your name on this
paper,' and mine was the third name on the paper, and I asked
her what she was going to do, and she said, 'We're going to carry
that paper from home to home, twenty of us. . . .' " [54]

Mrs. Croner thought of her own childhood and what she called
the "daily hardships" of her race. She remembered her own bitter reaction to this: "I done a right much reading and I'd repeat
some things that I wanted to say, out in the trees. . . . No, I
wasn't always angry when I went out there. I would very often
just say for my people, but I would speak out and pretend the
trees was listening. . . . Part of the time I was angry, yes, every
chance I would get I would get away and speak for my people,
justice for my people. . . . I continued to do that until I got
grown and married. Then I hoped my children would pick up
this speaking. . . . Well, I was married and had nine children,
five boys and four girls. Violet, Barbara's mother, was the second
oldest. Seven of them went through high school and one to
college. . . . Napoleon, now, he became a preacher but that
wasn't it. All had good jobs but still I didn't hear no speaking. I
gave the speaking up, left it off my mind. . . ." [55]

John Stokes remembers that the students were interested in
finding out how many of the parents would support them. Adult
advice they had sought impressed upon them the need for support of the entire community. Mr. Griffin made this point, and it
was reinforced by Robinson and Hill on Wednesday. John Stokes
recalls that early in the week the signatures indicated to the
students that something like 65 per cent of the parents were with
them, 10 per cent were neutral, and about 25 per cent were
opposed. [56]

Those opposed included Willie Redd, who says that he was
out of the county quite often during this period and did not
attend the PTA meetings before or during the strike. He takes
the position that the children, as minors, had no business insti-
tuting the action: "The parents should have done it. . . . I
guess they didn't because they had been turned down so often.
. . . I didn't think the children had any business striking. . . . I
don't like the word strike anyway. It's a demand. Some men
working for me strike, and I wouldn't think much of that, so I
don't think much of it when others do it. . . . Working with the
people I work with—I don't like to use the term white Southerners

but we know what I mean. . . . I have to depend a lot on approach. It's all in what kind of approach is used. . . . No, I don't think the approach was right."[57]

Another who was out of sympathy with what was going on was J. B. Pervall, who had been principal of Moton High School when it turned out its first graduates in 1931. He had remained principal of the school until 1943. At the time of the strike he was teaching at the A. G. Richardson School in Nottoway County. He heard about the strike over the radio and made up his mind to scout around Farmville, where he still lived, to see how people felt. He had some advice for those who would listen: "I told then that if they wanted to go in for a new school I would help them, but not integration."[58]

On Thursday night, April 26, the auditorium at Moton was packed with an estimated one thousand students and parents. This was the meeting that Hill and Robinson could not attend. W. Lester Banks, the state NAACP secretary was there, however, and Richmond papers covering the meeting leave little doubt that those who did attend understood that they were approving whatever action the NAACP saw fit to take to end segregation in the county's schools. The NAACP was requested by those present "to intervene in the matter," one paper reported. Banks's speech underscored the point. He told the audience that bulged from the high school auditorium where the strike had begun only three days earlier that a new school would not mean equality "if it were built brick for brick, cement for cement."[59]

Banks remembers that only one man in the audience rose to speak out against the new NAACP approach. This man, Banks said, felt that the students should have told their parents about their strike plans before they carried them out. Banks remembers his reply: "I told him as a parent I felt some agreement but that I was glad they didn't because if they had told their parents there wouldn't have been a strike."[60]

The man who had risen to question Banks was Fred Reid, one of the members of the more conservative wing of the Negro community. Five years later, Reid recalled his role: "At the first meeting called by the parents at R. R. Moton old school in May [sic], 1951, I sat as long as I could. After listening to many speakers on the floor, Mr. Lester Banks stated his condition of being here. He said that the reason he was here was because he was asked to be present. I arose to the floor addressing the chair.

'I have been listening to all who have spoken. I hope I will not be interrupted.' He said 'Proceed.' 'The first thing I want to know have your parents prayed over this matter, concerning the boys and girls who went on strike for a better school building. . . . The best thing for this body to do is to appoint twenty men and women from this meeting and meet the school board and tell them what we want. If they refuse the committee of twenty men and women, then we will put up a fight to the finish. . . . And if you go further than equal facilities count me out.' They would not listen. They wanted integrated schools. Now I know some who wish they had took my advice. The NAACP did not take any case on equal facilities. Mr. Banks said they take them on integration. So from that point the battle between the NAACP and Prince Edward County began, 1951." [61]

In view of the newspaper reports of Banks's speech, Reid's recollections, and the clear memory of a number of others who were present, it is strange that rumors persisted years later that some of the Negro plaintiffs who had signed the school desegregation suit were tricked into this action under the impression that they were seeking a new Negro school. The *Richmond Times-Dispatch* found some who would testify to this effect two years later.[62] The only explanation that makes sense is that in later years, discouraged by the slow processes of the law or elated by the completion of the new Negro high school, some of the original plaintiffs had lost account of their original intentions.

Hill and Robinson filed suit asking for desegregation of Pulaski High School on April 30. On that same day a mimeographed letter appeared in Prince Edward County over the signature of Principal Jones and members of the Moton staff. It arrived in the mail at the homes of patrons of Moton and was widely distributed elsewhere: "We, the staff members of Moton High School, have been authorized by the division superintendent to write this letter to you appealing to you to send your children back to school. As we stated to them last Monday, April 23, this was a very serious step to take. There are grave consequences which must be suffered by those who persist in violating the compulsory attendance law. . . . Aside from the fact that students remaining from school may incur punishment to themselves and their parents, it puts them at a tremendous disadvantage in their scholastic work and creates the wrong impression. . . ." [63]

The letter was distributed widely and swiftly. Out in Green
Bay, Mrs. Shepperson remembers getting it and reading it. Then,
she says, "I put it in the stove." [64]

But Mr. Griffin received a copy and realized that the letter
could divide the Negro community badly. He suspected that the
unanimity expressed at the meetings was more an expression of
the community's pride for the children and its desire for improvements in education than a total endorsement of the strike and the
NAACP goals. More work had to be done. He later said, "Of
course he [Jones] sympathized with the strike. . . . When I read
the letter he had sent, I knew it meant trouble. Jones had a lot of
influence, and I knew that a lot of people would send their
children back to school. So it had to be a test of influence at that
point. I got out a letter that very same day." [65]

Griffin mailed the mimeographed letter in a single big batch
at the Farmville Post Office. John Lancaster says that he ran into
Griffin and helped him mail off the letters. He traces many of his
future troubles to having been seen in the post office with Griffin
on this occasion. [66]

Griffin was afraid that the Jones letter would turn the will of
the Negro community and bring pressure to bear on the parents
who had signed authorizations. Griffin decided to call another
meeting while enthusiasm was still high. His announcement was
headed: "This letter is relative to the emergency at the Robert
R. Moton High School." It read:

> The National Association for the Advancement of
> Colored People has been requested to take action in this
> matter, and its attorneys are now working on the problem.
> You are requested to keep your children absent from the
> Robert R. Moton High School until you are further ad-
> vised to send them back to school. In making this request
> we are following the advice of our attorneys and no
> changes should be made in our plans until our attorneys
> advise us to make them. We must all co-operate fully to
> get results and this request must be followed at all costs.
> An important emergency meeting of the county-wide
> PTA will be held on Thursday evening, May 3, 1951, at
> 8 P.M. at the First Baptist Church, South Main Street,
> Farmville, Virginia. It is important that as many parents
> and patrons as possible be present at this important meet-

ing. Our attorneys, Hill, Martin, and Robinson will be
present to meet you and discuss with you the procedure
necessary for securing your constitutional rights.

It is necessary that all of us support the efforts being
made to get our just rights. We shall expect you to be
present and to bring others with you.

REMEMBER. The eyes of the world are on us. The intelligent support we give our cause will serve as a stimulant
for the cause of free people everywhere.

WE SHALL EXPECT YOU TO COMPLY WITH OUR REQUEST,
AND TO BE PRESENT AT THE FIRST BAPTIST CHURCH ON
THURSDAY EVENING MAY 3 AT 8:00 P.M.[67]

The division of opinion in the Negro community was in the
open. Whatever Principal Jones's desires, his words would be
given weight by some. J. B. Pervall, the former Moton principal
who opposed the strike, decided to go to the Thursday meeting:
"I felt that I had more than the ordinary right to be there as I had
been principal of the school so long. . . . all the parents had
been begging for a new school, and all the people I talked with
seemed to be leaning toward getting a new school. . . ."[68]

Mr. Griffin grubbed about the county and concluded that there
were few hesitators who could not be swung over in one, rousing
meeting. He was ready to play out his test of influence.

On Thursday, May 3, the firm of Hill, Martin, and Robinson,
representing some thirty students, petitioned the school board to
end segregation in county schools. Hill was quoted as saying
that with the Pulaski County case and the Prince Edward County
case, Negro leaders were changing their emphasis from "equal
facilities" to "abolition of segregation."[69]

With the authorizations for a suit secured, the meeting took
on the nature of a rally. Its purpose was to affirm publicly that
the Negro community stood together. Failure here could be ruinous for Griffin and the NAACP.

The church was "jam-packed," according to newspaper reports.[70] There were other speakers, but Barbara was the one most
mentioned in accounts the next day. She cited the student complaints against the shacks and spoke at length about efforts of
students to correct the situation.

But the meeting took its character from the results of the one
effort to turn back the tide. Spottswood Robinson was in the act

of instructing the striking students to return to their classes when Pervall stood up to speak: "I was under the impression that the students were striking for a new building. You are pulling a heavy load, Mr. Robinson, coming down here to a country town like Farmville and trying to take it over on a non-segregated basis." [71]

The audience sat as though stunned. W. Lester Banks reminded them of action taken at a previous meeting supporting the NAACP. Robinson asked, " 'Are non-segregated schools what you want?' There was 'applause from all corners.' "

Then Barbara stood up to speak again. In a picture taken at this moment, her head is thrown back, and the expression on her face is of one come to power too young to have learned its discreet use. The cutlines describe her as "the little girl with the sun-kissed coffee colored skin," and the headline on the accompanying story is "No Toms Can Stop Us." The reporter noted tears in the eyes of some in the audience as Barbara spoke. She turned at last and fixed Joe Pervall in her gaze: "Don't let Mr. Charlie, Mr. Tommy, or Mr. Pervall stop you from backing us. We are depending upon you." [72]

Barbara had caught the dominant note of determination in the meeting. With her reference to the despised system of Negro accommodation of segregation summoned up by the terms "Mr. Charlie" and "Mr. Tommy," she had utterly disposed of Pervall's complaint. The applause said that the student leaders would get their support. John Stokes remembers that hearing one man speak, he suddenly had the feeling that the students would win their fight: "Maybe it was because of the resonance of his voice, but I had that feeling. Then, there were some who had never had their pictures taken before by photographers. It must have dawned on them that it was all going to come true." [73]

Robinson told the crowd that retaliation against the striking students would not be tolerated, and Hill, described as "face red, voice booming with a trace of bitterness," advised the crowd to get rid of the superintendent of schools as quickly as possible.

Griffin's was the last talk: "Mr. Pervall has a right to speak. . . . Anybody who would not back these children after they stepped out on a limb is not a man. Anybody who won't fight against racial prejudice is not a man. And to those of you who are here to take the news back to Mr. Charlie, take it—only take it straight." [74]

The meeting ended with the students vowing to return to

school Monday, May 7, and with the attorneys promising that unless they received a satisfactory answer from the school board by Tuesday, May 8, they would file suit in federal court seeking action enjoining the board from practicing segregation.

Nobody in attendance at the meeting was more impressed than Barbara's grandmother, Mrs. Croner. She thought back to her wish of earlier days: "That meeting I went to . . . when I saw Barbara up there I got real frightened. . . . I thought did she know what to say, could she make the words. . . . She had a microphone and I thought my goodness she don't know what to say. . . . Yes, she was good. The people in the audience were nodding and saying 'that's good.' I felt real good. It was the result of my speaking. It came to me that it was my grandchild who was carrying on the speaking. . . . It often came to me to wonder why such a speaking came to me. It did seem like an unseen vision coming to me. Well, after Barbara spoke out, I felt like it was a greater power than me. I felt that God had instilled in her what I was trying to do. . . . I was very happy to know that God had used me to that extent. . . ." [75]

M. Boyd Jones, the principal of Moton, was at the mercy of the storm forces loose in the community.

Jones was a native of Gloucester, Virginia, a graduate of Hampton Institute on the Virginia Peninsula, a Virginian who planned from earliest recollection to remain in the state. He had been appointed to the Moton job in 1947 and was generally regarded as a good administrator. Superintendent McIlwaine thought him the best principal Moton had ever had.

White officialdom of the county might have had some early reservations about Principal Jones if they had considered just what he was teaching. Jones had an idea that high school, at least for the Negro student, had to serve as a training ground for democracy, a preparatory school for students who—as the white South should have known—would find segregation intolerable sooner or later. Mr. Griffin commented: "Jones's school was the most democratic thing that ever happened among the Negroes around here. His students participated in the administration and were taught to think for themselves and criticize and ask questions." [76]

Jones himself says that social as well as traditional aspects of education interested him. He testified in court that he had introduced a course called "Consumer Buying." "It was my hope that these children would at least get some of the language that is in everyday usage with members of the other groups. Looking at it this way, the average Negro parent has had so little background with this sort of language, whereas, with white children it is common language in the family." [77]

There is no evidence that the school board knew, or cared, that Moton was attempting to perform some of the functions usually set aside for the parent in white society. The concept was not revolutionary, though, and many white educators who favored segregation in their public utterances approved. McIlwaine and Jones had a falling out over something else entirely.

McIlwaine later testified that Jones was thought to have made some rude remarks about the failure of the school board to improve conditions at the school. This was about a year before the strike. McIlwaine said that when he and Board Chairman Maurice Large conferred with Jones the latter said that he had not meant his remarks in the way they were interpreted.[78]

In his testimony Jones, too, touched on this incident. He said that he was called to McIlwaine's office and told that McIlwaine had heard that he was an agitator and would not be re-employed. Later, Jones said, McIlwaine told him there was nothing to the rumor.[79]

Jones did push hard from time to time in his effort to get some action taken on a new school. Dr. Miller, then a member of the Moton PTA, remembers that Jones's aggressiveness on this subject began as soon as he arrived. He went before the school board to ask for a better building.

Jones himself concedes that he was unhappy about Moton's facilities and about other aspects of the segregated educational system of Prince Edward County. He testified to conferences he had had with McIlwaine and others concerning possibilities of a new school. He complained that the bus scarcity made it necessary to conduct football practice and games during class hours, that there was no place for the boys to change clothes or take showers after practice, and that despite reports that money was available to renovate the Mary E. Branch Elementary School across the street, so that it could be used as a high school, nothing was being done.

Jones was particularly annoyed by what he took to be the permanently disabling discriminations. He said that the Farmville Town Council talked poor and scraped the bottom of the barrel for a one hundred dollar contribution to the Moton library, then produced three hundred dollars for the Farmville High School library: "They would always talk about the Negro tax contribution being so low. Yet they expected us to raise our incomes without improving education. It was like the Egyptians telling the Israelites to make bricks with no straw, to do the impossible. . . ." [80]

McIlwaine felt that Jones was a chronic complainer. Because he felt this way, when the strike occurred, McIlwaine believed that Jones was in some way involved in it.

Jones insists that he was one in the Negro community who always called for moderation and patience in dealing with the school board. He testified that on one occasion he talked the Moton PTA committee out of filing a court suit against the school board because he had a promise that within six months something would be done. "My position on it had always been that if you get things through co-operative participation and understanding, we would all profit by them, and when we got through there would be no scars left." [81]

The characterization of Jones as a man who believed that the school board would take some action to improve conditions at Moton, and who did not favor legal moves on the part of the Negro community, is one that is supported by other PTA members. The Reverend Francis Griffin is positive on this subject: "It seemed to be the belief of Boyd Jones that if the right men went to the board, they would get results. It's ironic that he got caught in the thing. Actually, he had faith in them." [82]

Jones insists that he knew nothing of the students' plans until he discovered them in assembly upon his return to the school that Monday morning. He does concede that he thought something was going on among the students some time before the strike took place. He remembers that they talked a good deal in school about the tar paper shacks and expressed resentment. [83]

Afterwards, when it seemed clear to him the students were going ahead with their plan, the principal may have reached some accommodation with his staff—some of whom may actually have been advising the children. He will not say anything about this matter. [84]

His own position was greatly complicated by the happenings of Monday, April 23. He had married Miss Inez Davenport, the teacher Barbara Johns was so fond of, whose remark had set Barbara to thinking about taking some action on the shacks. His wife was then pregnant, and Jones saw in the strike a serious threat to his own security. He was faced with the ugly choice of failing to support a cause he believed in or, very possibly, losing his job. "I had no money. I had some insurance and small investments but no cash. We hadn't saved much although my wife had been working, too. It was foolish, probably, but we were just married and enjoying it a little and there was no cause for concern. I was healthy, and the job looked as though it would last." [85]

This situation could possibly have been what caused him to react so sharply against the strikers when he burst in on their assembly that Monday morning. The students were aware of the delicacy of his position. John Stokes remembers that the students decided that if the principal were fired before June they would strike again. Barbara writes of one specific occasion when the principal had expressed to her his real feelings about the strike: "As I mentioned before, we all admired and respected him, and I must admit I was disappointed in his attitude and that he shattered my image of him as a strong man of excellent principles and I must have showed this—because on one occasion on which I was in his office he whispered to me under his breath 'Keep up the good work. I am behind you 100 per cent but I must not publicly acknowledge this.' " [86]

The attitude of McIlwaine and other white administrators towards Jones accounts for some of the acts performed and those left unperformed during the early days of the strike. McIlwaine, for instance, did not come to Moton on the day of the strike. Jones testified that he had called McIlwaine and that he had been left with the impression that the school superintendent would come to the school.[87] About an hour and fifteen minutes later, he said, McIlwaine called to tell him that he had talked to Large and that he would not be coming to the school. This decision was made in the face of Jones's statement to McIlwaine that he had been taken by surprise and was unable to cope with the situation. McIlwaine thought it was all a trick: "What Jones wanted was that I come over there and make a fuss over my being there and get me involved in it, and I wouldn't do it. I told him it was his problem." [88]

Officially, the school administration had determined to treat the strike as a disciplinary problem. Students would have to return to classes before their grievances would be discussed. This approach was based in part on the concept that the strike had been directed by Jones and could be ended by Jones. This misconception colored everything the school authorities did during these crucial weeks.

On Monday, a week after the strike had begun, Principal Jones got out the letter Superintendent McIlwaine had "suggested," urging the students to return to school. Jones had no desire to send the letter, and no alternative either: "When you're not your own boss you do things that you can't help. I knew perfectly well what the situation was. That was just so much busy work." [89]

The pressures on Jones now increased from both sides. The school board clearly expected him to stamp out the rebellion. He could not do this even if he wanted to. His friends among the Negro leadership expected him to hold the school board at bay by some means, or at least not to play an active part in ending the strike. Only in the latter course had he any hope of keeping his job and the respect of his friends at the same time.

But McIlwaine and Large and others became more convinced each day that Jones was heavily involved in what was happening at Moton. A multitude of details added up. Jones stayed at 421 Ely Street in the home of a Daniel Brown. Oliver Hill and Spottswood Robinson were seen at this house on their trips to Farmville. Large's office window looked out on Lancaster's county agent quarters, and Large saw Jones with Griffin and Lancaster from time to time. School buses were being used to transport striking students, at least once to Mr. Griffin's church. Students were carrying placards on school grounds, apparently at the principal's sufferance.

Given earlier suspicions of Jones, circumstantial evidence such as this was certain to receive great weight. Some time during the first week of the strike, Large recalls, he asked Jones to prepare a report to be submitted at a meeting on May 2. He asked Jones to get this report to him well in advance of the meeting so that he could study it. The report was to have been in Large's hands by noon on the day of the meeting. At 5 P.M. that day, Large says, Jones handed over the report, saying that it had been finished only moments before. The fact that the mimeograph ink was completely dry persuaded Large that the report had in fact been drawn up in Richmond by the NAACP and that Jones simply had not received it earlier.[90] Jones denies this categorically.

The meeting between Principal Jones and the school board ended with the principal's issuing a statement to the press: "The first thing is to get the students back to class. . . . [Their action] is a rebellion against existing school facilities and is deep-seated. . . . This thing was thought out by the students who planned the whole scheme of the rebellion. I have talked to individuals and groups and have not been able to find in any way, shape, or form, any outside individual who had anything to do with the plan of this thing." [91]

The emphasis Jones was making on the rebellion as an internal matter was not casual. The white community leaders had begun to think in terms of a great conspiracy from outside. They could not bring themselves to believe that the strike could have roots in Prince Edward County.

News of the strike spread slowly through the white community on Monday, April 23. The *Farmville Herald* is on the streets on Monday and Thursday, and although news for the early week edition can be taken as late as mid-afternoon on Monday, the strike did not make that paper.

Publisher J. Barrye Wall, Sr., does not remember clearly when the paper learned of the strike: "Maybe we hadn't heard about it. It happened out yonder on the hill and nobody paid any attention to it. We had no alert, no idea the children would strike . . . I don't believe we knew about it. . . ." [92]

But Wall concedes that the paper might have heard about the strike and still ignored the story for the next day: "We didn't take it very seriously. That's how naive we were." [93]

The metropolitan newspaper circulated in Prince Edward is the *Richmond Times-Dispatch*. The *Times-Dispatch* had nothing on the strike on Tuesday morning either, but it did have the first story of the strike on Wednesday morning.

The story set the tone for much of the official white reaction to the strike that was to follow. It described the walkout of 450 Moton students but devoted a good deal more space to a version of the background of the strike that came into routine usage as the years went by. It went this way: The Prince Edward School Board had an $800,000 school in the planning stage at the time of the strike. The school already had been approved by the State Board of Education as a part of a four-year program in the county that was to produce $1,925,000 for Negro schools and

$675,000 for white schools. An application for funds was all that stood between the school board and the new Moton school.

The casual reader of this story might well have wondered why the students had acted at all. A Negro reader in Prince Edward would have been even more puzzled. Nothing had been said in print about this $800,000 school for more than a year. Nothing had been said at any time about construction of the school being approved by the State Board of Education. The implication that all the county school board had to do was to apply for state funds ran directly counter to what the Moton PTA had been told. Insufficient state money was available, the school board had said. That is why the board had suggested a bond issue—which it was afraid to press at this time.

First reaction to the strike by whites in Prince Edward was mild. It was 1951, and the idea of desegregated public education had not taken command of the public consciousness in the South. Only gradually would the whites of Prince Edward realize the meaning of the strike. With this realization would come the creation of a demonology of Negro leaders. An editorial in the *Farmville Herald* on Friday referred to the strike as "apparently student-inspired mass hookie" [94] and blamed lax discipline in the school, home, and church. The phrase "student inspired" seemed to take the students at their word. The interesting thing about this editorial, in the light of what later happened in the county, is Editor Wall's reflex action in blaming much of modern society —white and black—and particularly public schools, for what had happened.

The *Herald*'s first news story that day established the official white view of the strike as "a breach of discipline." It also picked up the long-missing $800,000 figure, possibly from the *Times-Dispatch*. It confirmed that the new Moton school had been "approved" by the State Board of Education but said nothing about the need for an application for funds. The school would be financed with Battle Fund money, the story asserted. Nothing was said of the fact that this source would provide barely one-fourth of the money needed. [95]

Stories in the Richmond papers during the next few days bristled with ideas dropped off like sparks by the Moton students. There would be a parade through the streets of downtown Farmville. [96] There would be a canvass of white sentiment on "nonsegregation." [97] The first never happened. Moton students later denied that they planned to take a canvass, but John Stokes remembers it quite well.

About forty-five Moton students took part, he says. They may have talked with three or four whites apiece. They simply went up and down the streets ringing doorbells and asking white residents of Prince Edward County what they thought of "nonsegregation." He recalls that some said that they would not mind integration if it came gradually. Most said less, many would not answer the door. There was no trouble, no seriously aroused tempers. Stokes regards it all now as a curiously anachronistic tableau, as undoubtedly it was. The white community had no monopoly on naïveté in those days.[98]

By May 1, the *Herald* was referring to the student action as a strike and commenting on news reports suggesting that the strike was intended to eliminate segregation from the public schools. "We do not believe this has any foundation in fact. However the so-called 'student strike' appears to have outside stimulus. If that be true it is even more important that we remember the principles by which we have made progress . . . to work together in mutual understanding seeking the best for our people." [99]

The filing with the school board of the petition for desegregation brought the attention of Virginia officials. Governor John S. Battle, responding to the tests of segregated education raised in Pulaski and Prince Edward, warned that such action could injure the public school system.[100] The *Richmond Times-Dispatch* on May 6 observed that the petition seemed sure to make a court case and quoted an editorial in the Richmond *Afro-American*: ". . . the howl we raise about equal schools is just a subterfuge to keep them on the move. We don't need more colored schools any more than we need a hole in the head. What we do need, however, are more modernly equipped schools for all. Just think what a fine educational system we would have if the money spent for 'separate but equal' schools went toward schools designed to accommodate all." [101]

At a time when the Negro students might easily believe that the tensions in the white community were rising, an incident occurred that could have confirmed their fears. John Stokes remembers that on a Sunday morning, while the strike was on, his aunt called and said that there had been a burning of a cross on the school grounds. The Stokes family got in their car and drove to the school. John Stokes remembers that a considerable crowd of Negroes had gathered around a cross about seven feet tall and wrapped in a sheet that had been burned to fragments: "That sort of aroused an antagonistic attitude. . . . As far as some of us were concerned it aroused anger, but others just joked it off as a prank because as far as we knew there were no members of any organization—like the Klan—no members of such an organization in the county. . . . I also feel there was a little fear, an aroused feeling, like a lot of us had heard a lot about this kind of thing elsewhere in the South but nobody thought it would ever come to their town." [102]

Stokes and others of the students went out to Barbara's house, to talk with the person they had relied upon so heavily. Barbara was calm and suggested that teenagers had been responsible. Mr. Griffin added his opinion that no organization had been at work. The story made the Richmond *Afro-American,* where the *Afro* reporter quoted the police as saying that some children were responsible and that the matter had been disposed of.[103]

The white community actually was taking the developments with calm and with a notable lack of rancor. James Samuel Williams, who was working as a janitor at the courthouse during this time, can remember no change in the attitude of whites toward him.[104]

The *Herald* observed upon the filing of the petition with the school board that "if the students initiated the movement, they are no longer in command of the situation." [105] But the *Herald* was not convinced. The *Herald* may have thought that the constant reiteration of the $800,000 figure for the new school was having a pacifying effect on the Negro community. Chairman Large was quoted as saying that plans were to go ahead with the school regardless of any action taken. But again there was no indication of how funds beyond the Battle Fund level would be obtained.[106]

As late as May 15, the *Herald* preferred to believe that the issue remained local. Editor Wall urged the school board to continue negotiations "which have been in the making for several months" to get a site for the school. The editorial contained hopeful mention of the absence of further NAACP legal action since the filing of the petition with the school board. Editor Wall remembered some years later that this was a period when hopes of white leaders for a compromise were buoyed by contacts with "our Negro leaders." The *Herald* even dropped the pretense that money to build the new school was on hand and stated that there were two possibilities of getting the money—first through the state literary fund and second through a referendum for a county bond issue.[107]

On May 23 the NAACP filed in federal court the petition for desegregation that had been rejected by the school board. Spottswood Robinson remembers filing the petition and getting in a car to drive to Clarendon County where hearings on that case were to begin within a few days.[108] The Prince Edward case was a legal fact.

With this fact, the struggle for the loyalty of the Negroes of the county reached a new intensity. The Moton students had returned to school, fulfilling their pledge. Noting this, the *Herald* called upon Prince Edward Negroes to express their disfavor towards the petition and reaffirmed its belief that the majority of the Negroes of Prince Edward did not want "nonsegregation." The villain in the *Herald's* view was now "a vocal minority, craftily led, agitated by outside influences." [109]

Elsewhere in the state the pressures intensified. The *Richmond Times-Dispatch*, which had predicted "friction, trouble, and even violence" if segregation ended,[110] reported that Attorney General J. Lindsay Almond said that the state would intervene and bring all of its resources into play against the suit.[111] State Delegate Robert Whitehead, noting a "great crisis" in the state, called for a correspondingly great effort towards equalizing the state's schools.[112] Whitehead was the recognized leader of the Democratic Party opposition to the leadership of Senator Byrd. And what did Senator Byrd think? From the apple orchards of Berryville came not a word.

In Prince Edward the white leadership was preparing one last effort to de-fuse the court suit. A meeting was arranged at Robert Crawford's laundry. Crawford and Willie Redd did the inviting. The meeting was to be off the record, with neither notice nor report in the newspapers. The white leadership hoped to be able to persuade the Negroes present to withdraw support for the suit in return for a new school.

Mr. Griffin was not invited at first. He heard about the meeting and managed to get himself invited. He remembers that the meeting was to be held on the same Sunday that he had set aside for a county-wide meeting at the church to get petitions to support Principal Jones, whose contract was coming up for renewal.

This would place that date at June 23—one month to the day after the suit had been filed, two months to the day after the strike had begun. Griffin recalls what happened: "Some of the people involved in the laundry meeting rode by the church and said come on to this meeting, that Jones was doomed anyway and that there was nothing any of us could do about it. I told them that I would finish up where I was and get over there later on. When I got there the meeting was in progress. There was all sorts of courtesy from the whites and this made me suspicious. Upon my arrival, I was called upon to give my ideas but I declined to do so at first as I wanted to get the drift of the meeting." [113]

Editor Wall was present. He recalls: "We opened the meeting and suggested to these people that the school board had plans on the drawing board for new schools. We suggested to them that this suit was brought against the school board and that none of them were here. We recognized the inadequacy of the present facilities. . . . They said all we want is good school facilities. Then after some discussion Mr. Griffin got up and said, 'I can't go along with you folks. At present Negroes have got as high an IQ as whites and the time has come for there to be no separation of the races.' " [114]

Mr. Griffin remembers that five or six members of each race were present. This was undoubtedly the first time in the two months since the strike began that whites and Negroes as a group had sat down to discuss the issues. But Mr. Griffin regarded the Negroes invited by Willie Redd to attend the meeting as "highly selected." He recalls that "several Negroes were willing to go along with the idea [the compromise]. I said I didn't come here to sell my people down the river—that's the term I used. I gave a little lecture about the evils of segregation . . . this was before all those psychologists had made all their findings on this. I told them about the fact that Northern whites were doing better than Southern whites mentally, and I remember one of the whites asked me where did I get that. At the time I remembered the book and I just told him. The meeting just fizzled out. . . ." [115]

Wall and Mr. Griffin are agreed that accord might have been reached if the preacher had not been there. They are agreed, too, that several of the Negroes present gave Griffin a sharp verbal lacing after it was over. Wall and other whites present felt that the Negro group invited would have been able to enforce an agreement upon the Negro community. Griffin and other Negro leaders close to the mood of the community say that this is nonsense.

The idea that the Negro community this late in the game would settle for a new school probably was nothing more than wishful thinking on the part of the whites. They were reluctant to believe that the leadership had passed out of the hands of the older generation of Negro leaders; they did not understand that to oppose the school desegregation suit had come to mean, in the Negro community, a betrayal of the hopes of the children.

Then, too, the battle shaping up over Principal Jones tended to unite the Negro community. On June 26—the same day the NAACP held its first national meeting in the South in thirty-one years in Atlanta and called for an attack on segregation everywhere—a petition was filed with the Prince Edward School Board bearing 493 names and calling for the retention of Principal Jones. The petitioners called attention to his good record and added that failure to reemploy him "can only be considered a reprisal against the Negro citizens of this county." The petition denied that Jones had anything to do with the school strike.[116]

On June 29, Jones appeared before the school board to answer some questions about his behavior before and during the strike. The exhaustive interview produced some evidence of friction on the Moton staff. Jones explained that he saw a good deal of Griffin because he and Griffin each had bought ten acres of land in the county and were talking about developing it jointly. He said that they did not discuss school matters at all. Jones also said that he had tried to break up the strike unsuccessfully by talking with some students on the Monday after it began.[117]

On July 3 the school board declined to renew Jones's contract. The action was described by the board as "in no way a reprisal as suggested in the petition presented to the board."[118]

Chairman Large explains the firing of Jones: "He may well have been involved in the thing against his will, for all I know. We think that after he became involved he did not act as he should have acted and that is why his contract was not renewed. . . . We felt that he did not deal with the situation the way we wanted him to. Either he was involved in what was happening or he was afraid to act because it would have made him unpopular. We felt that in either case we had to let him go. It was a failure of confidence."[119]

Reaction in the Negro community to the firing of Jones was a bitter, sullen silence. If white leaders hoped at this juncture to pacify the Negroes of the county with action on the new school, they were mistaken. The strike had loosened purse strings; the literary fund which had been "blocked" so long and so hopelessly that Prince Edward officials had never even bothered to apply, suddenly worked loose. On July 10, Superintendent McIlwaine was directed by the school board to prepare application for a literary fund loan of $600,000. McIlwaine commented later: "We knew [before the strike] that it would take a long time to get the money. But when the trouble began we were put way ahead on the priority list and could get the money right away." [120]

The loan was granted speedily, before mid-August. The money, added to the county's Battle Fund share of $274,214.77, would build the new Moton High School.

But it would not halt the progress through the courts of Virginia's only suit for desegregation of public schools. With the horse gone, the barn door had been securely locked.

Every valley shall be exalted, and every mountain and hill shall be made low; and the crooked shall be made straight, and the rough places plain; And the glory of the Lord shall be revealed, and all flesh shall see it together: for the mouth of the Lord has spoken it.

Principal Jones was not the only one to feel the pressures generated by the strike.

In his own church, Mr. Griffin felt, for the first time, menaced: "A small faction was involved, some members felt that the church was dissatisfied. Some members said this directly to me. There was a continuous contention about the matter. . . . My answer would be that I had to preach as I felt."

While Mr. Griffin knew that only a minority of his church was unhappy about his brand of social gospel and about his role in the school strike, he realized that complaints of this type travel far and wear many guises. He heard from as far away as Washington of trouble in his church. He correctly divined that the firing of Principal Jones provided an opportunity to draw the lines marking his position in an advantageous way. He chose the third Sunday in June, a Communion Sunday, the twenty-second, for the showdown with his membership.

Roger Madison, who was acting chairman of the board of deacons, considers that Mr. Griffin's opposition at no time was overwhelming. The sharpest opposition was on the board of deacons but even on this body Mr. Griffin had a majority.

The preacher's purpose, then, was to put to rout his critics, to silence the voices of discord within the church. To do this he worked hard on a biting sermon. Usually, he preached from sketchy notes; on this occasion he read the sermon he had prepared. He chose Isaiah 40:4 and 40:5 ("Every valley shall be exalted . . . ") as his text.

He wasted no time drawing the conclusions he wished to emphasize in the firing of Principal Jones: "Here we have an example of a person fired for doing a job correctly. Not only that, but fired without sufficient time to hunt other means of livelihood. Where are his friends? I had rather not have visible means of support myself than not voice my contempt for a school board or those in power for such brazen, inhuman treatment, because what happens to one colored citizen inevitably happens to all. It is not a slap at Mr. Jones primarily, but poison venom flung in the face of every colored citizen of the county. It is a method to tell us that we don't care what you think or want; you have no right to think. Who will dare to say that God is pleased with these actions? It is for these causes that 'every mountain and hill shall be made low and every valley exalted . . . ' "

The preacher turned to the subject of the school strike: "I would sacrifice my job, money, or any property for the principles of right. I offered my life for a decadent democracy, and I'm willing to die rather than let these children down."

A newspaper reporter present noted that the "amens" rocked the church and that an old lady sobbed as Griffin added: "What would we tell the millions of unborn colored babies when they reach school age? Can we say that we sold them out?"

Much of the sermon was sharply anti-white in tone. Whites were accused of playing up crimes committed by Negroes against whites and ignoring crimes committed by whites against Negroes. Griffin was trying to strike the highest emotional pitch possible with his congregation. "Because I know that God does not desire segregation and does desire equalization in its true sense—Because my heart is made sad when I think of the cruelty heaped upon colored men in slavery when white men raped their women, harassed their children, and brutalized their men, I must take my stand. . . . That is the past and might be forgiven were it not for the fact that the spirit of slavery still exists. . . . Everywhere poor colored men and women struggling to survive are being underpaid, underfed, ill housed, and exploited by a ruthless and heartless people. . . . Yet there are colored men and women who, because they themselves enjoy a measure of security, will continue to 'sell us down the river.' They would do anything so that their families might grow fat off the land. . . . These people are far worse than any white person. Like Judas who sold Christ for thirty pieces of silver, they are degenerated moral cowards who have no regard for human beings.

"Can we say, I had to sell you to survive? I, for one, will not be guilty. I must speak out against injustice any and everywhere I see it. I, for one, don't know where my next meals are coming from. I, for one, cannot give my family any of the things I desire. It matters not! I don't have a thing and never will have at the price of human dignity.

"Still I will have that which no man can take away from me, my individual right to think as I choose, and inner freedom. This is my belief, this is my conviction, this is my hope. It can be no other. Therefore, in the words of Martin Luther, I, too, must say: 'Here I stand, God help me. I can do no other.'" Griffin paused. The congregation was still: "No one's going to scare me from my convictions by threatening my job. All who want me to stay as head of the church raise your hands." [121]

The news account reported that "almost every hand in the church went into the air." Griffin recalls that the sermon had the desired effect. "The people swamped me at the end of the sermon, and many of them said that they didn't know what had been going on. The deacons took a vote to support my position and announced it publicly the next Sunday." [122]

4. MIGRANTS, I

Negro County Farm Agent John Lancaster was called on the carpet by his superiors in Blacksburg and charged with being too friendly with Griffin—with whom he had been seen in the post office mailing off propaganda letters—with contributing money to get the school suit started, and with holding a party at his house for NAACP lawyers. He denied each of these accusations and further denied agitating for social reform on state time. But he promised to be more discreet and returned to Prince Edward gloomily to await further developments.[1]

At that, Lancaster considered himself one of the lucky ones. With the strike over, Barbara Johns's people began worrying about her next year at Moton. Her name was too much on every tongue. There had been threats to her safety that might or might not deserve to be labeled crackpot. A decision was made to send Barbara to Montgomery, Alabama, where she would finish her final year of high school and, perhaps, go on to Alabama State College.[2]

Principal Jones, of course, had to get relocated. He had no money and no job. The Negro community, united more than ever by Griffin's electrifying sermon, was anxious that he be provided for as a kind of disaster victim of the strike. Jones, too, decided to go to Montgomery to do some teaching and to work for his doctorate at Alabama State College.[3]

The college was not Montgomery's sole attraction. The main attraction for Barbara was that her uncle, the Reverend Vernon Johns, lived there and preached in the Dexter Avenue Baptist Church. She had lived with the Johnses before and would be comfortable there, her parents agreed. Principal Jones promptly joined Mr. Johns's church.

In the story of the strike that already has taken the shape of folklore on the lips of many white residents of Prince Edward County, the master devil is Mr. Johns. Mr. Griffin, who is the only principal in the strike still around, comes in for more than his share of tarring, and the names of John Lancaster and Boyd Jones are remembered. But only Mr. Johns is credited with the diabolical skills needed to "invent" the strike.

Mr. Griffin and Barbara Johns confirm Vernon Johns's story that he was not in Prince Edward County immediately before or during the strike. Barbara has written: "Let me at this point dispel all rumors that my uncle was behind this strike. He was in Alabama at the time and knew absolutely nothing about it until he read it in the papers. He was too busy creating his own little private 'Hell' as pastor of the Dexter Avenue Baptist Church in Montgomery, Alabama. . . ." [4]

But of course Mr. Johns heard about the strike soon enough. He thought of his long, angry perorations against the stolid faces arranged in church pews. He had said, "Docility had its première in Prince Edward County." Now, in a moment, the Negro community had come alive. "It was a freak of nature," he later told journalist Carl Rowan, "like a fixed star leaving its orbit." [5]

It is true that this extraordinary man has had a knack for embroiling himself in unpopular causes and making his personal unpopularity exceed even that of his cause. Mr. Griffin concedes: "He is an advanced thinker. Nobody likes him. He could tell a person something and make them mad with him where somebody else would say the same thing and everything would be all right. He is inconsiderate of those who are not up to his level in thinking. . . . He is also one of the best speakers in the country, and I am his disciple. He called me that once, his disciple. . . ." [6]

Mr. Johns says that his family goes back to slavery days in Tazewell County. He is light colored and quick to point out that white families named Johns are scattered about this part of the country. He got his early schooling in Prince Edward schools and remembers that one of the most illustrious men in Virginia education—Joseph T. Eggleston—was superintendent of schools when he was attending a one-room school in the county. Mr. Johns remembers Eggleston coming to the school once: "He stepped it off. I have always wondered if he was saying to himself, 'This won't do.'" [7]

He remembers where his own defiance began: "It was watching fires in the tobacco barn and reading the New Testament. That was when I discovered Christianity. I discovered that Christianity was entirely different than I had supposed. I had been led to think that you couldn't do some things to folks because they were white. I found that Christianity didn't observe that distinction." [8]

Mr. Johns finished his education at the Virginia Seminary in Lynchburg and later, while he was pastor of the Court Street Baptist Church in that city, had a sermon included in Joseph Ford Newton's "Best Sermons of 1926." This publication brought him a letter from a white Philadelphian, obviously unaware of Johns's color, who was angry because friends with whom he had stayed in Lynchburg had not told him of this fine preacher of their city.

Mr. Johns preached in Prince Edward quite often, but only as a visiting preacher, usually in the elder Griffin's church. His father had left him a farm, and he became a gentleman farmer of sorts, whose wife, in the tradition of the educated Southern Negro of this century, taught. He became involved in a struggle with the county authorities at the end of the 1930's. The issue was school buses. Mrs. Johns says that this disagreement, more than anything else, earned her husband the enmity of whites in the county: "The children going to high school in Farmville had to be boarded out there, if they lived out in the county. There were no school buses at all for Negroes. Well, it was bad because if a family had several boys and girls and could afford to board out only one they boarded out one of the girls." [9]

It was the old Southern Negro story of the women's getting the education that would help them stay South and teach or go north and get jobs as secretaries. It was Grace Morton's story and Violet Johns's. What point was there in educating Negro boys for nonexistent jobs? By failing to provide school buses, the county forced the Negro parents to perpetuate the matriarchal society that kept the men on the farm and put the women in the position of chief wage earner.

The pattern infuriated Vernon Johns. He threw himself, heartily into the bus fight in Prince Edward. He managed to make most of the Negro community wince whenever he was among them, chastising them for their laziness, their bland acceptance of the status quo. He appeared before the school board, and they remember him. At one point, when rumors were prevalent that he wished to replace the principal of Moton at that time, he asked the school board if they believed the story. Told they did not, he responded, "I'm glad. I had prided myself that I could expect nothing from this board." [10]

Superintendent McIlwaine's figures show that the first buses for Negro school children in the county were furnished in 1938–39 and that 50 per cent of the Negro students were being transported by 1944–45.[11] As late as November, 1944, Vernon Johns was leading a delegation before the school board to protest the hand-me-down school buses assigned to Negroes and the overcrowding on these buses.[12]

Mr. Johns liked to cook up spicy sermon titles in order to shake his congregations out of what he feared was a constitutional lethargy. In Lynchburg, when the book "The Vanishing Virginians" was popular, he preached a sermon entitled "Some Virginians Who Ought To Vanish." Later, in Montgomery, he posted on the bulletin board of the church, which abutted the sidewalk, the eyecatching sermon title: "It's Safe To Murder Negroes." That Thursday morning he got a summons to appear before the grand jury. There followed a little dialogue in which the jury wondered why he had posted that title.

"That's my sermon subject and I put it up to attract attention, and it looks like it's going to succeed."

But why did he want to preach on such a subject?

"Because everywhere I go in the South the Negro is forced to choose between his hide and his soul. Mostly, he chooses his hide. I'm going to tell him that his hide is not worth it." [13]

The little inquisition ended inconclusively, but the sermon notice stayed up and Mr. Johns preached on schedule.

It may be that his hard-nosed sermons in Prince Edward County revealed in Mr. Johns a deep-seated feeling that some special fate awaited the county. After the strike he told the slavery-day story of the white master whose slave turned on him in the fields and beheaded him with a scythe or wheat cradle. According to the way Mr. Johns told the story, it all happened quite near the location of the old Moton High School.[14]

Several events of note followed the Montgomery sermon by the explosive Mr. Johns. A cross was burned in front of the church. A young Negro with a mild pastoral manner showed up at the church with a new degree and began his training to take over. He was interested in the problems with which Mr. Johns had grappled, and he had some ideas of his own on how some of them might be attacked. Principal Jones contrasts the newcomer with the older Mr. Johns: "Vernon is a man for making a frontal attack on race problems. He didn't preach this nonviolent thing. In general his attitude was to slug it out. Now, King was more of a traditional pastor." [15]

But the Reverend Martin Luther King had some unorthodox ideas of his own. He admired Vernon Johns who, in 1954, had decided to return to Prince Edward to raise livestock. But King put in a lot of time reading Thoreau and Ghandi and meditating. It seemed to him that nonviolent resistance would be put to good use in the Negro's struggle for equal treatment. It might even become the wave of the future, he thought.

PART TWO

MASSIVE RESISTANCE

5.   BLACK MONDAY

Monday, May 17, 1954: The Supreme Court handed down its school desegregation decision, and certain politicians in the South folded the corners of their calendars on the date, for opprobrious naming later on.

Friday, May 21, 1954: The Sheridan school board in Arkansas voted 5-0 to integrate twenty-one Negro students with six hundred whites in the upper grades.

Saturday, May 22, 1954: The Sheridan school board, having heard from some of the parents of the six hundred white students, voted 5-0 not to integrate twenty-one Negro students in the upper grades.[1]

Here was neither real resistance nor real compliance. The South, the many-faced South, groaning under a new burden, reacted with scattered reflexes. The Sheridan school board reacted naïvely, with those who thought that overnight was enough; actually it was too early even for the opportunist. A gubernatorial candidate in Arkansas named Orval Faubus proclaimed that the decision was the number one issue of the campaign. When the *Arkansas Gazette* objected editorially, Faubus decided to drop the matter.[2]

August 10, 1954: Orval Faubus won a run-off for the Democratic nomination equivalent to election as governor.[3]

Some Southern states were sure that compliance was out of the question. Alabama, Mississippi, Georgia, South Carolina, and Louisiana felt this way.

The Georgia legislature considered bills to abolish the Supreme Court and to remove all Negroes from the state; behind the foolishness lay a deadly serious manner. The feeling in the Deep South was very strong.

But the words of the men of the Deep South and the men of the upper South often masked different intent. Governor Byrnes of South Carolina said that he was "shocked" at the decision, and Governor Umstead of North Carolina said that he was "terribly disappointed." There they parted, Governor Byrnes to halt allocation of funds for school construction and Governor Umstead to appoint a commission to study a way out that would preserve public schools.[4]

Even in the South that thought of itself as immutable there was little talk of the court decision's being "illegal" or of the states' having the right, much less the duty, to resist. The day of the Southern Establishment was not yet.

The commoner assumption, particularly among schoolmen, was that the decision could be obeyed with a minimum of political complications. Yet the Sheridan school board in Arkansas was not alone in discovering a hesitancy among the people to follow the counsel of sudden change; politicians, sensitive to such things, sniffed the air and speculated.

Some Southern states were sure that compliance was possible. These included Arkansas, Delaware, Maryland, Kentucky, Missouri, Oklahoma, West Virginia, and the District of Columbia. The doubtful states were North Carolina, which was already showing signs of a willingness to comply; Florida, which was probably going to waver between the two camps; Tennessee, which was getting moderate leadership; Texas, which was cautious but not defiant; and Virginia. Of the states that might have been expected to supply a thrust of leadership in one direction or another, Virginia was the most difficult to read.

May 17, 1954: Governor Stanley said that the Supreme Court decision called for "cool heads, calm study, and sound judgment." He promised to consult "leaders of both races" in the state.

May 17, 1954: Officials of Richmond, Henrico, and Chesterfield county schools said that they would sit tight until a nonsegregation policy pattern was formulated by the state.

May 17, 1954: The division superintendent of schools for Gloucester and Mathews counties said that the decision was law. "If we use good judgment, integration will take place smoothly and will be carried to a successful conclusion."

May 17, 1954: Senator Harry Flood Byrd, leader of the Party, said that the decision "will bring implications and dangers of the greatest consequence." [5]

The press around the state called for calmness, dignity, probity, reasonableness, graciousness, and—although only by implication—obedience. The *Richmond Times-Dispatch*, a kind of bellwether, even suggested that the Supreme Court set a definite time limit for its order to go into effect.[6]

Yet for all the spirit of co-operation in which these things were said, for all the Gloucester schoolman's optimism and the *Times-Dispatch's* good manners, doubts prickled. Senator Byrd's utterances were ominous. Governor Stanley, a loyal if unimaginative Byrd attendant, may have blanched when he read that Francis Pickens Miller, an old anti-organization foe of Byrd, praised his May 17 statement.[7]

May 18, 1954: Governor Stanley announced that he had modified his plans to call a conference of state leaders of both races. The court's decision no longer seemed to him to require such immediate action.[8]

The brakes were on. A delegation of political leaders from the Southside's Fourth Congressional District met with Governor Stanley. They undoubtedly talked about political soundings they had been taking. They undoubtedly talked about Senator Byrd. They undoubtedly talked about Prince Edward County.[9]

May 19, 1954: Governor Stanley said that he would appoint a study commission (no mention of "both races") and that the present policies of segregation would remain in effect for the coming year.[10]

May 20, 1954: Governor Stanley asked Southern governors to meet in Richmond on June 7 or thereabouts for a pow-wow, "without contemplating any organizations or adoption of any group plan." [11]

June 20, 1954: Fourth District leaders met in the Petersburg fire house and declared themselves "unalterably opposed" to integration in the schools. The meeting was presided over by State Senator Garland Gray, a high Byrd official who was to be appointed to head Governor Stanley's study commission.[12]

June 25, 1954: Five weeks after his moderate statement on the Supreme Court's decision, Governor Stanley declared: "I shall use every legal means at my command to continue segregated schools in Virginia." [13]

The state was committed, not to do something, but to do nothing for the time being, to wait. The locks of massive resistance had not yet been fashioned, but the spirit of noncompliance was abroad. This spirit had found its guidance in the leaders of Prince Edward's Southside and in Senator Byrd.

Governor Stanley had not called in for consultation "leaders of both races," and he never would.

6. DEFENDERS OF STATE SOVEREIGNTY

The Southside architects of the resistance movement to the Supreme Court decision are agreed on one thing—it was a primary purpose of the organization they had in mind to see to it that no violence occurred.

There was extreme talk in the South, and, according to those most interested in preserving segregation, there was danger in Southside Virginia, right in Prince Edward. Robert B. Crawford, the laundry owner who served as chairman of the school board, remembers that after a meeting of his Bible class in May, 1954, shortly after the decision, a friend came to him: "He said, 'Mr. Crawford, I work a lot of men and they're not saying much, but I can see [here Crawford puts his hand over his heart in recounting the story] that they've got a lot pent up here. They don't like this thing,' he said, 'and I'm afraid of an unfortunate incident.'" [1]

The suggestion was that leadership would be required, if only to keep the peace. Crawford remembers another kind of appeal from an individual who was concerned with more than just the possibility of an "unfortunate incident": "Barrye Wall came to me on the street one day and said, 'Bob, the Negro organization of the NAACP has made right much progress in recent years. It's not the type of progress that we like but it's done in an orderly way, legally, and with plenty of money and smart lawyers. We ought to organize the same way and see what we can do.'" [2]

Little evidence is offered that the man on the street and the man behind the plow reacted sharply to the Supreme Court decision. There were a few letters to the editor. The men who began to meet to form an organization of resistance have a common recollection of attempting to palliate a spirit of violence, but the record deals more with their efforts to harness and energize a spirit of legal rebellion.

The *Herald* had begun by regretting the decision and reaffirming its belief in segregation.[3] In this period after the Supreme Court decision, Editor Wall remembers attending meetings in Farmville, and he remembers that a group of Prince Edward people drove to Petersburg, the nearest sizable city, to talk about what might be done.[4]

The gradual stiffening of determination against the court's decision cheered these Southside leaders beyond measure. To some extent their own feelings may have contributed to Senator Byrd's gradually evolving decision to fight the court to the end. But it is far more significant that political leadership of the resistance movement flowed down, from the summit at Berryville.

On June 20, that important meeting was held at the Petersburg fire house. The meeting plainly had high sanction, perhaps even the nature of a political obligation. Some twenty state senators and representatives from the Fourth District were on hand, including State Senator Garland "Peck" Gray, thought to have hopes of being governor and soon to be appointed to Governor Stanley's commission. With Senator Gray presiding, the sense of intimacy with Richmond and Washington was strong, as two legislators from central Virginia who did not attend recognized by going to the trouble of sending excuses.

Among the fifty "guests" invited to the meeting were Wall and Crawford. Wall recalls that the Prince Edward group, with its special position under the gun, urged the larger body on to a determined stand: "I listened and they called on me at the last. They weren't going fast enough to suit me and I said so."[5]

The outcome of the meeting pleased the Prince Edward delegation. The politicians expressed their unalterable opposition to school integration and pledged "determined purpose" to keep the schools segregated. They also decided to mail circulars to the governing bodies of all Virginia counties and, in the weeks following, sixty-one of them responded by adopting resolutions urging the continuance of segregated schools. United States Representative Watkins Abbitt, who was to become one of the stoutest leaders of the resistance, suggested that a convention might be needed to amend the Constitution of Virginia to preserve segregation.[6]

Five days after the Petersburg meeting Governor Stanley issued the statement that he would use every legal means at his command to preserve segregation. The resistance movement was a thing of substance, not yet massive but viable.

Back in Prince Edward, Editor Wall pulled out the stops. The first statement in the *Herald* beyond a simple declaration of faith in segregation had come from United States Senator Willis Robertson who was not likely to be out of step with Senator Byrd on so basic a question. On June 4 the *Herald* editorial page had contained remarks by Senator Robertson to the effect that the decision had invaded the legislative field.[7] A *Herald* editorial had picked up this motif on June 18, but it was a week later—after the Petersburg meeting—that the full orchestration was sounded: "We therefore conclude that public education as it is presently constituted has been undermined and toppled to fragments by the general decision of the Supreme Court. We submit that Virginia had not abandoned public education; the Supreme Court has abolished it. What will be put in its place of necessity will be a far change from the successful system developed in the past. In counties where there are a few Negroes it is conceivable that schools can be desegregated without harm to the students or to education. But in Southside Virginia, where the school populations are about equal, desegregation will present problems incapable of solution." [8]

On July 9, the *Herald* rounded out what was to be its judgment of the Prince Edward school matter. An editorial set forth the theme of an NAACP conspiracy, probably of long standing, against Prince Edward County, which had been selected for an experiment in desegregation before the Moton strike, possibly because of the independence of its Negroes.[9] The *Herald*, thus, editorially bade farewell to public schooling in counties with heavy Negro populations and blamed this turn of events on an NAACP plot and an "unconstitutional" decision of the Supreme Court. The editorial accurately outlined the course of state policy under Senator Byrd's guidance. It was not yet massive resistance—since it conceded the possibility of some limited integration in the state's public schools—but it was in that direction.

Robert Crawford remembers that in this period the resistance group in Prince Edward was casting about for a national figure to provide leadership and to give the organization respectability. They tried former Governor John S. Battle, a much respected man in public affairs. Crawford reports that "[Battle] said, 'I would rather have a hundred members who represented real leadership than five hundred people you couldn't count on.' He was responsible for our charging membership fees, to get quality folks. We wanted him to do the job for us or get Jimmy Byrnes to do it. I wouldn't say we got a flat refusal from him; he was cordial . . . but before anything could come into being we found that other states were doing the same thing we were. We had thought we were the only ones." [10]

More meetings were held in Farmville and Petersburg. Barrye Wall remembers that the little group was enlarged by the process of having each of five members choose five more for the next meeting.[11] At least one meeting was held in the Weyanoke Hotel in Farmville.

Crawford credits J. Barrye Wall, Jr., the editor's elder son and a practicing lawyer in Farmville, with suggesting "Defenders of State Sovereignty" and the Petersburg contingent with adding "Individual Liberties" to the name of the new organization.[12]

It was in Blackstone, in neighboring Nottoway County, that the organization became a reality on October 8. Editor Wall credits State Senator Charles Moses of Appomattox with bringing an organization out of this meeting. The press was barred, but Wall remained as a "private citizen," fuming at the footdragging in the meeting and "just about disgusted" by the time the main business of the meeting was settled three and one-half hours later.[13] Representatives of eighteen counties were at this meeting and what emerged was the framework of an organization to be designated "Defenders of State Sovereignty and Individual Liberties" and destined to be called, simply, the Defenders. Its pledge was to maintain states' rights, individual rights, and to preserve segregation in the schools.[14]

Crawford was out of town when the meeting was held: "When I got back I found that Senator Moses, Watt Abbitt, and Barrye Wall had been appointed a nominating committee to select a president. Barrye Wall came to my house before I even had time to eat a sandwich and said 'I want you to be president.' I was surprised because I thought they were looking for a national name but Barrye said this was just temporary." [15]

Robert B. Crawford may not have been the inevitable choice to head the Defenders' organization, but no one else was much surprised when he was chosen. He describes himself as a man who is always being elected to head something and tells of discovering once in the *Herald* that he had been elected to head a five-county fair committee. Crawford's fans, and these number some who disagree with him heartily, say that he is chosen for these activities because he is a man of indomitable zeal. A critic tempers praise for his energy and resourcefulness: "Bob is the sort of fellow who would like to lead any parade that came to Farmville. Even if it was a convention of nudists. But the minute he wasn't the leader any more he would be all through."

The news that Publisher Wall brought Crawford was more than pleasing to the laundry owner. He had been present at the birth of the Defenders' organization, and he recognized in it the germination of a potent political energy. Here was a cause that meant more than an opportunity for routine administrative success. Crawford believed what the Defenders believed. Here was an affair of real passion to him.

Crawford is a tall, thin man with a lantern jaw; raw-boned, with something of the look of the zealot about him tempered by a relaxed, smiling manner. He is full of charm and persuasiveness, the kind, as well, that people call a good mixer. Unlike many of the Defenders who would be under his administration, Crawford was not a native of Southside Virginia. He was born and reared on a farm near Staunton in the Shenandoah Valley. Augusta County was cattle and orchard country, a different agricultural world from Southside's tobacco monoculture. It was also Senator Harry Flood Byrd's political home ground. Crawford recalls, "I used to go to the senator's office and get two or three barrels of apples and distribute them around on this apple a day keeps the doctor away business, among the farm families of the area. I also held pruning demonstrations in his orchard. I subscribed to his political conservatism." [16]

Crawford had been to Virginia Polytechnic Institute in Blacksburg, Virginia, by then and had earned a degree in agronomy. He had behind him a year of military service and some time in Alabama managing a twelve-thousand-acre cotton, hay, and livestock farm. He was county agent in Warren County when an opening, with better pay, came up in Prince Edward. He showed up with a wife and two children and bought a house because this was the only way to get adequate living quarters in the county. This was in 1925. The Crawfords settled in.

County agent Crawford brought some progressive ideas with him: "I realized that this one-crop system was a curse. I used to watch these people coming into town to sell tobacco to buy hay to feed the mule to plow up some land to plant some more tobacco." [17]

With the help of an interested banker, N. B. Davidson, Crawford initiated the "Living At Home" loan program designed to shake the county loose from the toils of the single crop. Crawford applied the crop rotation practices that he had learned in the Shenandoah Valley to Prince Edward County. No agricultural revolution ensued, but Crawford made something of a name for himself. The program was widely touted in Virginia and North Carolina in farm trade journals.

But if Crawford's agricultural ideas were progressive, his political ideas were staunchly conservative, even by Southside standards. His favorite reading was Bernard McFadden in the old *Liberty* magazine. He was a Byrd supporter who had even more trouble than the Senator in backing the Democratic ticket. He voted for Herbert Hoover against Al Smith partly because of a friend who had worked with Hoover in food administration and who had a high opinion of him. From the beginning Crawford had little respect for Franklin D. Roosevelt, whom Byrd supported in his first presidential campaign.

Crawford had struck up an interest in the American Legion that would last the rest of his life. It was motivated by more than the pride of service and desire for companionship that brought so many others into the Legion; Crawford was one of those zealously interested in Americanism with a capital *A*. By 1935 he was distributing a book written by the director of the Legion on how the other "isms" detract from Americanism. Crawford became convinced that what he perceived in the country's government and society as a dilution of American ideals of free enterprise could have a ruinous result. The turn of government that the New Deal took shocked him; the social fabric seemed loosened dangerously by new and alien forces.

A strong Presbyterian, Crawford found symptoms that depressed him within the church: "I became convinced in the very early thirties about a trend in our churches that I did not like. I was concerned about it in the Presbyterian Church, my church, and I learned that it was in all the Protestant churches. I'd say that it was when preachers began talking about religion instead of Christianity, when they started saying that instead of salvation, religion was a matter of right living. . . . It was then that 'brotherhood' became popular. It's been variously labeled as social gospel, behaviorism. . . ." [18]

Later on, he found reason to blame "religionists" with their "pouring out of propaganda against segregation," for the racial difficulties that beset the South.

During these early years Crawford was interested in what had not yet come to be called race relations. As a county agent, before he purchased his laundry business in 1927, he had had practical field experience in a county in which the population was almost 50 per cent Negro. He knew John Lancaster's father, who was Negro County Agent, and, vaguely, his son, who would follow in the father's footsteps with results none could imagine then. Crawford got along well enough with Negroes like the elder Lancaster.

His ideas on race were the strange and compelling blend of contradiction that at once enrich and complicate Southern life. The idea of the Negro as a human dependent, in need of the white man's service and patience was one he had from his father: "I remember my father listening to white hands say the nigger is no good and replying 'the Negro's soul is as dear as the white man's in the eyes of the Lord.' " [19]

But if this was equalitarianism, it was the equalitarianism of the hereafter. Crawford's ideas of the proper relationship between the races in his America were not confounded by such considerations. The white man and the Negro could be close in human contact as individuals, but, as races, they were divided by truths more unassailable than anything Jim Crow might write into the law; by the structure of Southern society, by economics (perhaps economic necessity); and, more importantly, by the gulf of a past seen in terms of fear. The educated white man's role was that of a kind of missionary, and the risks were missionary's risks. Crawford said, "I remember, when I was in Alabama, on that cotton farm, after work I would lay down in the farm boss's shack and I would be the only white man among eighteen Negro families. I wouldn't even latch the screen door. I would come and go among them. I remember that an old

Negro woman died once. The doctors in those days charged a dollar a mile and a doctor had to be called to the place. I dug down and paid for this." [20]

Crawford's father did not express his central fear to the white hands whose outright bigotry he tempered, but he told his own son. Crawford remembers that "he would take me aside from time to time and tell me that he was afraid that it would all end up in amalgamation." [21]

Here was what lay hidden below the surface, but could be raised as a final, irrefutable argument for segregation. A single word, it covered a multitude of doubts and fears, the real and the imaginary. Amalgamation. It must not happen.

Years later, Crawford would reflect this view in an interview with Haldore Hanson in the *New Republic*: "Mixed children in school is the beginning of the end for both races.... It is inevitable that children who play together from the age of five will not stop at eighteen. There will be intermarriage." [22]

But intermarriage was hardly a live question in the world of Prince Edward County in the 1930's. Crawford's impulse was to assume a position of leadership in his community. He wanted, too, to help the Negro—that is the way he would put it. He was elected to the county school board in 1931 and would remain a member until 1946, the last seven years as chairman. In 1944–45 he was named Outstanding School Trustee of the Year in Virginia. Of no service in his career is he more proud than his years on the school board, and in no area more than that of education for the Negro: "I had two pet projects, separate high school and lower school for Negroes and vocational training. Not many of them were going to college in those days. I felt that when they finished high school, they had to do something with their hands." [23]

His economic and social conservatism, however, served to limit these ambitions rather strictly. He did not believe in floating bonds for education. He was a pay-as-you-go Byrd Democrat, and his inclination was to trim expenses wherever possible. He thought public schools capable of unconscionable waste unless kept under strict surveillance. When Moton High School was built in 1939, he considered that the school board had achieved an ultimate triumph. "We were so proud of that. At last we had gotten the big children separated from the little ones and in their own high school. I used to go out to the auditorium and hear their musicals. I'm fond of Negro music. We thought we had things all set." [24]

Crawford's fondness for Negro music had put him in contact with certain members of the younger group of Negroes in the county. In reminiscing, he said that "when this preacher Griffin's brother was just a school boy, he had a terrific bass voice. I used to invite the boys in the quartet he had around to sing at the opening and closing of Sunday School. They'd come to me when they wanted anything, like uniform jackets, things of that kind, and I'd try to help them get up the money." [25]

Both young Lancaster and Mr. Griffin concede that Crawford was the one in the white community to whom Negroes would turn most readily for help. Griffin recalls how this situation led many Negroes in the county to a curiously naïve assumption: "Back when he was chairman of the school board he was always supposed to have been such a liberal, always plugging for the equal in separate but equal. When all this started [the strike], Negroes thought he would be in favor of the Negro position. . . . When he became a Defender leader, they really were disappointed." [26]

The truth was, of course, that Crawford's real contact in the Negro community was with the older leaders who accepted the separateness of the races. Until the strike took its anti-segregation turn (until, as Crawford says, "the NAACP took over"), it was hardly possible for him to think of a serious division of opinion between him and the leaders of the Negro community.

Like virtually all of the leaders of the white community whose visits to Negro functions were necessarily ceremonial, and whose observations of Negro life were consequently superficial, he was quite out of touch with the changing current of Negro opinion. He was unreservedly for Negro progress within the limitations of what he could imagine as legitimate goals. He had even attended some meetings of an interracial group associated with Will Alexander's Commission on Interracial Relations back in the 1930's. He remembers in particular one meeting at St. Paul's Church in Richmond when he remarked, to the huge amusement of two Negro educators sitting on either side of him, that the trouble with the group was that its membership included too many teachers and preachers. He remembers bumping into some prominent men in state government in the Hotel Richmond afterwards and telling them that they ought to attend such meetings.

But Crawford recalls that his old devil, the Council of Churches, got in the organization and he got out.

So the new Negro leaders arising out of the World War II years were strangers to him, and their ideas of the new American society—had he known them—would have seemed to him outlandish. The single, most important thrust in Negro life generated by the war—the desire for an education indistinguishable from that of whites—was a mystery to be unraveled in his mind only in reflection, years later.

At the time of the war, personal matters preoccupied Crawford. Although he says that he visited Moton on many occasions, he does not remember even being conscious of the overcrowding problem. During these years of his chairmanship of the school board, distractions were multiplying. His old predilection for 'leading the parade' was beginning to stretch his physical resources thin. He was in Washington all of 1941, representing the National Laundry Owners Association. His interest in politics led him to consider running for the state legislature in 1943 (he finally decided against this, after 'walking' for about a month). He was vice-president of the American Automobile Association in Virginia and on the board of the Blue Shield hospitalization insurance system. In 1946 his service in the American Legion culminated in his election as Virginia department commander.

He was cut off from his school board work, too, by his conviction that the county's educational system harbored inefficiency and encouraged waste. This belief led him into conflict with others on the school board. Crawford's constant criticism alienated him from the men with whom he had to work, and he decided that it was time for him to quit.

One of his last acts on the school board was the raising of money for an athletic field to be built around Moton. He got twenty-five hundred dollars each from the board of supervisors and the Farmville Town Council. Reflecting on it later, he remembered having applied to this act a social commentary: "I put it to them [the board of supervisors and town council] as an investment in the future, to keep down juvenile delinquency." [27]

He was as surprised as any other white leader in the county at the Moton strike and the suit that followed. He was surprised to learn that the old leadership of the Negro community, upon which he had depended, was in default. The friends he had prided himself upon among Prince Edward's Negroes were those leaders now out of power—men like Willie Redd and Joe Pervall. He did not speak the same language as men like Lancaster and Griffin. Everything he believed was based on the continuance of segregation; everything they believed was based on the ending of segregation. He concluded that the new influence in the Negro community was foreign to those it held in thrall, and he said, "By that time [1951] the NAACP had taken over." [28]

Crawford was then entirely remote from the school board. He had become more interested than ever in the movement of conservatism, now in the hands of one of its most successful practitioners, Senator Joseph McCarthy. The issue of Communist infiltration of the government was one that had seemed live to Crawford for many years. With the postwar liberalism of the Truman administration, he was convinced that the country was in danger of falling to the radical left.

In the years that followed, with the Supreme Court's desegregation decision of 1954, it seemed clear to Crawford as to other conservatives of like thinking, that the race issue could be understood as a Communist plot to divide Americans. The theory accounted for the widespread unrest along racial fronts in the country. It even accounted for the inability of white community leaders to speak the same language as the younger, more radical Negro leaders in their community. To these white conservatives, the old Negroes remained the real leaders of their people, and the new Negroes became either the conscious or unconscious dupes of world Communism.

The idea of the Defenders had a powerful appeal for him. It was plain that such a body, properly run, would have important political support. He says that no overt effort was made to enlist Senator Byrd to the Defenders' ranks, but that he never doubted that the Senator's dominant political organization would support them wholeheartedly; as it turned out the Defenders came to carry the expression of the organization's sentiment on racial affairs. Crawford recalls, "We didn't think much about Senator Byrd when we were organizing. But it was a natural for him. The Byrd Democrats were the ones who took the leadership in it. It was just a case of birds of a feather flocking together."[29]

The fact that important politicians were involved in the Defenders' movement gave it a prestige and a potential it would not otherwise have had. The membership of two thousand when a state charter was granted in October, 1954, did not begin to suggest the group's true strength.

This fact made it all the more important that the Defenders' goal be lofty and their motives above reproach. It is impossible to tell, reading the four-page, single-spaced Certificate of Incorporation filed with the State Corporation Commission that the Defenders stood for anything more controversial than liberty. Segregation is not so much as hinted at; education is mentioned only once, and then almost apologetically as a kind of domestic practice indulged in by the states and best regulated by them. Another Defenders' document—a statement of beliefs—goes on for almost a full page about states' rights, strict interpretation of the Constitution, private enterprise, and the dangers of concentration of powers—with segregation mentioned only at the end, almost as an afterthought. In a speech to local Defenders in November, 1954, Editor Wall listed the objectives of the organization as "sovereignty of the states according to spirit and provisions of the Constitution," "salvation of our Republic," and "preservation of segregated schools, the immediate object"—in that order.[30]

What the Defenders could not stand for was as important as what they could stand for. Crawford, Wall, and other Defender speakers bore down on the theme that violence would mean ruin for the movement. Benjamin Muse, in his *Virginia's Massive Resistance,* makes the point that the Ku Klux Klan was completely discredited by the Defenders and that the White Citizens Councils that were beginning to spring up in other parts of the South were treated with great suspicion.[31] Reporter Hanson quoted Crawford: "If this community should suffer just one incident of Klanism, our white case is lost. No matter who starts it, the whites will be blamed. We must not have it." [32]

With the instincts of some of the state's ablest politicians working for them, these men realized that the slightest taint could doom the organization in the eyes of the proper Virginians they must count upon for support.

But violence was not the only enemy the Defenders saw on their right. The White Citizens Councils and other racist organizations were spewing forth the seedy literature of race hatred, playing on the uncounted fears of ignorant white Southerners. The material, quite naturally, poured into the Defenders' offices.

Crawford says that he threw it out as quickly as it came in. The Defenders officially shunned the use of such materials, although members as individuals undoubtedly did use them, particularly as the organization expanded.

The Defenders' organizers in Prince Edward combed the ranks of the county's staunchest segregationists to find officers of unquestioned propriety and standing in the community. Crawford's own personal reputation was high. A liberal like Muse was able to write about him later: "Crawford was typical of many previously little-known individuals who have come into prominence and no little power in the South by leading movements of extreme segregationists. A man of integrity, and as it developed, of considerable ability, Crawford impressed many with the sincerity of his segregationist views." [33]

The list of officers and directors of the local Defender chapter included tobacco manufacturer J. W. Dunnington, Mayor W. C. Fitzpatrick of Farmville, Dr. S. C. Patteson, J. G. Bruce of the Board of Supervisors, former school board chairman Large, and, of course, Publisher Wall. There could be little doubt at this point that the Defenders had control of the organs of government in Prince Edward County.

The Defender leaders in Prince Edward and elsewhere did not agree on all major planks. The desire to preserve segregation was, at all levels, the cement of the organization. Yet the leadership was, with Crawford, much more acutely concerned with states' rights, with the constitutional issues. Crawford indicates why the Defender leaders might accept for themselves different priorities from those accepted by the general membership: "You can't explain the real conspiracy to a man in a tobacco patch or a peanut patch. But if you tell him that they are going to make his children go to school with niggers he knows what you mean plain enough. I hoped to get the man in the tobacco patch to move from the emotional involvement with the race issue to broader issues." [34]

The conspiracy was, of course, the most fascinating thing. The theme of mysterious internal subversion was always present in the background. The *Herald,* for instance, devoted several editorials in 1955 to praising Senator Eastland of Mississippi for his charge that the Supreme Court had fallen under the influence of the Communist conspiracy in its 1954 decision on schools. Crawford thought the conspiracy involved some intellectuals, teachers, agitators of assorted backgrounds and, of course, some churchmen.

Crawford felt himself at the head of the biggest parade of his life. What he had thought, what he had stood for, suddenly was becoming an important issue in the intellectual life of a region—who knew, of a nation? He was determined that the battle would be joined on what he took to be the proper grounds.

Speaking before the Charlottesville Defenders one evening, he touched several of his favorite themes. He berated the leadership of the Southern ministry ("The worst obstacle we face in the fight to preserve segregated schools in the South is the white preacher"), he called for restraint ("Nothing could hurt our cause more than bloodshed"), and he identified the real villains of the piece as "International Socialists and Communists." [35]

What worried him most was the danger that the struggle to come would divide the South along lines of race hatred: "This must not develop as a clash between the white man and the Negro. We would be jumping on the wrong man if it did." [36]

There was nothing artificial about Crawford's concern over allowing the issues to reduce to racial hostility. As a practical man he saw that this reaction would be the disgrace of the Defenders' movement and its political ruin. As a Southern segregationist, he wanted to preserve the old and easy relationship between the races. He resented keenly that the political crisis left an opportunity for that relationship to be misunderstood: "The thing I hate most about it is that it has given the white man a sense of race guilt." [37]

The "it" that Crawford spoke of was, of course, the Communist conspiracy. Its greatest attraction to men like Crawford was not only that it placed the villains outside the pale of Americanism but that it placed them outside the South. It cleansed the Southern white and Negro of any real responsibility for the crisis. It left the white Southerner free to maintain that it was not the Negro Southerner—not "our" Negro—who was agitating for social change.

The relationship between the Southern white and the Negro— the terrible and beautiful bonds of contradiction—had to be preserved, then. But what exactly was this relationship? Even segregationist leaders like Crawford did not stop to analyze its implications. They simply attributed all the good in this relationship to segregation and ignored all of the evil in it. Segregation could not be evil because segregation, to them, was nothing more than the Southern way of life; they could not imagine the South without segregation.

In April, 1955, a delegation appeared before the Prince Edward Board of Supervisors to ask that no funds be appropriated for integrated schools. The supervisors, dominated by Defender sympathizers, voted to delay the school fund appropriation until the last legal moment—May 31. By a coincidence, this was the date that the Supreme Court chose to hand down its decree calling on district courts to implement its school desegregation decision.

The courts and the board of supervisors were evidently on a collision course. But how much time remained for maneuver? Would a district court order the Prince Edward schools desegregated in September, 1955?

Prince Edward School Superintendent McIlwaine and School Board Chairman B. Calvin Bass drove to Richmond that afternoon to ask these questions of their attorneys, the firm of Hunton, Williams, Gay, Moore, and Powell. The decision had not surprised the lawyers, and they were of the firm opinion that it meant that the county had at least another full school year of grace before having to make its decision on school desegregation. They felt that the schools could be operated safely on a segregated basis the next school year. Implementing the court's decision would take at least this long.

McIlwaine and Bass hurried back to Prince Edward County to present this opinion at the crucial meeting of the supervisors scheduled for that night.

The courthouse was crowded before 8 P.M. when the meeting was scheduled to begin. The atmosphere was tense.[38] Speaker after speaker urged that the supervisors refuse to appropriate money to operate the schools under this threat of desegregation. Many of these speakers were leading Defenders in the county organization. Bass chose a spot between them to speak his piece. He told the crowd that he and McIlwaine had conferred with their attorneys that very afternoon and that they were assured that the court decision would permit continued operation of the county schools on a segregated basis for another year. He pointed out that no applications from Negro children to attend white schools had been received. He said that if an order integrating schools did come down, the school board could refuse to act on it and resign. He cautioned that if money were not appropriated for the schools, teachers would find jobs elsewhere. After a year's operation, the county could look at the situation anew: "By that time the Legislature will have met again and we may have some new laws. At least we'll know where we stand."

The *Richmond News-Leader*'s account of the meeting the next day described the reaction to this statement by Bass: "'That's not good enough for me,' one man in the audience shouted. A burst of applause and another round of comment endorsing his complaint followed." [39]

The mood of the heavily Defender-dominated crowd at the meeting clearly was favorable to action cutting school appropriations. It may be that Supervisor John G. Bruce, himself an ardent Defender, was right in his assessment of the situation: "There was nothing else we could have done even if we had wanted to." [40]

And the supervisors clearly did not want to. Their attorneys were advising them that the only way they could be sure that a school board would not allow school desegregation was to refuse to appropriate money for the schools. In theory, they were protecting the school board from the courts by denying it funds to do the courts' bidding. Actually, they were tying the hands of a school board whose loyalty to segregation at all costs they could not insure. They did not believe that the courts could force them to appropriate money for public schools: This was to be the bedrock of the supervisors' legal position for years to come.

Bruce offered the motion to vote only the legal minimum for schools—$150,000—nothing like enough to operate a school system. It meant, in effect, that the county stood ready to let its schools close. As the *Richmond News-Leader* put it: "... it could be said that the courts ruled at noon that Negroes must be admitted to Prince Edward public schools, to which the county responded at 8 o'clock there will be no public schools." [41]

Much has been made of this action. Benjamin Muse recalls a talk with Dowell J. Howard, then State Superintendent of Schools, who said that Virginia would be all right in the school desegregation business if it could avoid sensations. Muse observed: "Alas, here was a major sensation within hours after the announcement of the Supreme Court's 1955 ruling. The news flashed across the nation and Prince Edward at once became famous, in a sense which was tragic for the little county, for Virginia, and for the South. Prince Edward became the symbol of the application of the Supreme Court ruling to an 'impossible' situation and an early symbol of resistance to it." [42]

This was precisely the symbolism that the Defenders wished the county to assume. They did not share the South's general belief in the "breather" provided by the court's latest decision. Delay had no appeal for them. They wished to see the issues joined, and in Prince Edward they could establish a pattern of action to be adopted wherever school segregation was threatened.

The pattern they had in mind was gradually evolving into a public statement. Editor Wall had said that public education would have to be replaced. The supervisors had taken a mighty step in this direction by refusing to appropriate funds for public schools. On the day after the meeting of May 31, Chairman Edward A. Carter of the supervisors released a statement that was intended to draw on the broadest possible base for support: "I believe in equal but separate schools for the children of the South as interpreted by the Supreme Court in 1896. I believe in states' rights. I believe that if we are left to work this question of schools out we will evolve a system acceptable to both races and in the best interest of all children. I believe we, of both races, should work for the mutual good of all. The citizens of Prince Edward have provided for Negro children a high school second to none in the country.

"I don't believe integration will serve to elevate or make better citizens of either race.

"In view of the above facts, we shall use every legal and honorable means to continue the high type of education we proposed to give the children of both races in Prince Edward County." [43]

This was talk designed to have appeal to the whites in Prince Edward County who might be uncertain of where they stood. After all, the county had built a magnificent, $800,000 Negro high school. The new Moton, built swiftly on the Hanbury property, had been in use since the fall of 1953. It had an auditorium, gymnasium, cafeteria—everything a modern high school should have. Carter was appealing to the broad mass of Prince Edward whites who might be expected to ask at this point why their Negro children should be entitled to more than had already been done for them.

These were words for Prince Edward. The Defenders were at work on a "Plan For Virginia" that would be presented to the Gray Commission, deliberating on the problems raised by the court's decisions, in a matter of days. This plan called upon the legislature to prevent expenditure of any funds on racially integrated public schools, to authorize use of public funds for private schools, and to remove all mention of compulsory education from state law. This was a plan to preserve segregation by state law *everywhere* throughout the state. This was massive resistance, as yet unnamed. The state was not quite ready for it yet, but the Defenders were paving the way.[44]

It was necessary in Prince Edward for the Defenders to solidify the gains they had made through the action of the board of supervisors. The community was not entirely unified behind the board's position. School board members were unhappy about what had happened, and their unhappiness could spread. School Board Chairman Bass recalls this feeling: "The board—several of us—felt that we had been kind of let down when the supervisors took their action, as though we had been slapped in the face." [45]

What the Defenders needed most now was a major expression of community harmony. The action of the supervisors on May 31 suggested how this might be accomplished. With no money appropriated for the public schools, the teachers would have to seek employment elsewhere as Bass had said—unless their salaries were guaranteed in some way. A public meeting to guarantee white teachers' salaries would be more than useful.

The one organization that could be used to turn out a good public showing over the issues of schools and teachers was the Parent-Teachers Association. The president of the Farmville Elementary PTA at the time was personable, influential B. Blanton Hanbury, scion of the prosperous Buffalo Shook Company. Hanbury was a solid supporter of resistance and an ideal man to line up the meeting.

It was decided that the PTA's should be kept out of the business officially, in deference to their nonpartisan status, but that the presidents of the PTA's and certain other "interested citizens" could meet to make plans. Hanbury remembers that the group in final form numbered about forty-five and that it met on the Saturday following the May 31 supervisors' meeting in the Town Council: "We concluded that something on the order of a corporation or foundation ought to be organized to set up a makeshift private school system." [46]

The supervisors' meeting had stirred the Richmond press, and stories on the activities in Prince Edward were in the papers every day. The *News Leader* reported that the PTA group would seek $200,000 to pay the salaries of the county's white teachers. [47] A mass meeting would be held on the following Tuesday. A committee under Hanbury was chosen to make the presentation to the public. In this same issue of the *News Leader* there was a story quoting Oliver Hill and other Negro leaders as saying that the NAACP had plans to petition all school boards in the state to end segregation.

Defenders' President Robert Crawford emphasized that the mass meeting was necessitated by the position in which the teachers found themselves. "Naturally they are as jittery as they can be. We felt we owed it to them to assure them that we would take care of them. This is white only—which is tragic of course. We are interested in educating all of the children of course." [48]

The churches of Prince Edward County on Sunday announced the Tuesday mass meeting which was to be held in Jarman Hall, Longwood College. Hanbury remembers that there was some discussion among the organizers of the meeting of how much usable space would be available for private schools in the event they had to be put into operation. [49]

The Defender leadership was aware that everything depended upon the outcome of the meeting. Editor Wall recalls the uncertainty: "We didn't know for sure what the people would do. We had heard rumors of some opposition." [50]

But there was much to stir the Defenders to optimism. Prince Edward's special position in the line of the court's fire had been amply described in the press. The people were aware that their county would be among the first in the country to be forced to integrate its schools. They were aware, too, that the NAACP would press its advantage wherever it could: any doubts about that were dispelled by Oliver Hill's statement. Finally, it was hard to believe that the people would not applaud the ostensible purpose of the meeting—preserving the county's white public school teaching staff.

Now was the time for the Defenders to consolidate their leadership. They had come a long way from the previous summer. The organization begun by a handful of men meeting on sidewalks had become a strong, well-integrated force that effectively controlled the main organs of community action in the county. Membership in Prince Edward County was estimated at about six hundred at this time;[51] but the total represented only organization leadership—broadly based on businessmen and farmers— rather than its following.

More importantly, by now the reaction against the Supreme Court decision that had spawned in Prince Edward was launched, full-flight, on the state. Much later, Publisher Wall recalled, the men who had summoned up this new symbol of resistance realized from what place in the past it had arisen: "Someone noticed one day that the name 'Defenders of State Sovereignty' is on the Confederate monument on High Street up yonder. I guess we just unconsciously lifted it from that." [52]

> Keep it, widowed, sonless mothers,
> Keep it, sisters, mourning brothers,
> Furl it with an iron will;
> Furl it now, but—keep it still,
> Think not that its work is done.
>
>   From "The Conquered Banner."

The Confederate monument in Farmville stands just back from the tree-lined sidewalk of High Street, across from the cool columns of Longwood College, in front of the red-brick Farmville Methodist Church. It is a statue of a soldier at the ready. The stone on the east side bears the legend "Erected by Confederate Veterans and the Daughters of the Confederacy, October 11, 1900"; on the west side is a list of the companies formed in the county in 1861; on the north a Confederate flag; and on the south, "Confederate Heroes 1861–Virginia–1865," and "Defenders of State Sovereignty." Cannonballs are perched on all four corners of stone.

The monument is more than simply a reminder of The War. It is a symbol, gathering about it the strands of legend and tradition that make Southside Prince Edward the place that it was and is. The Defenders would not need to look consciously to the monument for their past; they would, and did, remember that past in the words engraved on the monument.

From about 1895 the county's veterans of The War gathered annually to celebrate the cause, and in that year the United Daughters of the Confederacy set about to raise money for the monument. After the unveiling, the thinning ranks of gray would assemble at the monument annually, listen to speeches, and repair to the Eaco Theater (now the State, with the inevitable popcorn machine in the lobby) for entertainment. All this was not just for the veterans, whose rheumy eyes were turned toward each other in fading recollection; these were major occasions of public entertainment when old Tom Booker played the banjo and sang "I Ain't Never Been Reconstructed and I Don't Give a Damn" (after first asking permission of the giggling ladies to utter, in their presence, a cuss word), and then prizes were awarded to the high school youngsters for essays on historical subjects. An inspirational speaker would be on the program, and then the ladies of the UDC would serve dinner. Today's Defenders would have been young men in 1925, when Dr. Douglas Southall Freeman spoke; the reunion and, through it, The War and the monument, were all part of their memory.[53]

Defender President Crawford remembers a state-wide reunion in 1926. He had just come to Farmville. He recalls driving a couple of the veterans to Sailor Creek and that two from Staunton later came out to the Crawford house for supper: "They were pitiful old fellows. They were bewildered because what they remembered as a field had turned into woods at Sailor Creek."[54]

Only the young, who had not been there, could avoid these ugly little conflicts with reality. In Prince Edward County The War was a presence vivid enough to tempt youth to languish forever in the fields of the past.

The fighting had been almost over when it reached Southside Virginia in the spring of 1865. The county saw the last of it; the weary, bloody last of it then, but now, in the glory of defeat made more honorable with each passing year, the magnificent last of it. The Confederate Army, retreating northward, was caught in the Sailor Creek area and utterly crushed. Dr. Freeman describes the melancholy scene the next day when Lee stood with aides at the scene of the battle in what the historian has called the last rally of the Army of Northern Virginia. On

April 7, Lee arrived in Farmville and stopped at the home of an
ardent secessionist, Patrick Jackson; by early afternoon, he had
crossed over to the Cumberland side of the river and Farmville
was in federal hands. From the Randolph House that same day
General Grant dispatched the first of the surrender notes that led
to the meeting at Appomattox Courthouse two days later.[55]

The monument recalled all this. But there were tangible evi-
dences that the people of Prince Edward had grown up with—the
Hillsman House, with its honeysuckle and the fresh, scrubbed
look of preservatives; the Randolph House, now the Prince
Edward Hotel, and next to it the Whitfield Building, with its
scar from a Confederate shot intended for General Grant on the
hotel porch; the home of Patrick Jackson, still standing on Beech
Street where children play; and always, near at hand, Appomattox, honor out of defeat.

But the monument was more than a symbol of a defeat grown
resonant with the years. It also meant an attitude of independence, fiercely attained, fiercely to be defended. The Defenders
were not merely standing off the Yankee batteries, but all that
was alien as well; they were citizens of a South that remembered
far back before The War and the monument represented them,
and their South, as different, apart.

The Scotch-Irish and English settlers who divided up land in
what was then Amelia County south of the Appomattox River
in the mid-eighteenth century were a hardy lot, typical enough
of the frontiersman, quick to praise and quick to fight.[56] They
developed the strain of independence and the tendency to orient
to the family that typified Southern out-settlement. When the
time came to break the ties with Great Britain, men like these
marched with Captain John Morton in 1776 from Prince
Edward Courthouse for eastern Virginia, Suffolk, and Portsmouth, to skirmish with Dunmore's forces. Even more were home
when Cornwallis sent Lieutenant Colonel Banastre Tarleton with
his raiders into Southside counties in the summer of 1781.[57]

The monument stood for this too, the birth pains of a nation in
Virginia, where towering men were born into service.

The habit of unreflective action spilled over into this Southern
society. Prince Edward historian Bradshaw notes that slaves
were not the only ones to answer in court for assaults: "One of
the most surprising discoveries in reading the court order books
of the period is the number of times Scotch-Irish settlers were

involved in such charges. Some of them seem to have been contentious and hot-headed, quick to anger and prompt to strike." [58]

The same might be said along any frontier. But this part of the South was not to experience the flood of immigration that washed out or diluted the old frontier ideas. The real as well as the spiritual descendants of these days of drums live in Prince Edward County today. They do not find reason to take issue with John Hill, the only Whig to represent Prince Edward in Congress, who said after his election in 1839—"My most ardent wish is to lessen the powers of this government—and if it cannot be done, I believe that within twenty years it will be an absolute despotism." [59] Jefferson's agrarian, least-governing society lingered and is remembered yet in a county where 99 per cent of the population are native-born Americans.

The habits of independence were brought to the slavery issue. Citizens of Prince Edward not in sympathy with slavery felt that Virginia would emancipate eventually if left to herself but feared the consequences of outside forces exerting pressure. It was perhaps as much against the pressure as for the institution that they reacted. For them, John Brown's raid was the torch in the sky, the signal. As early as December, 1859, Bradshaw records, able and distinguished members of the Virginia bar gathered at Prince Edward to draw up resolutions: ". . . if the Abolition or Black Republican Party wins, the time may have come for the South, by proper regard to its interests and rights, to withdraw." [60]

By 1861 secessionist feeling in Prince Edward was described by the *Richmond Enquirer* as perhaps the most unanimous in the state.[61] Virginia was relatively late to secede; but in counties like Prince Edward in Virginia's Southside, the secession of the spirit came early. The old habit of independence, the economic orientation of the area to the Tobacco South, the presence of two Negroes in the county for every white contributed to this. Since 1831, when Nat Turner's slaves had revolted and slaughtered whites in Southampton County, seventy-five miles from Prince Edward, the sense of violence had hung over the South in which the white man was a minority. After John Brown this was clearly the peril to be answered.

The peril, the answer to it—these, too, are represented in the monument in the minds of some.

Then The War and then the end. Prince Edward, occupied

before Appomattox, later under military rule, later with the Underwood Convention represented in Congress by an English-born Yankee and a Negro.[62] The peril of rebellion was replaced by the peril of Negro rule, carpetbag-scalawag-Yankee-Negro rule; the hand of the stranger was in command. It was with this same hand that the public school system was built and closely associated with all that was alien to the South. It was another creature of the Occupation, a work of invaders.

The Occupation went on, resisted in the main by political means. The Conservatives (Democrats) fought for home rule against the hated Radicals (Republicans). Once snipers were stationed in second-story windows on Main and Third Streets (where groups of whites and Negroes walk and stand now in spring evenings, under the facades of commerce) and were instructed to shoot down certain white Radicals participating in a street celebration of "Union League and Emancipation" day. They did not shoot, perhaps never intended to shoot, but they were there, with guns, the avengers.[63]

A nation ready to embark on the Gilded Age was also ready to forgive the South and forget the Negro. The Compromise Election of 1877 indicated the kind of turn that lay ahead. As C. Vann Woodward has observed, the politicians who had elevated the Negro as a political convenience were willing to let him fall as a political convenience.[64] In 1901 the literacy test for voting in Virginia became law, and the *Farmville Herald* estimated that not over 10 per cent of the Negro vote remained by the next year.[65] The Conservatives were back in power at the sufferance of a nation tired of contention.

With the peril past, the White South set its mind to find a place where the Negro would be useful but neither a political nor an economic threat. The old, personal relationships of slavery were no longer possible; the new relationships would continue to be on the white man's terms. Lines would be drawn that could not be crossed. By the end of the century, Negroes who were members of white churches would have left. By 1896 this impulse would be established as doctrine by a Supreme Court that laid the groundwork for separate but equal.[66] With this decision segregation was recognized officially and soon would widen and tighten its grip on custom.

There was an attempted lynching in Prince Edward County in that year of 1896.[67] For some, the Negro's place needed constant definition and explanation. By 1902 "Sufferer" in the *Farmville Herald* called for state legislation bringing segregation to depots as well as moving trains to preserve whites from "filth of body, filth of tongue, bad whiskey and bad pipe odors." [68]

Was this part of a spirit to be memorialized or simply remembered?

By the time the men who would become the Defenders of State Sovereignty and Individual Liberties were boys, listening to old Tom Booker's banjo and Dr. Freeman's sonorities, the monument had come to take on different meanings from any that could have reposed in the minds of its builders.

Booker sang:

> Oh, I'm a good old Rebel, Now that's just what I am,
> For this "Fair Land of Freedom" I do not give a damn!
> I'm glad I fit against it, I only wish we'd won,
> And I don't want no pardon for anything I done . . .
>
> I hates the Yankee nation and everything they do,
> I hates the Declaration of Independence too;
> I hates the 'glorious Union,'
> 'Tis dripping with our blood,
> I hates their striped banner,
> I fit it all I could.

Bradshaw reports that these words invariably were greeted enthusiastically. "The theater never echoed greater applause than that which broke forth as Booker twanged the last note from his banjo." [69] The Confederate Major Innes Randolph's bit of folk poetry, sardonically dedicated to tough old Thad Stevens, still brought shouts of approval half a century after it was written. There was simple high-spiritedness, even humor, in the approval. But if the song had meaning, what was that meaning?

The twentieth-century Defenders who looked to the monument for their name and their inspiration might not have been in agreement themselves. Perhaps it meant something different to each of them; certainly it meant little, consciously, to many of them. But just as they lifted their name unconsciously from its inscription, they honored its spirit without having to think about it. If they did think about it, they said that the monument stood for a way of life that had been born with the striking away of the tyrant's hand at the end of Reconstruction. Long years after the last soldiers fell came the rebirth of the South that they celebrated and meant to defend. It was a South that had been forced to accept the proposition that all men must be free but that had made its own rules for that freedom. In the end, the rules came to be a way of life: they could not imagine the South without segregation.

7.   THE DISSENTERS

Among the spectators at the meeting on May 31 at which the supervisors refused to appropriate money for public schools was one who kept silent with some difficulty. The Reverend James R. Kennedy, the pastor of the Farmville Presbyterian Church, had come merely to listen, for information. He left after the meeting shaken at what he had seen and heard. He pondered later the "mob spirit" present at the meeting: "It was implied rather than actual. There was a great deal of zeal and fervor, rising and shouting. . . . Then I remember later someone saying 'I would rather my child grew up in absolute ignorance than go to school one day with a black child.'" [1]

Mr. Kennedy concluded that the board of supervisors had little choice of action in the face of this demonstration of sentiment. His own concern was that this high feeling would spill over into a public community act that would later be regretted. He was afraid for the public schools. With the announcement later of the Tuesday mass meeting at Longwood College, he had to ask himself what he should do.

Here was no simple question to be answered blandly with a biblical allusion. Mr. Kennedy had never looked upon himself as a man free of prejudice. There had been a time—and he remembered it clearly and well and not unpleasantly—when he had accepted the separation of the races as ordained by God, or at least, immutably, by man. He could remember when he had not the slightest taint of doubt that this was right, and even now he could not think of those days except in terms of innocence.

Moral judgments on the validity of segregation did not impinge on life in the small South Carolina town of Chester, where

Mr. Kennedy grew up. His father was a dentist and a Presbyterian elder, a man more than ordinarily devout. The Kennedy family enjoyed simple Christian bonds and secure ties to the community. The fact that the Negroes who flocked the streets and worked the farms did not go to school with white children or sit at counters with whites in public eating places was entirely without significance to young Kennedy. Segregation was not something imposed by one race on another, but something as natural as people, as natural as black and white.

Mr. Kennedy marks his years at Union Theological Seminary in Richmond as those in which doubts about segregation arose. These were theoretical doubts, the stuff of a minister's training, not the kind to send the young South Carolinian into the Negro streets of Richmond where he would find, in any event, nothing that would shock him with the urge to reform. But a passage in the Bible seized him. It was from Ezekiel. The prophet, stricken with his vision of the wheel in the air and the four figures, had been ordered by the Lord to go to the children of Israel. Ezekiel 3:15 tells of his going: "Then I came to them of the captivity at Tel-abib that dwelt by the river of Chebar, and I sat where they sat, and remained there astonished among them seven days."

The passage, with its sense of revelation, haunted the young minister. It had a message in terms of discovery among one's fellow men. He related it to the white man and the Negro, and its mystery worked on him in succeeding years.

His early pastorates were in Spartanburg, South Carolina, and Whiteville, North Carolina, where segregation was hardly being questioned. He left an associate pastorship in Norfolk, Virginia, for Farmville in January, 1950, arriving only a few months after another young minister, Mr. Griffin, had returned to live with his people. If Mr. Griffin came on a mission of social reform, Mr. Kennedy did not. He remembers that ensuing strike at Moton dimly; his sentiments were for better school facilities for the Negro children, but he did not think that the school suit filed by the NAACP was a good thing or, at first, that it would succeed.

But as the years went by without a decision from the Supreme Court, he became convinced that it would succeed. He made an effort to prepare the community, only to find that resistance was deeply rooted. He found the atmosphere for discussion unbelievably poor. He found that the other ministers in town could not agree on an approach to the problem. Members of his own congregation could not agree on how to meet the problem. Worse, he found that the subject could not be discussed without vehemence. Most of the members ridiculed the idea that the Supreme Court would rule in favor of the Negro plaintiffs.[2]

Not long after the court's decision of May, 1954, the Presbyterian Synod of Virginia met in Staunton and voted its endorsement. Mr. Kennedy came home to a disturbed congregation and elected, on the following Sunday, to discard a prepared sermon and preach on the church's decision. His effort was to try to allay fears that had arisen, but the net result was that the congregation became even more disturbed. Mr. Kennedy feels that 95 per cent of his congregation would have been satisfied only with his direct opposition to the Synod's action. This he could not give, because he had voted for that action.

Criticism of the minister rose in a tide. Staunchly Presbyterian Farmville numbered some of its first citizens in Mr. Kennedy's church. These included, as members of the church Session, School Superintendent McIlwaine, and more ardent segregationists such as Fred H. Hanbury and Crawford. The latter found in the Synod's action confirmation of his worst fears about the liberal tendencies of the new churchmen. The opposition to Mr. Kennedy's role also included some who did not care to speak to him face to face: he received anonymous telephone calls and letters on the subject.

The ordeal fired Mr. Kennedy's personal position in this matter: "It was quite a struggle for me to know what sort of position I as a pastor should take. I had gotten rid of most of my prejudice. . . . I still have some, I don't think I'll ever get rid of all of it." [3]

One of the chief criticisms of the Synod's action was that it called for integration of youth conferences of the church. This outraged many of Mr. Kennedy's congregation. He considered the action somewhat hasty, but he would not renounce it. He elected to go along with the church's view, beginning with the words of the General Assembly resolution—"enforced segregation of the races is discrimination which is out of harmony with Christian theology." He was not out to integrate; he placed great emphasis on this opposition to "enforced" segregation.

The board of supervisors' meeting of May 31, then, had special significance for Mr. Kennedy. He would have to make a different kind of decision now. He would have to decide whether to take up this fight on the local level, whether to take this occasion of public fervor to fly in the face of an already aroused congregation. Segregation was not the only issue here. It was plain to Mr. Kennedy that public education was in some danger. He could imagine jerry-built private schools for whites and nothing for Negroes. As one who had attended public school, he felt a strong commitment to public education. He wrote later: "My people have always believed in education and have seen to it that their children received what public education offered, as well as private or church-supported higher education. Education —both public and private—is a part of the Presbyterian heritage." [4]

On the Tuesday of the mass meeting, he had not yet made up his mind what to do. He spent the day in a fever of activity, telephoning people he thought or hoped would be opposed to the establishment of private schools. He recalls that he was interested only in discovering what he should do and how he might be effective: "I was accused later of lining up everything. It was all laid at my door. But I didn't know what I was going to do. As I walked in I met at the door a professor of English and another professor, Foster Gresham. It was Gresham who said that he was prepared to offer a motion such as the one that was passed in Nottoway County to insure all the public school teachers their salaries for the coming year. I said I would second the motion." [5]

The one thing that people who attended the June 7 mass meeting at Jarman Hall agree upon is that a sense of crisis was in the air. The very size of the crowd pressing in from High Street was evidence of that. Jarman Hall, a new building on Farmville's Longwood College campus, was built in 1950 after a fire, and its seating capacity was 1,250. As the hour for the meeting approached, it appeared that there might not be seats for all.

School Board Chairman Bass remembers his reaction to this midweek turnout: "If you can pick up some 1,500 people in a county this size for a meeting, you know that some pretty deep feelings are involved." [6]

For himself, Bass could not view the swelling crowd with anything but concern: "I was under considerable pressure because I had to make a statement that I was expecting to be unpopular." [7]

Some others who were not on the speaker's platform felt keenly that the works of this night would be of moment. Dr. Dabney

Lancaster, within a month of retirement as president of Long-wood, had not come prepared to speak; yet he experienced a sensation of apprehension that he does not remember as pleasurable. He was not a Defender. He was a public school man. He looked about him, and up at the platform, and what he saw and heard was not reassuring.

Nobody from the college was on the speaker's platform. The school board was not represented, either, nor the school board's attorneys. The dozen people on the platform were heads of local PTA's and other "interested" citizens. They had been chosen at the Saturday meeting of PTA heads, but they were not representing the PTA's, and the state organization had nothing to do with the meeting. They were, for the most part, staunch Defenders. All were in favor of the plan that was to be presented.

Chairman B. Blanton Hanbury called on Maurice Large, the former chairman of the school board. Large asked that the topics of integration and segregation be set aside and that the group turn its attention to a single problem—the necessity of keeping the county's white public school teachers. The supervisors had appropriated no money, and the school board could guarantee the teachers no pay. Large proposed the creation of a non-profit organization to solicit $233,550 to guarantee the salaries of the county's sixty-nine white teachers: "In your discussion please bear in mind that this meeting is called for one purpose and one purpose only, namely to attempt to insure that our teaching staff will be available to our school board this fall, provided our school board comes into a position where it can operate the schools." [8]

And, if the school board could not operate the schools—that is, if the courts did order desegregation? Large's speech was utterly silent on this point. But the money, having been pledged to the teachers, would have to go to the teachers—in a private school system. This thought was unspoken; but it lay in wait before every step taken at the meeting.

Hanbury called upon speakers from the platform. One by one, they rose to offer support of the proposal. It was the only way to keep the teachers, their remarks implied. Could anyone oppose keeping the teachers? Individuals in the audience began to speak on behalf of the plan.

Observers friendly to the dominant view spoke later of the spontaneous action that was the night's work. Others regarded the results as engineered skillfully by the choice of speakers. Dr. Lancaster recalls his own reaction: "I went to the meeting without even expecting to make a statement. Then, by George, I found that Blanton Hanbury had Mayor Fitzpatrick and Barrye Wall and all the representatives from the PTA's lined up, and they produced a parrot-like performance, each one making the same speech. Impromptu speakers from the floor joined in, some of them very radical. It was apparent that they were willing to close the schools." [9]

Closed public schools. Here was the issue in the bottom layer, below the explicit purpose of raising money to hold the teachers and the implied purpose of using the money for a private system. A private system meant the death of the public system, closed schools, did it not? Some in the audience thought so; but the big majority, gathering its slow assent to the performance of the platform speakers, probably thought in simpler terms, of the threat posed by an alien court's despicable decision and of the way the community had come together to answer it.

Dr. Lancaster stood up and waved to get Chairman Hanbury's attention. As he took the platform to speak, the big crowd hushed. Here was a figure from the world of education whose presence commanded respect—former state superintendent of instruction, even now concluding a popular term as president of Longwood, among the state's most respected educators. And few in the hall that night were sure just where Dr. Lancaster would stand. Those in the audience whose minds were not made up looked for guidance. The Defender organizers of the meeting, whose minds were made up, leaned forward in their seats expectantly. Upstairs in the balcony, Defender President Crawford, who was not scheduled to speak that night—he has recalled since that the reason he was not was that the organizers of the meeting wished to preserve its local nature—got up and began to pace about in the foyer.

It was a curious speech, full of the conflicts of the day. Recalling it much later, Dr. Lancaster spoke of his purpose: "I told them that I was in full sympathy with what they had in mind on integration, thought it bad for both races, but that we could not afford to close the schools, that that would be bad for the whites and that we could not afford to have Negroes running in the streets. . . . Some good friends of mine said that if they didn't know I was leaving, they would assume that I would be run out. But some Negroes also said that I'd made an inflammatory speech against them. It was damned if you do, damned if you don't. But the people I knew and had respect for I felt would understand what I was saying." [10]

The newspapers devoted considerable space the next day to his remarks. He was quoted as believing that the schools could be run on a segregated basis for the coming year and that the Supreme Court's 1955 decree was a retreat from its earlier position. He was also quoted as saying that closing public schools would "open the way to dictatorship." But he delivered himself of a stirring defense of segration too: "We'll fight it [integration] from the housetops, from the street corners, in every possible way. We are going to maintain our way of life." [11]

Upstairs, Crawford listened with feverish interest. Furiously pacing the foyer as Dr. Lancaster's voice dipped and raised with his emphasis, Crawford ran into J. Barrye Wall, Jr., the publisher's son and Defender attorney. Crawford remembers the exchange: "I said, 'What's he doing?' and Bo said, 'He's ruining us.' Lancaster was talking about fighting integration from the housetops and alleys and all this, but he said that if this country ever gave up public education the Communists would take over. He even fooled John Steck who was covering for the paper. Hell, he was talking about saving public education." [12]

It was not surprising that opinions later were so divided on Dr. Lancaster's speech. He was expressing approval of the money-raising plan only as it might work to hold the public school teachers. This was his immediate concern. But he was also recognizing that the money could be used to substitute private for public schools, and this he opposed.

Dr. Lancaster's dilemma was not merely one of making himself understood, though. At this point, words meant nothing if they could not persuade. Dr. Lancaster was enough of a Southsider to know that the Jarman Hall crowd was aroused and that he would have to use strong words—and some words they wanted to hear—to carry them along with him. Dr. Lancaster's real dilemma was one that was to confront Southern moderates more than once in the years to come: How far ahead of the people can leadership march and still lead? Dr. Lancaster wrapped his support of public schools in a garb he hoped would be acceptable to his audience.

Opinions later reflected differences of temperament. Mr. Kennedy was deeply disappointed that Dr. Lancaster had chosen to speak "like a politician." [13] Others who did not favor the private school idea thought that he had made his point successfully. Some of those who did favor the private schools—Editor Wall among them—thought that Lancaster's talk actually backfired on him and helped their cause. [14]

When Dr. Lancaster sat down there was a polite silence but no applause. Professor Gresham stood up and offered a motion. In substance it called for a petition to the board of supervisors asking for a public declaration of the board's intention to honor teacher contracts the following years. This was the action the Nottoway County supervisors had taken. What Gresham was asking was for the Prince Edward supervisors, in effect, to reverse themselves.

Chairman Hanbury declared Gresham's motion "entirely out of order," but Mr. Kennedy rose to second it anyway. He insisted that the motion was in order. He did not make a speech, contenting himself with saying that he thought Gresham's motion would protect all teachers.

The audience stirred restlessly. Some confusion existed over what the intent and scope of Gresham's motion was. Did it contemplate guaranteeing salaries for white teachers or for all teachers? he was asked.

For all teachers, he replied.

A chorus of "no's" and "boo's" swept the hall. Like nothing else that happened that night this response betrayed the depth of rift between the Negro and white communities. If the Negroes wanted to keep their teachers, this motion said, they would have to do so on their own. [15]

School Board Chairman Bass remembers the sensation of rising tension. The meeting was trembling on the brink of disorder. "I don't think I've been in so large a meeting when the tension was so high. You might almost have expected a riot." [16]

From the audience a man arose to challenge Mr. Kennedy. He asked the chair if the preacher would state whether or not he was an integrationist.

Mr. Kennedy remembers putting down his anger and responding that he did not think that the question was to the point of the meeting: "I said that if the speaker would meet me afterwards I would state my position." [17]

Chairman Hanbury ruled that the question was out of order.

At this point, the private school group desperately needed something to turn the meeting back to its original purposes. Then Mayor W. C. Fitzpatrick provided a substitute motion for the Gresham motion, which had not received recognition from the chair. The Fitzpatrick motion called for the establishment of a private corporation to raise funds to guarantee the salaries of the county's white teachers. Here was the plan that Large had outlined in his opening address. The Fitzpatrick motion was quickly seconded, and the Gresham motion passed into limbo.

But the contention was not over yet. School Board Chairman Bass, under wraps by order of the board's attorneys felt that the public schools could be operated "as before" (the accepted euphemism for "segregated") for at least another year.

Once again this simple statement of the attorneys' opinion drew fire. Mrs. C. W. Glenn, wife of a Defender officer and member of the platform group, objected to the phrases "they thought" and "probably" that Bass had used in restating the attorneys' opinion. She expressed her view: "That is not good enough." [18]

And once again, this sentiment was applauded. Ideally, from the Defenders' viewpoint, this would have been the time for a vote on the Fitzpatrick motion.

But James Bash, the personable principal of Farmville High School, had a prepared list of questions he wished to ask the platform group. They were questions that he said bothered members of his teaching staff. If salaries were paid by the private corporation the following year, would teachers get credit for that year's teaching experience in any other school division in the East? Would they lose membership in teachers' professional organizations? To whom would they be responsible? What work would be expected of them? Assuming that private schools ultimately were formed to make use of the teachers, could public buildings be used? If not, where could classes be held? What equipment would be provided? Would pupils get credit for their work? What accrediting standards would exist?

For himself, Bash spoke out plainly: "I am a public school man. I would be unable to accept a check from a private corporation of this kind." [19]

In the discussion that followed this battery of questions—few of which were, or could have been, answered with any assurance—one teacher said she would do her duty to the county children regardless of where the money came from. Robert Gilmer, coach at the high school, stood up: "If some of you will feed me next year you don't have to worry about giving me a dime to look after your kids." [20]

Gilmer's statement was greeted with thundering applause. The one thing that almost everyone present could agree upon was that this audience of whites had a duty to try to keep white teachers. Here was one of them offering to stay under any conditions. Gilmer, a husky, friendly man, had captured the spirit of the meeting, which was that sacrifices had to be made in the name of the good—and the good could be education as well as segregation. With this mighty, if vague, consensus called into being, nothing remained but the vote.

When Chairman Hanbury called for those favoring the Fitzpatrick resolution to stand and be counted, the hall seemed to rise up in a body. Nervous laughter broke out as those standing contemplated their virtual unanimity. Then Chairman Hanbury called for those opposed to stand.

One account of the meeting put the majority vote at over 1,250 and the minority at about 25.[21] Some who were opposed to the plan probably elected not to single themselves out against such a formidable majority; if so, this merely confirmed the majority victory. Some later criticized the procedure by which the dissenters were made to identify themselves. Superintendent McIlwaine described it thus: "It was a kind of 'look at em' thing, utterly unfair. Many people went along with the majority who were not sure." [22]

Editor Wall counted 15 votes against the Fitzpatrick motion, including in that number one drunk who spent the next day walking the streets of Farmville apologizing to one and all, more for his vote than for his drunkenness.[23]

After the meeting had adjourned, a reporter corralled Mr. Kennedy and Professor M. H. Bittinger of Longwood College, who also had stood with the minority. The next day Mr. Kennedy was quoted as saying: "I think the action of the board of supervisors was hastily taken without fully realizing the consequences of their action. . . . The answer to our problem definitely does not lie in the abolition of our public schools." [24]

And Professor Bittinger: "[The supervisors] should have waited for some pattern of action on a state-wide level . . . . [There is] tremendous danger that the plan proposed here now might be out of step with the state's policy." [25]

But this was happening on the fringe of the dissolving meeting. The important thing that was happening was that printed pledges were being distributed among the audience committing those who signed them to support a nonprofit organization that would be chartered to hold funds aside for educational purposes. A total of sixteen thousand dollars in these pledges was collected at the meeting, according to later reports. The *Richmond News Leader* reported that fifty-five thousand dollars had been collected by the next day.[26]

What would the next step be? Most of the members of the Jarman Hall audience could not know this, but any who thought that they were voting nothing more than support for public school teachers were deluding themselves sadly. For they were doing two other things that were more important and worked directly against the maintenance of public schools. They were establishing an organization that could pay the white teachers privately, and they were making a distinction between these white teachers and the Negro teachers whose salaries thus were not guaranteed.

Whatever the Jarman Hall audience thought it was doing, the Defender strategy was clear. The pressure on the Negro community to withdraw the demand for desegregation was implied by the threat to close schools. But the threat was no empty one, and the Defender strategy was based on the assumption that the Negro community would not withdraw and that the courts would at some future date order desegregation. Some of these men may have hoped to see that day—at least that is the charge that has been leveled at them by those who have regarded their support for public education as less than devoted. Certainly they were clear in their minds that they would scrap the public schools in a minute rather than accept any desegregation.

The stated purpose of the meeting—the protection of the white public school teachers—actually was something of a paper issue. Despite the validity of Bash's questions, there was little likelihood that many of these teachers would leave the county for employment elsewhere. Most were not professional educators like Bash who could be expected to use a wide range of choice in deciding where to teach. Most had local roots; they were natives of the county or were married to men well established in the county. A knowledgeable source estimated later that the private school people might have counted on 70 to 75 per cent of these teachers remaining regardless of an advance guarantee of salary.[27]

The real Defender victory had little to do with "keeping the public school teachers" but everything to do with the method to be employed to this end. The real Defender victory was the establishment of an organization—the Prince Edward Educational Corporation—empowered to collect money for private education and supported on the record by a massive display of public sentiment. From this point on the Defenders in Prince Edward County are synonomous with the private school foundation leaders for all practical purposes. With the powerful running start supplied by the Jarman Hall meeting, the educational corporation had collected $180,000 in pledges by mid-July.[28] It was a going concern from the moment of its birth.

The corporation was no accident, just as the private school corporation was no ad hoc body thrown together in haste at the Jarman Hall meeting. The private school corporation was merely the end product of a plan that the Defender leadership had been hatching almost from the inception of this resistance group. It was a plan that looked to the likelihood of private, rather than public, schools at some point in the future. To succeed, this plan required an organization, and the Prince Edward Educational Corporation was the organization. All this took careful planning.

One of those in attendance at the Jarman Hall meeting noted that the pledges' being distributed from the speaker's platform after the meeting were not scraps of paper, but legal, binding documents. Editor Wall threw some light on the meeting: "It was a meeting in which a big decision was made by the people. But a considerable amount of preparation had gone into it. You could tell this because two days after the decision the charter was granted to the group set up." [29]

The significance of the Jarman Hall meeting was lost, too, on the Negro community, despite the fact that the meeting itself—ironically enough—was integrated. Fred Reid, the retired railroad man who enjoyed Crawford's confidence, had asked if he and other Negroes might attend and was told to come ahead. He complained later that little interest was shown by Negroes in the community.[30] In any event, only Reid, Dr. Miller, the former Moton PTA chairman, and one other man attended. Dr. Miller recalls that because of the size of the meeting they were thoroughly integrated into the seating at the hall. But the one thing that Dr. Miller recalled later was that Dr. Lancaster had told the whites not to close the schools. At the time, that seemed to him to be the important news.[31]

The crisis over the public schools of Prince Edward County in 1955 lasted just long enough for the private school group to make a success of it. On July 18 a three-judge federal court, following the precedent set in Clarendon County, South Carolina, a few days earlier, ruled that Prince Edward County would not have to desegregate its schools in September. The court did hold that desegregation must take place at some future date, but set no time limit. The decision meant that public schools could be operated on a segregated basis once again. By this time, however, it was a simple matter for the private school group to applaud the outcome as a well-needed "respite" from the court's pressure and continue to hold the pledges.

The county's public school system was in danger. Some of those in attendance at the Jarman Hall meeting recognized this fact. Supervisor Bruce remembers overhearing one woman leaving the meeting expressing her fears for the public school system in a motherly way. " 'Just think of the poor little children', she said. 'They won't get hot lunches anymore.' " [32]

Bruce was amused.

In June, after the court's decision permitting the county to operate its schools on a segregated basis for the time being, reporter Homer Bigart, then of the *New York Herald Tribune*, came to Farmville. He interviewed a number of the principals at the Jarman meeting, among them Mr. Kennedy.

The Jarman Hall meeting had left a bitter residue for Mr. Kennedy; the preacher was in serious trouble with his own congregation. But the brunt of public opinion at large was not directed at him until publication of the two-part series Bigart wrote. Robert Crawford, described by Bigart as one of the prime movers in the efforts to unseat Mr. Kennedy, significantly blamed "religionists" for "pouring out propaganda against segregation." But the real cutting edge was supplied by the quotes attributed to Mr. Kennedy himself: "As a Christian, I can't defend segregation. . . . You can't take the Gospel with its great message of His love for every one and defend enforced segregation." [1]

In territory usually regarded as Bible Belt in sentiment, these were hard words indeed. At least one person who wished the preacher no good had copies of the article distributed widely throughout the county. Several of these copies were mailed to Mr. Kennedy with what the senders considered appropriate comment. One passage in Bigart's story described Mr. Kennedy's dilemma lucidly: "I haven't been under any persecution, but some individuals would like to see me move on. Some folks who had been rather warm friends have been cool. But the Lord has given me a feeling of peace. I'd do it all over again. In weaker moments I think I ought to go, but I don't want to." [2]

One letter writer merely bracketed this passage suggestively. Another typed the comment: "For the good of all concerned you would be wise to find another church." [3]

Mr. Kennedy's mail volume picked up sharply. From California, Philadelphia, and Boston came letters supporting him, written by people who had seen the stories. From New York came a denunciation. The local mail contained nothing but criticism. Those whom the preacher believed agreed with him kept silent. The telephone's ringing could mean some new unpleasantness.

Mr. Kennedy knew that he had friends in the county, inside and outside the church. But he could see the beginnings of real, internal trouble. Robert Crawford was a power in the church and word came to the preacher that Crawford was making his position an issue among the congregation. Crawford says that he never took overt action to see that the preacher was removed, but that he did believe that Kennedy ought to go: "It might be a bit strong to say that his position ruined his chances of having a good ministry in Farmville. But it certainly hurt him. He realized after that that he had better find someplace to go. He certainly could not be as useful to the church as if he had remained neutral." [4]

Others in positions of importance in the church agreed with Crawford. Some disagreed but they were less vocal than the others. The matter came to a head, as far as Mr. Kennedy was concerned, in August. He was scheduled to go on vacation to the orchard country in Linden, Virginia, near Front Royal, and he was uncertain what might happen while he was away. Was it not possible that the dissension over him might break out into the open? Could this disagreement not do serious damage to the church before he returned?

Some considerations might have persuaded Mr. Kennedy to stay. Far from being unorthodox, his views on race matters were demonstrably in harmony with those of the Presbyterian church. On the same day that the Jarman Hall meeting had been held, for instance, the General Assembly of the Southern Presbyterian Church meeting at Montreat, North Carolina, voted 236 to 169 for a report from the Council of Christian Relations, which said, in part, "enforced segregation of races is discrimination which is out of harmony with Christian theology." [5] This statement was no less than what Mr. Kennedy had said. The church was with him rather than with the unhappy members of his congregation. He had ammunition with which to remain and fight, if he chose.

But the fight would be ugly. Mr. Kennedy, a slight, bookish man, describes himself as a man who hates to fight. He could not, then, look forward to a fight from a personal standpoint nor could he persuade himself that the church would benefit from a clash that would certainly place neighbor against neighbor and stir enmities that would stand to divide the congregation for a generation. Against this recognition he placed his conviction that he was right—that the General Assembly of the church was right—and that his duty required that he stay.

He had not planned to stay in Prince Edward County indefinitely. He had thought in terms of a stay of five or six years, and he had been there that long already and had turned down several calls to leave. If he stayed on for an indefinite period now it would be in some part to wage a kind of crusade on the race issue. He felt that he had to consider whether this would be justified, what it would do, for instance, to the church's building program and other measures for growth. He struggled mightily with his conscience over these questions. In the end he could not justify the fight: "I love the church too much to see it divided. . . . I don't feel that I was pressured into resigning. I went to the Session when I felt animosity against me was rising. I told them that for the good of the church it would be wise for me to consider moving, sometime between then and the close of school in June, 1956, that I would leave then. I told them to keep it to themselves. . . . I believe there was a genuine searching of the hearts on the part of the Session." [6]

But the decision to leave following the graduation of his son, David, from Farmville High School did not entirely relieve Mr. Kennedy of personal pressures: "The real impact hit home when my boy David . . . began to be subjected to some rather unfortunate incidents. He was playing basketball and one boy in particular made it rough on him under the excuse of ordinary contact. He made some snide remarks that made it plain that this was because of my stand on segregation. He began to feel the pressure there. Later, at the close of his senior year, I felt he was thoroughly eligible for the Beta club, having the honors and the position in his class. He didn't make it and I felt that was definitely attributable to me." [7]

Word got around that Mr. Kennedy might be available elsewhere, and a number of inquiries came from congregations in the East. One was from Charlotte, North Carolina. "I realized that anywhere I went in the South the issue would be with us. After a year of it I had gotten into a rundown state of mental and physical exhaustion. I longed for a respite." [8]

In April, 1956, Mr. Kennedy told his congregation that he was leaving for a church in Hinton, West Virginia, in June, after David's graduation.

The congregation seemed surprised at this announcement, Mr. Kennedy recalls.[9] Some of the congregation resist to this day the idea that he was forced out of his ministry there. When reporter Lucy Daniels was doing a story in Prince Edward County, she came across such a parishioner, a woman who pointed out that when Mr. Kennedy left Farmville a grateful congregation gave him five hundred dollars and a sterling silver tea service.[10]

Of the four other individuals who had singled themselves out as dissenters at the Jarman Hall meeting, three decided, for different reasons, to say no more publicly. Professor Gresham, who says that he simply did not understand what was at stake at the meeting, became a supporter of the private school position;[11] Chairman Bass, for reasons of health not entirely dissociated from the pressures on him in the school fight, resigned as chairman of the school board; and Professor Bittinger decided to keep his thoughts to himself.[12]

The fourth, Principal Bash, posed a special problem to those who liked him and wanted to keep him in Prince Edward. Among those was School Board Chairman Bass, who has said since then, "I feel very bad about that whole thing. He sat right there where you are sitting that day and told me what he was going to say. I didn't put any words in his mouth but I didn't try to talk him out of it. I didn't foresee the reaction that he would get. . . .The feeling was high against him and Kennedy. They seemed to blame those two." [13]

School Superintendent McIlwaine also had high regard for Bash, a Midwesterner who had graduated from the University of Virginia and was in his first year as principal of the high school. McIlwaine says that there was pressure on Bash as a result of what he had said on June 7, but that some members of the principal's teaching staff did what they could to persuade him to sign papers sent by the foundation people to the school indicating that he would teach in the private schools if and when they were established.[14] Bash would not sign.

He may have represented a special problem to the private school forces. For if what he had said at Jarman Hall were taken as the sentiment of the teachers in general, all the subscription money in the world would not create private schools in Prince Edward. The story of the meeting, in the *Herald*, made no mention of Mr. Kennedy or Professor Bittinger, but it did devote considerable space to Principal Bash. It quoted his statement at some length but only after reporting a statement signed by fifteen teachers at Farmville High School: "We, the undersigned teachers and staff of Farmville High School, do appreciate and endorse the action taken by the patrons and citizens of Prince Edward County at a mass meeting at Jarman Hall, June 7, 1955." [15]

A spokesman for the teachers, not named, was quoted as saying that only one member of the staff definitely was opposed to the Jarman Hall action; others were away on vacation and could not be reached. No telepathy was required to determine who this one dissenter was, for Bash's statements that followed made this clear enough.

So Bash was publicly isolated from other teachers at the high school. He had set his course, perhaps irrevocably, at the Jarman Hall meeting and he did not deviate from it. He handed in his resignation, basing it on the uncertainty of operating public schools in the years ahead. On August 8 the school board accepted this resignation along with Bash's thanks to the board and to Superintendent McIlwaine for their support.

In October, 1955, the Prince Edward County Board of Supervisors passed a resolution abolishing the job of Negro county farm agent and cutting off all payments of salary and expense under this heading as of December 31.[16] A notice was duly sent to John Lancaster informing him that he was out of a job.

John Lancaster figured that it had taken them a while to get him, but they had done it.

The salary of county agents in Virginia is paid by the counties, but the men are supplied by the extension service of Virginia Polytechnic Institute in Blacksburg. John Lancaster drove to Blacksburg to talk over this new development with his supervisor. He told the people at Blacksburg that he was sure that the county leaders were merely taking punitive action against him for what they fancied to be his part in the 1951 strike. He was told to sit tight.[17]

Back in Prince Edward he went to his constituents, the Negro farmers of the county. They supported him wholeheartedly. He got up a petition with over five hundred names on it asking that he be retained. This petition was presented to the board of supervisors which took it under consideration [18] and voted soon afterwards to reaffirm their decision.[19] The job would be abolished.

Nobody doubted that Lancaster had lost his job as a result of his activity during the strike. He was widely regarded in the white community as little more than an agent of the NAACP. To this day, he denies this feeling towards him. He was in favor of the strike, and he spoke for it when his opinion was asked, he says. But he did not use his position to agitate for the strikers or the law suit.[20] Mr. Griffin says that Lancaster hated to leave his native county, but would have hated even more a row involving the state agricultural extension program which he hoped to return to later on. In December, 1955, he went to Richmond and took a job selling insurance. Two years later he got back into agricultural work, taking a job as Negro county agent in St. Mary's County, Maryland.

In October, 1956, a year from the time it abolished John Lancaster's job, the Prince Edward Board of Supervisors voted to choose six members from the Negro community to serve as a committee to determine whether a farm agent and a home demonstration agent were needed.[21] The committee recommended that these jobs be filled, and they were filled the next year.

While John Lancaster was busy looking for a new job in October, 1955, James Samuel Williams of the Moton strike class of 1951 was getting out of the Army. He was twenty-one years old and had no notion of the kind of life he should make for himself. "I still hadn't even made up my mind what to do. I even started to re-enlist. But it was between that and going to work, and so I went up to Newark to work with Donald Coles at Curtis-Wright as a machine operator." [22]

Some of his fellow students had thought at first that Williams was a reluctant striker back in 1951. The reason they thought so was that he asked many questions and expressed much doubt in the auditorium meeting when the strike was announced. His mother, a teacher in another school, had not been in favor of the strike, and her feelings may have made Williams seem cautious. But he says that he was entirely in favor of the strike in principle:

"What laid the groundwork for me was a course I took in the seventh grade in Negro history. . . . I was so impressed with that course . . . the main thing was how my foreparents had been treated. I had heard about this but this went into detail. Yes, about slavery and about the figures of the day: Harriet Beecher Stowe, Harriet Tubman, Nat Turner. It laid bare on my mind." [23]

After graduation from Moton the year after the strike, Williams went to Atlantic City, New Jersey, to work as a chef. In the fall he enrolled at Maryland State College. He remembers, "I was not too satisfied. I didn't want to go to school. My mother wanted me to stay in but I was not too settled about it." [24]

The army did not help settle him. He spent his service time in the headquarters corps stationed at Fort Jackson, South Carolina, and Camp Gordon, Georgia. He found life in an integrated military enclave in the heart of the deep South generally uneventful. His only revelation was the discovery that Negroes from the North were curiously unaware of the actuality of segregation in the South.

After the Army, he stayed with Curtis-Wright for two years. He was laid off work in April, 1957, for almost a year. During that time, he worked for a friend who had an automobile laundry, and did janitorial jobs. His close friend of Prince Edward days and an old Moton classmate, Donald Coles, was overseas at the time. Williams explains how this friendship led to his returning to school: "I was visiting his mother. I hadn't been in church in about a year. There was some gospel singing at the Abyssinian Baptist Church in Newark that caught my attention. It affected me and got me thinking about the ministry. I had started to go to Shaw in September, 1957, but I still needed time to think things over. There was no need to apply for school because I figured my mind would change again." [25]

In September, 1958, James Samuel Williams enrolled at Shaw University in Raleigh—Mr. Griffin's old school—to study for the ministry.

9. FOOLERY TO INFAMY

When Carl Rowan of the *Minneapolis Tribune* visited the Reverend L. Francis Griffin in Farmville in 1953, he found a confident leader, apparently respected by his congregation and full of a jaunty and poetic pride in his work. The dissension that had torn the church after the 1951 strike was nowhere evident. After all, the new high school had been built—an $800,000 school, as modern as any in the state—and the suit was given a good chance to win in the Supreme Court. To members of the congregation of the First Baptist Church, it seemed that the preacher had been right all along.

One of them told Rowan: "That preacher may not look like much, but he's sure got conviction. Sure is different from his pappy, who figured the only way to get anything from the white folks was to beg 'em for it." [1]

And Griffin, now grown somewhat stouter, wearing a moustache, smiling his deceptively lazy smile, responded to the renewed faith of his congregation with the airy demands of leadership: "Pray, pray 'til your knees get sore. Then get up and let's fight for our rights." [2]

In December, 1955, Rowan returned to Prince Edward County in part of a swing through the South to assess the new spirit of defiance that was animating the segregationist forces. He reported what he and a photographer found when they visited Griffin's house: "Our rap on the door produced a far different figure from the confident leader I had met in 1953. Here was a sad-faced man, coughing, and wheezing, his eyes betraying a wish that we had not caught him in such circumstances.

"Inside the house, I stood puzzled. Where were the rugs? Why were the walls bare? What happened to the furniture that was in the back bedroom when I telephoned from there two years earlier? Why was the house so bitter cold?

"I looked at his children, their faces marked by what I was sure was ringworm. One child ran barefoot on the floor. The girls' hair was uncombed. Their clothing bore patches that now showed a need for patches. Over the wailing of the youngest child, who stood with tears streaming down a face marked with eczema, I asked the minister: 'Well, how are things going in Prince Edward now that you've won the big court case?'

"Mr. Griffin rubbed his hands as if to warm them. He breathed heavily and noisily like an overweight man with respiratory trouble. Then he smiled and said facetiously, 'I tell you foolery has turned to infamy.'" [3]

Rowan learned that the white community had begun to exact a toll from the preacher for his radical leadership of the Negroes of Prince Edward. He pressed the point, and Mr. Griffin told him that three white men had given him some information on the subject: "They said they wanted to tip me off as a favor that I would be wise not to buy anything else on credit. But like many other people, I already was carrying credit to my full limit. Suddenly I was faced with demands for full payment. I strained in every direction to find cash.

"Take the fuel companies—they always have made it a practice to sell oil on a yearly basis: you buy what you need this winter, and if you pay for it by the following September you can get the following winter's oil on credit.

"Suddenly I was notified that I had fifteen days to pay my fuel bill. When I went to buy clothes for the children or food for the family I was told I had to have cash. All of a sudden . . . this place and that place and places I can't even remember were serving warrants on me." [4]

The men who told Griffin to be careful of extending himself on credit were merchants who held more or less liberal views of the racial dispute that had fired the county. Griffin remembers that they used the phrase "gentleman's agreement" in describing how other merchants had determined to freeze him out of the community.

The point remains much in contention. Many whites in Farmville, including some who do not agree with the militant segregationist position, say that no real economic coercion was applied.

Some of Mr. Griffin's friends say that he always had been careless in money matters and that he was capable of working himself into a hole. The verdict of at least one merchant not unfriendly to the preacher was that he was a poor credit risk. Plainly, with feelings in the white community rising against leaders of the Negro rebellion, there were some white merchants who were not interested in helping this "radical" Negro preacher out of any trouble, self-made or otherwise.

And Mr. Griffin probably was a poor credit risk, as much as a result of the economics of his life as of lifelong disdain of bookkeeping. His financial position was grave. He was drawing about $150 a month from the church, and membership had declined sharply from its peak in the days before the court's decision.[5] Now, with the threat of closed schools hanging over the Negro community—and especially over the Negro teachers—there was not much likelihood that Mr. Griffin could improve his position materially.

Mr. Griffin says that he ignored the warrants against him and strove instead to pay back the debts as systematically as possible. Friends point to the warrants as evidence of coercion; merchants had not resorted to them before, and they were regarded by the Negro community now as harassment. Mr. Griffin's car was repossessed. The heat was in his home only when he could afford to pay for the oil that he once had been able to get easily enough on credit.[6] He walked about cold rooms, rubbing his hands and worrying about the running noses of his children and the sad, infinitely deep detachment of his wife. In this condition, he appeared to the visiting reporter, Rowan.

Mr. Griffin was further embittered by what he took to be direct pressures exerted on him by the white community through some members of his church. He describes the congregation during this period this way: "They were nervous. At meetings everything that was wrong with the church was blamed on the school situation. If we had a financial lull, or anything, this would be the cause."[7]

This "nervousness" took the form of direct or indirect pressures brought to bear on him. One of his congregation who is convinced that some white merchants were trying to drive the preacher out of the community remembers that the treasurer of the church was frequently asked at the bank why the congregation bothered to keep a pastor who caused them so much trouble.

Some members of Griffin's congregation would have been glad to see him go. They worked through those they believed had influence on him. One of them summoned his brother in Norfolk. When Mr. C. E. Griffin got to Farmville to answer the call, he was told that he should try to persuade his brother to desist in his reform efforts. "He appealed to me as the oldest child and through his regard for my father to try to get my brother 'straightened out.' I told him that my brother was his own man." [8]

Some members of the white community encouraged bringing this type of pressure to bear on the preacher. Griffin picked up the method here: "They would go to a man not even a member of the NAACP and tell him they had heard that he was Griffin's right hand man. He would say that if this was so he [Griffin] would be in another place by now." [9]

The fact was that in these times Griffin had become a dangerous friend to Negroes as well as the symbol of the enemy to many whites. If white opposition had driven him to the wall economically, this could not have been done without the defection of Negroes he once had been able to count on. He recalls that "it was no longer considered the thing to do to come to this church. You would be branded a supporter if you did." [10]

Close observers of the Negro community point out that while the movement against Griffin was aided by some of his own people, others remained steadfast. Even the teachers, who were vulnerable to white displeasure and who stood to lose out in the eventual course of desegregation, offered Griffin, for the most part, their quiet support.

But Griffin needed more than this. He expressed it to reporter Rowan in an odd paraphrasing of Gray's "Elegy," spoken even then with a wry humor and, in later years, recalled with the preacher's rumbling chuckle:

> Chill penury has repressed my noble rage,
> and froze the genial currents of my soul. . . .[11]

Griffin needed more money, first of all, if he were to survive. He went to his board of deacons. A member of this board remembers the situation clearly: "The only thing we did do was he took on two other charges. We didn't have it within the economic set-up of our church to raise the salary any. . . . He took on two extra charges which abbreviated two of our services some-what. The congregation agreed that he would do this at the same salary." [12]

Mr. Griffin took two extra country churches in Cumberland County and hustled out into the pines to spread his mission on Sunday mornings. "Fortunately it was the custom of these chur-ches to pay on the day of the preaching, so that I would have some money, and I would come back to town, often, and buy food. . . . Yes there were times when I did not know where my next meal was coming from. There were weekends when I didn't know whether my kids would be eating or not until I took the rural churches. I would rush home and buy food, oftentimes skipping the visiting altogether." [13]

The pressure built up in less subtle ways. Mr. Griffin remembers a few insulting phone calls, anonymous notes, intimidating re-marks. "It would be . . . How would you like to attend a necktie party and you be the honored guest? Some whites would ride by and call out nasty things. Once someone called me up and said that if I went by the Confederate monument on High Street I would be killed. I don't know how, but it got around my congre-gation and there was considerable fear. I decided I had to go because of this fear. I wanted to restore some faith. . . . I re-call several people bringing me shotgun shells and leaving hastily. I used them for hunting." [14]

There was a homemade bomb, a clumsy, childish thing that fizzled out on the Griffin doorstep. And there was an abortive attempt to start a fire from the outside of the brick parsonage and a more successful case of arson across the street that just might have been mistaken identity. But these seemed the works of child-ren or incompetents. For the most part the community offered Griffin no threats. People he knew of both races greeted him with a frayed cordiality; the amenities of rural Southern living were observed. [15]

The threat of the minority within his church was something else. Mr. Griffin suffered more than a narrowing of his economic horizons. The dispute over his tactics had become, to some degree, public. Willie Redd told reporter Homer Bigart that his position was "poles apart" from that of the preacher. Mr. Griffin des-cribed the division in the church to Rowan: "Two members of my church board are putting pressure on me. The trustees met the other night and didn't do a bit of church business. They spent the whole night squabbling over my activities in the NAACP." [16]

But Willie Redd also conceded that the majority of Mr. Griffin's church was with him. Mr. Griffin had every reason to believe that he would win this fight, as he had won the one back in 1951, if the matter ever came before the deliberations of the congregation. Yet the dissension was an irritant.

His lack of funds was more than an irritant. Still another matter troubled him even more deeply. His wife, who had suffered mental distresses in the past, now plunged toward a complete breakdown. Rowan observed in his story the drastic change that had come over her: "When [Griffin] left the living room, his wife spoke: 'I used to think I was courageous; now I'm afraid to stick my neck out.' Mr. Griffin was back and she was quiet now, staring into the distance strangely. What had happened to Mrs. Griffin? The charm, the attractiveness were gone. She seemed but a tired, distraught woman." [17]

The five Griffin children were under their grandmother's care soon afterwards, and Mrs. Griffin was in the hospital.

Now the pressure on Mr. Griffin seemed to him to be too great. He talked with the psychiatrist who was treating his wife: "He said that while the school situation wasn't to blame for all this, it had triggered it. . . . Yes, she knew about the homemade bomb and the other things, and that bothered her. . . . Most of all, though, was the ostracization. At that time it was not considered the right and proper thing to be seen in my presence. She was cut off, in a way, from others she knew in the community." [18]

Mr. Griffin took counsel where he could. He spent long nights brooding in his study, trying to think his way out of a dilemma that got worse day by day. Members of his congregation remarked that the preacher's usual good humor took on an edge of bitterness and that his preoccupation was deep. Among those he talked with was his older brother in Norfolk. The Reverend C. E. Griffin remembers: "I did go up to see him, and I told him that if he could not take it to remain out of the church and let them work it out." [19]

Mr. Griffin had offered his resignation to the deacons. He describes himself in this period as "depressed." A board member recalled: "He presented his resignation and said that he had an opportunity to get another spot that would help his family. The reaction was that we were surprised and we called him in and found that it was with great reluctance that he was leaving. He asked us to give him three months' notice. . . . It was presented to the church and reluctantly accepted. There wasn't anything they could do about it. Afterwards we got to him and asked him to reconsider. . . . Whatever he was expecting didn't materialize. We asked him if he would be willing to stay and he did." [20]

Griffin remembers quite well his "reluctance" to leave. He remembers, too, the NAACP's reluctance to see him leave. With Griffin gone, the battle in Prince Edward could easily have been lost for lack of leadership. The NAACP and some members of his congregation pressed Griffin to stay. One argument for his staying unwillingly was advanced by some who wanted him to leave: "There was a statement made—I don't know who made it—but 'twas something about to the effect of 'why follow that preacher. He can leave you any time he wants to and you can't leave.' I wanted to show that it wasn't my intention to lead folk into trouble and then leave them." [21]

Griffin actually was officially working out his notice for a couple of months, and for a short time he followed his brother's advice and stayed away from the church in Farmville altogether. In the spring of 1956 he told a reporter that he still planned to leave by June 1. "I'd have gone long ago if the kids hadn't started this thing with their strike. I've got four young children and I need more income. My service in Farmville has been sacrificial from the beginning. . . . 'Chill penury has repressed my noble rage. . . .'" [22]

In the end, Griffin decided to stay. He persuaded himself that his wife could remain out of the county for some time if necessary and that her condition in any event would be no worse if he stayed than if he moved.

His economic situation gradually improved. He reflected, with wry humor later on: "This is the last time I will ever resign from anything in the winter time." [23]

10. THE IMPOSSIBLE PRINCE EDWARD CASE

The three-judge court's July decision that Prince Edward need not begin desegregating its public schools by September, 1955, meant that schools would open. But the private school forces were convinced that a day-to-day threat of an integration order existed. They asked the board of supervisors accordingly to make funds for public schools available on a month-to-month basis. Each month thereafter the supervisors shifted money from some other budgeted source to pay the previous month's schooling bills. Public education in the county had been given a renewable, thirty-day reprieve.[1]

The private school forces had no intention, either, of abandoning their subscription drive. Some $190,000 of the $212,830 goal in pledges already had been collected. In writing about the situation, the *Herald* saw a firm future for the Prince Edward Educational Corporation: "The Corporation, we trust, will continue its activity through several more years. . . . The Corporation . . . has a definite place in guiding the future educational program in Prince Edward County. Its work has not ended, it has just begun. . . . Only the first emergency has been met, we hope, fully. A respite for maybe a session has been granted."[2]

A wider sampling of the opinion of leading Defenders in the county supporting the private school corporation was obtained by a reporter who showed up directly after the decision had been handed down. Nobody he talked with quarreled with Blanton Hanbury's caution: "My reaction is to sit tight. We are going to hold on to those pledges. We want to be awful sure where we are and where we are going."[3]

The only division of opinion occurred over whether the court's decision was a good thing. Robert Taylor took the position that it was a reprieve for a year against integration, but T. W. Brooks, local Defender secretary, feared apathy, and Supervisor Bruce and C. W. Glenn told Bigart that they wished the court had been specific on whether the schools could be operated in the usual segregated manner for the coming year.[4]

Prince Edward, at any rate, had committed itself to a policy of all-out resistance to desegregation. Elsewhere in the state a struggle was going on over what Virginia's policy should be, and in this struggle the Defenders' movement born in Prince Edward was to play a key part.

In November, 1955, the Gray Commission appointed by Governor Stanley to study the school desegregation problem recommended a program that would make state policy one of seeing to it that no white child attended integrated schools against the will of his parents. Schools could be closed to avoid integration by community choice, and when schools were integrated by community choice parents objecting could secure grants to send their children to private schools.

For a time this or similar programs of "freedom of choice" enjoyed political support in Virginia. Editor James Jackson Kilpatrick of the *Richmond News Leader* supported the idea. Hard resisters like former Governor Tuck and Representative Abbitt made proposals that would permit integration by local referendum. Senator Byrd, himself, in a statement in November, threw his support behind the idea: "Such referenda on a local level would in no wise conflict with the Supreme Court decision. I do not see how any reasonable person could deny the local units— counties and cities—the right if desired to ascertain the will of the qualified voters in each locality. If the vote is for integration, then segregation can be abolished in any locality so voting. If the vote is against integration, then the locality with backing of the state government can take action in accordance with its best judgment."[5]

But another, conflicting idea was being born at about this time. A Virginia attorney named William Old produced a pamphlet on "interposition," the theory that a state may interpose its authority to render a Supreme Court decision null and void. Editor Kilpatrick picked up the idea and began an exhaustive editorial campaign for it. The Defenders, growing more powerful almost daily, gratefully adopted it as the true intellectual expression of the will to resist. The *Herald*, which had favored a fight along ideological lines to prevent desegregation anywhere in Virginia, could give its unqualified support to this approach.

All over the South this will to resist was stiffening. New resistance groups were springing into existence, furiously waving gaudy banners. The Citizens Councils' day was dawning. Historian C. Vann Woodward later pointed to this rising tide, fixing January, 1956, as the month when it became readily visible. By this month, he wrote, the meaning of the Supreme Court's May 31 decree in the hands of the NAACP had become clear. Nineteen court decisions had gone against the South on a district level, and in the summer of 1955 Negroes had petitioned 170 school boards in 17 states for desegregation. Woodward observed that something like a panic seized many parts of the South.[6]

In Virginia the Defenders called on the General Assembly to pass a resolution of interposition. Other states would be asked to join in this effort. Senator Byrd praised editor Kilpatrick for his service to the state.[7] To this background the General Assembly set a January date for voters to pass on a constitutional amendment that would make possible the use of public funds for private schools. Moderates like Dr. Dabney Lancaster favored the amendment because it was part of the "freedom of choice" Gray plan; the Defenders favored it in spite of this.

By this time, though, it was becoming obvious that the "freedom of choice" features of the plan were doomed. Senator Byrd said that he would vote for the amendment to use public funds for private schools but added significantly that he would not comment on other features of the Gray Plan.[8] The fear was that under some form of local option Virginia communities would not hold the line against desegregation. This fear was given substance in January, 1956, when the Arlington school board approved a plan to begin integration of the community's schools the following fall. Arlington was in Northern Virginia, under the dominance in the view of rural legislators of that urban pestilence, Washington, D.C., which was even now being described as a hell-hole of integrated schools. In many things Northern Virginia was allowed to go its own peculiar way, unadvised and unsupported from Richmond. But this was different.

Events moved swiftly. The January vote heavily favored the constitutional amendment. The vote in Prince Edward was 2,835 for and 350 against. A couple of weeks later, in Richmond, Governors Stanley of Virginia, Timmerman of South Carolina, Griffin of Georgia, and Coleman of Mississippi met to endorse interposition. The Virginia General Assembly passed an interposition resolution and then rudely stripped Arlington of its right to elect a school board in punishment for that body's desegregation announcement. In March the constitutional convention called by the voters gave the Defenders what they really wanted—a state constitution amended so that public funds could be expended for private schools. The rivets of legal resistance had been forged.

March, 1956, marks the flowering of the resistance movement in the South as well as any month. The Southern Manifesto was introduced into both houses of Congress March 12, signed by eighty-two representatives and nineteen senators, decrying the Supreme Court's encroachment upon the rights reserved to the states and commending those states declaring their intention to resist by all lawful means. Senator Byrd and Representative Howard Smith of Virginia introduced the resolutions. The Senator spoke of the action as part of a plan of "massive resistance" to the court's decree. The Autherine Lucy case in Alabama had whipped up sentiment for resistance, and a furious state senate there went so far as to petition Congress to provide federal funds to move Negroes out of the South. Interposition resolutions passed elsewhere in the South. By the end of March, at least forty-two prosegregation measures had been recorded for the first three months of the year in Alabama, Georgia, Mississippi, South Carolina, and Virginia.[9]

In Prince Edward County the resistance movement took heart. To talk that the county should take steps to assure the court that it intended compliance, the *Herald* replied: "In all honesty and good conscience there is but one answer to give the court, namely that Prince Edward has made no progress toward integrating its schools. Prince Edward has no plans for integrating its schools." [10]

When the NAACP went to court in April, 1956, seeking an order to desegregate the schools by the following fall, the county responded quickly. Defenders began circulating a "statement of affirmation" of the county's intention to close schools rather than to desegregate.[11] On April 25 a delegation from the county informed Governor Stanley of this intention, and on May 3 the "statement" with 4,184 signatures (the 1950 census puts white population including children at about 8,460) was presented to the board of supervisors, which for its part reaffirmed its intention not to appropriate money for integrated schools.[12] The board went further. It laid down a legal bedrock that was to be the foundation of the county's defense for years to come. It affirmed in somewhat sententious language the "first tenet of American liberty—that men should not be taxed against their will and without their consent for a purpose to which they are deeply and conscientiously opposed." Stripped of its bogus political imperative, this statement meant simply that the county did not think any court could make it appropriate money for schools. In May the *Herald* declared pithily: "Prince Edward rests its case. There is nothing more which can be done by the white people to make known their wishes." [13]

In the next months the state plunged into its final decision to resist. Perhaps a vital moving force behind this decision was what appeared to be the beginning of action by the NAACP to carry out its threat of pressing desegregation to the utmost in Virginia. New suits for desegregation were filed quickly in Newport News, Charlottesville, Arlington, and Norfolk. No longer was Prince Edward a lone bastion; targets were being selected all around. W. Lester Banks, the NAACP official in charge in Virginia, says that the organization was merely responding to the sense of the Supreme Court's order.[14] But plainly the NAACP had decided that multiple suits in Virginia courts was the way to compliance. Just as plainly, at least in the short run, the suits accelerated the resistance movement.

The report of the Gray Commission was set aside, and in September, in accordance with a decision made quietly by Senator Byrd and his chief lieutenants to make Virginia the front line of resistance, the General Assembly enacted the package of laws that would activate massive resistance. These were laws supported by—in some cases first suggested by—the Defenders. They created a State Pupil Placement Board to take over from localities the job of assigning pupils (the board during the years of massive resistance never found it necessary to assign a Negro child to a white school); a provision to close any school that was ordered to desegregate by a court; a provision to let the governor take over that school and reopen it segregated, if possible; and a tuition grant program to provide public funds for private, segregated schools, if public schools so closed could not be reopened segregated. This same General Assembly enacted a package of laws designed to drive the NAACP out of business.

At his annual apple orchard party in Berryville, Senator Byrd made clear how he felt: "It's no secret that the NAACP intends first to press Virginia. . . . If Virginia surrenders, if Virginia's line is broken, the South will go down, too. . . . Why can't we fight this thing with every ounce of energy and capacity? I think we are on sound ground." [15]

This was Defender talk. The Defenders had control of the full political machinery of the state. And as the state prepared to resist, the Prince Edward case moved toward some new climate. The county asked the three-judge court to reject the NAACP's motion seeking desegregation by fall. Grounds cited for the motion included a statement by the sheriff that serious racial tensions existed in the county and the argument, more suitable for the front porch than the courtroom, that Prince Edward's 50 per cent Negro population paid only 14 per cent of the county taxes.[16]

The NAACP by this time, however, had found reason to revise its timetable in Prince Edward. In view of the action on the legal front elsewhere, the NAACP amended its request to the court and called for a beginning of desegregation in 1957. The three-judge court dissolved itself and appointed Judge Hutcheson to hear the arguments, which were held in November.

Extremism was loose throughout the state. As Benjamin Muse observed: "The flood of political oratory, the inflammatory editorials and the bold words from respected leaders had done their work. Extremists were in the ascendancy, and not only 'integrationist' but 'moderate' had become a term of reproach." [17]

President Eisenhower carried Virginia in the 1956 elections, but the winner in Prince Edward County was the states' rights candidate, T. Coleman Andrews. As a reminder of the growing power of the militant segregationist vote, Robert Crawford announced that the Defenders might put up a candidate for the gubernatorial campaign of 1957 if any other candidate took a "weak" stand on segregation.[18] Attorney General J. Lindsay Almond promptly threw his hat in the ring, announced his fidelity to the cause, and waited hopefully for a sign of approval from Washington. Senator Byrd, assessing this brash bid carefully, decided finally that the attorney general would have to do, and gave his blessings.

Judge Hutcheson pondered the Prince Edward case as 1956 drew to a close. The judge was a gentle, much-beloved figure who had shown real mettle with county school boards who failed to provide equal facilities for Negro school children when this was the issue in court. The son of an astute Southside politician, Judge Hutcheson once fined a school board for failure to support a bond issue for Negro schools.

But while Judge Hutcheson was not surprised by the Supreme Court's desegregation decision, he was out of sympathy with it as a social mechanism: he believed that the equalization process should have been pursued further. He saw tensions rising around the state and took account of some reports that violence in Prince Edward might be possible.[19]

It did not seem to him that this was the time for drastic change in the county. In his opinion, he noted: "In the present state of unrest and racial tension in the county it would be unwise to attempt to force a change of the system until the entire situation can be considered and adjustments gradually brought about. This must be accomplished by the reasonable, clear-thinking people of both races in that locality. . . . I believe the problems to be capable of solution but they will require time and a sympathetic understanding. They cannot be solved by zealous advocates, by an emotional approach, nor by those with selfish interests to advance." [20]

Judge Hutcheson's decision set no deadline for desegregation in the county but did allow plaintiffs to review progress after the county had been afforded a reasonable time to effect a solution. The county would have to cease segregating its schools; this much the judge made plain.

The decision was applauded, not only by fully committed segregationists but by many who customarily took issue with this racial view. Delegate Robert Whitehead of Nelson County, leader of anti-organization Democrats and one of the state's most respected men in politics, hailed the decision as "a realistic opinion by an understanding judge." [21] In his book, Benjamin Muse, who had served in the state Senate, commented: "Many people, including to my knowledge many Negroes, would have been happy to see the 'impossible' Prince Edward case left with that admirable observation of this federal district judge . . . but the NAACP attorneys noted an appeal." [22]

With the appeal, the county's delight in the Hutcheson decision was destined to be short-lived. As the case proceeded back up to the appellate court, it was all too easy for both sides—the NAACP leaders and the segregationist leaders of Prince Edward—to forget the heart of the Hutcheson decision, the judge's unwillingness to see schools closed, the process of education arrested.

The judge had stated: "An interrupted education of one year or even six months at that age places a serious handicap upon a child which the average one may not overcome. It is my belief that at this time a continuation of present methods could not be so harmful as an interrupted education." [23]

But the judge's prophecy was quickly buried away in the musty files of his clerk's office where it would not trouble consciences—yet.

PART THREE

THE SCHOOLS

11.   WITH PROFOUND
REGRET

On June 2, 1959, without a great deal of ado, the board of supervisors of Prince Edward County announced its intention not to appropriate money to operate public schools for the coming year.

The board issued a statement meant to cover its action:

> The action taken today . . . has been determined upon only after the most careful and deliberate study over the long period of years since the schools in this county were first brought under the force of federal court decree. It is with the most profound regret that we have been compelled to take this action . . . it is the fervent hope of this board . . . that we may in due time be able to resume the operation of public schools in this county upon a basis acceptable to all the people of the county.[1]

In other words the supervisors were closing the schools rather than agreeing to operate them integrated; they would open them only if and when they could operate them, once again, segregated.

The "force of federal court decree" mentioned by the supervisors finally had come to bear on Prince Edward County. The county was under orders to desegregate its public schools by September.

Behind this action in point of time lay the torn body politic of massive resistance. This state-wide policy which Senator Byrd had hoped would set the pattern for total resistance in the South to the Supreme Court had been invoked in September, 1958, when under state law some twelve thousand children were locked out of schools under desegregation decree in Norfolk, Charlottes-ville, and Front Royal. In January, 1959, the courts struck down the massive resistance laws passed by the Virginia legislature in 1956, and Governor Almond capitulated—much to the displeasure of Senator Byrd's loyalists, who wanted the governor to show his defiance by going to jail.

In February, 1959, some thirty Negro children attended formerly white schools in three Virginia communities. Massive resistance was dead. The crisis in Virginia was over before the crisis in Prince Edward had begun.

Massive resistance was dead; but resistance burned fierce in the hearts of the segregationists of Prince Edward. The courts had told the state that it could not operate a school system and close select schools that were threatened by desegregation. But what if the initative for school closing came from the county? What if a county simply refused to tax its people for public schools to be integrated? Could a court make that county fork up money for schools? The Southside strategists did not think so.

The hour of testing had come swiftly. Judge Hutcheson's decision setting no timetable for desegregating Prince Edward County's schools had been overturned by an appellate court. In a second look, Judge Hutcheson set the date of desegregation in 1965—ten years from the time the Supreme Court's implementation decision had been handed down. This decision, too, was overturned by an appellate court that was at pains to point out that the county had not taken a single positive step toward eventual desegregation. The court ordered desegregation that following September, and the board of supervisors provided its answer in June.

Despite the supervisors' refusal to appropriate money for schools and the plans of the Foundation leaders to renew the $200,000 in pledges and open private, segregated schools for whites in September, many in the community could not believe that the public schools would not open. The school board had tried in vain to persuade the supervisors that their action was premature.[2] No Negro applications for white schools had been received. The board's attorneys felt that they had secured another year's delay.[3] With appropriations on a month-to-month basis anyway, what had the county to lose by continuing its public schools until the last moment?

School Board Chairman B. Calvin Bass worked to see that

viewpoint prevail. When the school board failed to convince the supervisors, Bass arranged a conference with Attorney General Harrison in which it was proposed that the Foundation receive "gifts" equaling the county's regular contribution to schools and that state matching funds be applied to keep the public schools open.[4] The Foundation's answer to this proposal was an editorial in the *Herald* dispelling "rumors" that the public schools would operate for another year.[5]

Bass was not alone in his efforts to rescue the public schools from their plight. A Longwood College professor named C. D. G. Moss and a colleague of his had gone to work. Their idea was to collaborate with Negro leaders to effect some sort of agreement that would permit the schools to continue in operation. Whom should they choose to talk with? Dr. Moss remembers: "We had concluded that we should find some Negro men to go over with us to Richmond if we could get an audience with the governor. We approached Willie Redd just because we knew him and assumed he was a major leader of the Negroes. He said he would be glad to go with us . . . ."[6]

The two college professors knew nothing of the workings of the Negro community, actually knew no Negroes well. Dr. Moss had talked with Mr. Griffin at some length at a funeral for a member of the preacher's congregation and he recognized that any agreement would have to have this man's approval if it were to stand up among the Negroes. They chose Mr. Griffin and an influential and respected member of his congregation. They began exploratory conversations, slipping off at night to Mr. Griffin's church or some other safely secluded meeting place.[7] The date for the opening—or rather the non-opening—of the schools was fast approaching, and all four men worked with some sense of urgency. They became convinced that a compromise was possible. They thought that it would be possible to get the Negroes to agree to a three-year moratorium on pressing desegregation of the public schools in return for an agreement to accept the Supreme Court decision in principle and to establish bi-racial committees charged with preparing the way for its eventual acceptance in fact.

The document drawn up as a result of these talks was to become controversial. In a speech in Charlottesville some years later, Dr. Moss indicated that the plan had the complete approval of the two Negroes taking part in the discussions. Mr. Griffin has since denied that the agreement was this complete: "I went up to the point of saying that we would call representative Negro citizens together to discuss it. . . . I wanted to know what steps would be taken to prepare the people for what was coming. Are we going to get human relations experts? What makes you think people would be ready three years from now if no concrete plan is drawn in the interim? It all stopped for me with questions and I don't know if they could rightfully answer them, because we all were fishing in the dark." [8]

Whatever the status of the agreement, Dr. Moss and his colleague felt that they had enough to go on to try to make contact with Governor Almond. They knew that his administration would co-operate in any reasonable plan aimed at keeping the schools open. By this time, they had learned that Willie Redd was regarded as a member of "the older generation" of Negroes and would not be a suitable representative. Still, they planned to go to Richmond with some Prince Edward Negroes. Dr. Moss remembers that when they wrote a letter hopefully suggesting that a compromise might be worked out, Governor Almond had an aide telephone his approval of a conference. [9]

Dr. Moss recalls that the Governor suggested that it would not be wise at this point for Negroes to be included in the Richmond conference. Dr. Moss went to Governor Almond's office in the first week in September, with the shadow of closed schools perceptibly lengthening almost by the hour. Dr. Moss remembers the Governor's reaction: "In the conference he said that if we could bring the leaders of the white supremacists—that's what I call them—to him about continuing the county schools that he would be more than glad to do it. He thought he could find funds for running the schools despite the supervisors' action. . . . We did suggest that he take the initiative in appointing a state bi-racial committee. Apparently he had talked about this before because he turned it down quickly. . . . I thought the Governor was abrupt, almost angry, when he did this." [10]

The two professors were heartened nonetheless by the Governor's willingness to try to work out a compromise. They returned to Farmville and hurriedly set about to secure an agreement. They thought that the Negro leaders would go along with the substance of the plan. They called on Editor Wall to meet with them to discuss a way to keep the public schools open.

These men were not strangers in spite of the different positions they had taken on the school issue. Dr. Moss and Wall were fellow members of the Episcopal church, and all three men were in a discussion group that met regularly to talk about current events. A fourth member of the discussion group was included in the conference as a kind of familiar "neutral" on the school issue.

The conference was a complete failure. The professor's idea was to get Wall to agree to bring five Foundation leaders to negotiations with five Negro leaders and five "neutrals" in an effort to work out a compromise along the lines of his three-year moratorium plan. But the conference idea never got far enough off the ground to test their ability to find acceptably neutral neutrals. Dr. Moss recalls what happened: "Barrye said that he wouldn't sit down with Griffin and Madison to discuss anything. We asked him if he would discuss with other Negroes the idea of public schools. When we pressed him on what Negroes, he wouldn't name one specifically." [11]

Wall thought that further talks would be pointless. He was typically direct on this subject: "They said Griffin would use his influence to keep schools clear of integration for three years. I told him I wasn't interested because if we were going to integrate the schools we'd do it now rather than three years from now. I also asked how they knew Griffin would be able to control the situation." [12]

Dr. Moss had to write Governor Almond of the failure to get Foundation leaders to discuss the situation with the Negroes. In contrast with the telephone call reaction to the earlier communication, Governor Almond never answered this letter at all. [13]

As September arrived, it appeared that the forces pressing for desegregation of Prince Edward schools were disposed to compromise as never before. No final order had been entered by the district court calling for the act of desegregation. No Negro children had applied for white schools. The Negro leadership in the county was apparently fully prepared to try to reach some accommodation, and nothing in the actions of the NAACP indicated that it would try to block this move. Active white moderates were at work.

Yet for all this it was apparent to anyone who wished to see that the public schools would not open that September. The private school Foundation was busily preparing makeshift accommodations for the white children. The Foundation leaders were too deeply committed to this experiment to turn back, and there is every indication that the average Prince Edward citizen, caught up in the whirlwind preparations going on, supported the Foundation's position. At the moment of the most feverish effort to save the schools, it was plain that the schools were doomed.

The Foundation leadership is left facing the charge of being deaf to all talk of compromise and even of desiring to see the schools closed—although the evidence on the latter point is scanty. Yet given the determination to block integration of the county's schools forever, the Foundation leaders were the only ones who viewed the situation in its total reality. They could not believe that the NAACP, having gone so far in court to win this case, would settle for segregated schools for long. Wall pointed out editorially that Mr. Griffin had said that he expected some applications from Negroes to white schools.[14] If they did not come this year, in the Foundation view, they would come next year, and whenever they came would be too soon. Subsequent statements by NAACP leaders left little doubt that this would have happened.

Why should the Foundation stall its accelerating drive for funds and facilities merely to begin again the next year?

It may be that Editor Wall's intransigence was very much in the spirit of the thinking of Prince Edward whites. They would bar the doors of their schools to Negro children forever. They would be part of an effort in the greater South to render the Supreme Court's Brown decision historically ineffective. Editor Wall felt that he did not have to test the temper of the community with the illusive compromises of Dr. Moss. He thought he could speak without hesitation for that part of the community that wrote the rules and articulated its opinions. When the board of supervisors cut off the funds for public schools, Editor Wall had exhorted the people of the county to "stand steady."[15] But how long could the private schools with their haphazard financing last? a critical editor asked. "Always," stormed back Editor Wall. "Because the people of Prince Edward County will not submit to integrated schools."[16]

Wall was as much the creator of that opinion as its principal reflector.

Opponents of the Prince Edward County school closings liked to say that all that was needed to reopen the schools was five funerals. Hastening to add that they were speaking figuratively, they nevertheless supplied similar listings of candidates, most of them community leaders and former Defenders who later gravitated to the Foundation power structure. These were solid citizens, all, and at the head of every list stood the name of J. Barrye Wall, Sr., perhaps the solidest citizen and certainly the pivotal figure in the county's long struggle to maintain segregated schools.

Wall hardly agreed with the "five funerals" thesis. He has maintained all along that the *Herald's* rigidly segregationist position was merely a reflection of the dominant thinking in the county. But of course it is impossible to set a community's principal organ of communication on the course of a strong opinion and hold that course for more than ten years without creating opinion. The opponents of the school closings were right to regard Wall as their principal adversary; he was the bulwark for those who wished to hold the line against any compromise.

But these critics do not at all agree on Wall's goal. In his Charlottesville speech, for instance, Dr. Moss accused Wall of desiring to close the public schools.[17] The editor replied frostily that his record was one of favoring public education "under conditions conducive to the learning process."[18] Is it then that Wall merely loves segregation more than education (having accused the NAACP on every conceivable occasion of loving integration more than education)? Is the clue to his fiercely held convictions to be found in his attitude to the Negro himself? Or is he merely—as a former employee puts it—"death on expansion of Federal government?"[19] Wall likes to elevate the debate, in private or public discussion. He told me once: "I see the thing as the usurpation of the rights and powers of the states. If you take this principle out of it, I have no interest in the matter at all."[20]

Wall comes from solid, Southside Virginia tradesman stock. His maternal grandfather, a dentist like his son, fought in the Confederate Army and later settled in Farmville after marrying a Buckingham County girl. The Wall side of the family settled in Surry County and migrated to Lunenburg. In the 1890's Wall's father came to Farmville and became one of the town's pioneer merchants, establishing a dry goods and clothing business on Main Street, where his name is still on the sidewalk in large gold letters. He married the dentist's daughter, twenty years his junior, and Wall was born in the apartment right over the store. When Wall was only five years old, his father died.

Wall's entire schooling was in Prince Edward, in Farmville elementary and high schools and at Hampden-Sydney, where he managed a degree and the usual collection of extra-curricular activities including editing the yearbook. He graduated in 1919 and came back the next year to establish a book and cigar store on the campus. He boomed a fifty-dollar investment into a fifteen-hundred-dollar sale in one year's time, operating the store and an auto jitney to and from the college. He established the *Hampden-Sydney Tiger,* a weekly college newspaper, in 1920. After a brief stint selling automobiles on Virginia's Eastern Shore he returned to Farmville looking forward hopefully to the town clerkship, which his mother had worked to line up for him. When his job fell through, he worked briefly in the textile mills of Danville. At about this time James L. Hart, a printer who had bought the *Herald* in 1892 from the Farmville Iron and Coal Company which had founded it in 1890, died and the business came up for sale. Wall bought the *Herald* on March 7, 1921, and has published it ever since.

Two significant things about Wall are apparent in this thumbnail sketch. He is, first of all, very much from and of Southside and has had virtually no experience outside these parochial confines. Additionally, he is a merchant first and a newspaperman second. He bought the paper in his own account simply because it was the only business that had come open in Farmville.

In these circumstances it was natural for Wall to make of the *Herald* a paper dedicated to "boosting" the county, interested in expanding the trading area of Farmville, and steeped in the traditional thinking of the small, middle-class merchant.

In this respect Wall's thinking departs significantly from that of Crawford, with whom he is largely in agreement. Crawford's background is rural, rather than small-town urban, and his fiscal conservatism is deeper than Wall's. The editor, for instance, found it possible to call for more expenditures for education and to support Walter Mapp in his gubernatorial race against Harry Flood Byrd because the former favored highway building bonds. Wall has long regretted this vote and styles himself a Byrd Democrat of the sort who still stands with the Senator on Franklin D. Roosevelt's 1932 platform; but in fact he belongs to the more progressive wing of this political oligarchy where fiscal matters are concerned.

Not so, in matters of government. Here, Wall's position is closer to Crawford's. He, too, talks a good bit about the Communist menace at home—although he seldom writes in this vein. He takes second place to no man in his conviction that the states are being stripped unnecessarily of their powers by an ever enlarging federal government, which is assumed to be malevolent by definition. He calls the Brown decision of 1954 "unconstitutional" and talks even to this day about mounting a national tide to sweep its effects away.

But where Crawford plunged into state politics in an effort to be part of a wider movement of Southern resistance, Wall contented himself with fighting the good fight at home. A friend remarked accurately: "Barrye is no politician." Wall has none of Crawford's warmth or charm and additionally has a positive distrust of politics that links him with the merchant middle class of an earlier day. His thirty-five years on the Town Council he writes off as civic rather than political duty.

Wall's views on race are, on the surface, traditional. He shares the commitment to segregation common throughout the South. Within these limits he represents himself as being in favor of progress for the Negro as well as for the white. He is surprised, however, to be asked whether or not he wrote editorials calling for bettering the Negro's lot before the school strike of 1951: "No, we didn't have any subject of race before this. I mean we carried editorials on better education or better roads or whatever for everybody." [21]

In a general way, this is true. Yet all during the long years of negotiations with the school board over the conditions at Moton, the *Herald* remained silent. Wall's explanation is that since the paper then did not cover school board meetings (it has since reformed in this and other ways), he was not aware of the growing pressure in the Negro community.

It is entirely possible that he heard nothing of it. For Wall has not felt a newspaperman's curiosity with regard to the Negro. Throughout the school crisis he was often the most ill-informed of all the journalists who tracked through the county on the subject of plans in the Negro community. The failure of Willie Redd to remain in power in the county cost Wall his best contact with the Negro community.

Actually, even in a segregated society where contacts between the races are necessarily few, it can be said that Wall is peculiarly insulated from contact with Negroes. He likes to tell visiting journalists that he has a Negro as a next door neighbor, as an example of how friendly relations are between the races (outwardly, relations are reasonably friendly, but the fact that Negro homes back up to white homes does not in the least affect Farmville's rigid segregation). Despite this geographical proximity, observers say that Wall has had very little to do with Negroes and that he wants very little to do with them. Although he has attended a few meetings in which Negroes were present as participants, he has declined invitations to various bi-racial meetings.

Possibly because of the editor's remoteness from the scene of the problem, The *Herald* has not understood the nature of the attack on its segregated schools. In the days of the school strike, the *Herald* at first concluded that a simple misunderstanding was at the root of the trouble. When the incident developed into a court suit, the newspaper took the familiar Southern position that this was all the doing of outside agitators. This position it maintained through the long years during which—it is true—"outside agitators" in sufficient numbers showed up, but, more importantly, during which the Negro community underwent a complete revolution of leadership and willpower. By refusing to comprehend that the Negroes of the county were not the same people, with the same desires, as ten years before, the *Herald* closed off its most useful channel of understanding.

Instead, Wall made the *Herald* into an instrument of the will of the Foundation's attorneys. Editorially, the *Herald* adopted the tone of an advocate advising his over-zealous client. It called repeatedly for calmness and courtesy in dealings between residents of the county, white and black, and above all counseled against resort to violence. In this respect the *Herald* undoubtedly performed a real service to its community. These amenities aside, however, the *Herald* was consistently and ardently in favor of closing the schools and keeping them closed. It developed a formal line of argument that changed but little through the years: the courts ought to be allowed to settle the issue of whether the federal government or anyone else could order a county to appropriate money to run its schools; until this issue was settled, the county should hold the line against the possibility of school desegregation by maintaining its private schools for white and—if they elected to accept them—for Negroes too. This purely legalistic argument was buttressed on occasions by simple statement of the satisfactory nature of segregated schooling and the unwillingness of the community (the *Herald* came to speak as though in the voice of the community) to accept integrated schools. Most of the time the *Herald* simply assumed that its readers understood the underlying issues and concentrated on repetitious expositions of the legal soundness of the county's position and the danger to the state and the nation of the trend toward judicial encroachments. The oft-repeated injunction to the county to "stand steady" seemed to mean to resist any temptation that might arise to smash things and to keep the schools closed until some court ruled finally that they had to open.

In the early years of the school closings, it could be said at least that a live question existed of counties throughout the South joining Prince Edward in a protest movement that would replace segregated public schools with segregated private schools. Later on, when the fever of massive resistance had abated somewhat in the South, and it was apparent—even to the ardent segregationists—that no general school closings would take place, the legalistic argument lost its effect. What good would it do to prove that legally counties could raise money and close public schools in favor of private schools if none wished to do this? Yet the *Herald* clung stubbornly to the concept that Prince Edward was a great testing ground and that it would amount to a kind of legal genocide to drop the case in court and reopen the schools.

Wall's personality is stamped into this position. Short, rotund, cigar-smoking, Wall has the expression of a man who does not easily change his mind in the face of argument, however compelling. He is a study in fascinating contrasts. Something of a raconteur and a creditable after-dinner speaker, he is entirely humorless on the subject of segregation. He can appear obstinate, wrongheaded, and even arrogant, as on one television program, "The Crippled Generation." [22] After watching himself on this program, the editor was so upset that he wrote an editorial saying that he would stick to his own medium from then on and implying that he had been edited down to his worst by the film clippers.[23] Other reporters in Prince Edward noted that Wall shared with others involved in the segregationist cause the kind of burning zeal that made it impossible for him not to expound the cause at some length and with some heat whenever the subject was raised.

Yet, in spite of this enthusiasm and in spite of the voluminous files of correspondence and news clips which he kept in loose-leaf notebooks in his cluttered first-floor office, he never exercised the full editorial curiosity to discover what was going on among the county's Negroes and dissident whites.

It can hardly be doubted that the issue of the county's schools became something of a crusade to him. He was extremely sensitive to criticism and would seize upon any written or spoken attack on the county's position to engage in a long editorial rebuttal. A friend, commenting on the energy and thoroughness with which Wall attacked his task, added almost regretfully that his favorite of the editor's utterances was a hurriedly written front-pager that summed up the longer editorial flights in three paragraphs.

Wall's energetic devotion to the cause of the private school Foundation was not confined to the writing of editorials. During periods of crisis, as when a fund drive was on, he spent most of his waking hours on matters of Foundation business. He could be found in its offices directing the mailing of enclosures or helping to plot campaign strategy far into the evening.

When Wall talks of his unstinting service to the community over the years, he is not exaggerating. Before the emergence of the school issue, his restless energies were consumed in a multitude of community activities, all directed to the purpose of "boosting" Prince Edward. He was one of the original founders of Southside Community Hospital, for instance, and will tell you that Negroes are admitted as well as whites, although there is some doubt that a qualified Negro doctor would be admitted to practice there. He has said, "When you've got all those white nurses, you've got a problem. It's hard enough to keep nurses at these county hospitals as it is." [24]

A good deal of the Jaycee remains in the editor's makeup and shows in the flashes of bitterness he exhibits at the way events have conspired to "tear down everything I've tried to build up." [25]

Yet his unflinching parochialism will not permit him to despair for long. He was heated in his defense of the county's potential even with the public schools closed for so long. He is equally insistent that race relations in Prince Edward are better than in the larger cities of Virginia or the Northeast: "I wouldn't live in Washington, D. C., where you would be afraid to go out of your door." [26]

Wall likes to walk during the humid early afternoons when he has a break from his labors in the tiny office walk-in (newsroom upstairs) where he writes editorials, sells advertising, and takes orders for printing work from the customers who come in off the street. He is a man who says that he has no hobbies besides people; he can be seen strolling downtown, tipping his hat, pausing for a brief exchange of words with acquaintances. Like many men of this type, he is essentially a loner who says that while he tries to be friendly with everybody, he has few close friends.

Except for an annual vacation at Myrtle Beach, South Carolina, the editor's relaxing apparently consists of reading several publications (five newspapers a day; two weekly newsmagazines). He rarely reads books and never reads fiction: "I'm not interested in something that's not happening." [27]

His influence in the community is great. He is not a newspaperman who has achieved influence, but a businessman who uses his newspaper to augment his influence. The power attaching to the voice of that newspaper has been broadened by Wall's encouragement of key personnel to take part in civic affairs. Managing Editor John Steck, the author of a long apologia for the school closings, is a member of the county board of supervisors. Wall's second son, Bill, listed as general manager of the paper, is a member of the Farmville Town Council. The newspaper's influence on the affairs of the private school Foundation is enhanced by the position of Wall's elder son, J. Barrye, Jr., who is attorney for the Foundation and a frequent adviser to his father on the legal aspects of editorial strategy.

The *Herald* had put this little opinion-making machine to work for the cause of private schools early in the day. Thus it was natural that the newspaper would rise to the occasion when, in the summer of 1959, it appeared that in four short months the public schools would fail to open for a new term.

In May, 1959, the Prince Edward Foundation had $11,000 in cash, $200,000 in three-year-old pledges, no teachers under contract, no buildings, no school buses, and no other tools of education. By September, the Foundation had to be ready to provide private education for approximately fifteen hundred white children in the county.

If the task seemed Herculean, the county had the extraordinary good luck to find a man willing to undertake it. He was Roy

Pearson, a high official of Standard Oil Company with many years of administrative experience overseas. Pearson had decided to settle down in his retirement in Farmville, the home of his wife. They arrived in 1957, and Pearson soon afterwards was appointed to the school board. An energetic man only fifty-three years old who wished to keep his hand in activities, he was the obvious choice to run the private school Foundation, especially as he had a stake in its success in the person of a school-age daughter. He believed fervently in segregation. His sole previous experience in education came to one year of coaching and teaching in a rural school after his graduation from North Carolina State College, but this was not considered a fatal defect. The job he was called on to perform was administrative, not educational, in the Foundation's view. Pearson had a persuasiveness with people, great personal force, and the ability to make gears mesh. He was a godsend to the Foundation.

In the seven weeks that remained before school opening Pearson produced and directed an effort that galvanized the county. He drove himself tirelessly. It was through his presence that the county's white people purposefully gave of their time and efforts as well as their money toward the goal of adequate schooling for their children. A close observer recalled those days: "It wasn't any eight-hour day for Pearson. His lights were on every night. He turned out to be quite a businessman. . . . He went into this thing like it was a hobby. . . ." [28]

The major consideration beyond money was buildings to house the children. The public school buildings themselves could not be used without giving the Foundation effort a public coloration that might be fatal in court. Field trips by Foundation officials to Front Royal, Charlottesville, and Norfolk, where segregated private schools had been set up hastily alongside public schools, confirmed that churches were the logical buildings to house emergency education. Most churches had educational buildings or otherwise suitable rooms. Furthermore, the white clergy either was in sympathy with the private school effort or—perhaps recalling the case of Mr. Kennedy—thought it prudent not to oppose that effort.

Pearson's first organizational task was to find handy, well-established social institutions through which to get adequate church housing around the county and to see that the buildings were put in shape to serve as schools by September. The PTA organizations, used so successfully in the Jarman Hall meeting of 1955, were the logical organs for the establishment of a county-wide private school system. Committees were set up in the various districts, consisting of a Foundation director for the district (invariably a solid, highly respected citizen), the president of the PTA, and the local school principal.[29] Their task nominally was to take applications for the Foundation schools—applications, incidentally, that were filled out by the vast majority of white school-age children—but they accomplished far more than this. The enrollment meetings turned out to be effective pep rallies at which those in attendance learned first-hand what was being done elsewhere in the county and were exhorted to do as well. Responsibilities were divided between the district committees, which were entrusted entirely, for instance, with the task of arranging for school transportation, and a central committee in Farmville, charged with surveying buildings, collecting textbooks, recommending school hours, and the like.

The system worked admirably. Throughout the county occurred what one visiting reporter described as "an outpouring of community zeal." [30] There was a boom in church building. A rural Methodist church built a fellowship building containing two rooms plus rest room and kitchen, which became a part of the "schools" in September. A similarly intended four-room addition to a Baptist church was begun with volunteer labor in mid-August with six thousand donated cinder blocks piled high on the church grounds. A Presbyterian paused from his labors of hand long enough to express public delight to be working on this Baptist church.[31] All over the county, churches blossomed out with fire escapes whose purpose was to satisfy fire laws pertaining to schools.

An acute need for chairs, desks, wastebaskets, blackboards, fire extinguishers, and the like was filled, bit by bit, almost entirely on a volunteer basis. Robert Redd, one of Pearson's assistants, remembers having about a week to make desk top attachments for some six hundred folding chairs. He set up an assembly line production and telephoned volunteers—lawyers, salesmen, carpenters—for work in day and night shifts. Out of conduit masonite and inexperienced but willing help, they finished their task.[32]

A football field was needed. In August the Jaycees took it on as a project. They leveled a field adjacent to the city dump, planted grass, acquired bleachers, and somehow got enough volunteer, skilled help to set up the lighting system. One observer recalled that one night the lights and poles were up around Farmville High School and the next morning before daylight they were up around the Foundation field.[33]

The zeal of the county's effort was reflected and given encouragement in the pages of the *Herald*. Feature stories of group and individual efforts were common. Editor Wall's "where there's a will, there's a way" editorials ran in almost every issue during these hectic weeks. But even the general run of gossipy, small community news was permeated with the local story that dwarfed all others. A civic league news story might tell of approval of two school buses and an invitation to any and all to show up at the "school" any Saturday to join neighbors carpentering, moving books, and so on.

The effort inside the community was supplemented by an impressive, scarcely organized effort from without. News of the Prince Edward experiment traveled far and swiftly. Stories in state and out of state papers spread the word; the Foundation officials saw to it that all organizations that might logically help —whether because of sympathy with segregation or simply a humane desire to see some form of schooling continued—were notified.

Donations of all imaginable kinds turned up. A Silver Springs, Florida, man sent along 250 pounds of chalk. Old school buses, suitable for reconditioning and use in the private school system, were donated. Surplus school equipment of one kind or another was acquired from public school systems elsewhere in the state. A Midlothian man loaded his truck and drove it to Farmville to deposit gifts of that most badly needed necessity of schooling— books.[34]

Great emphasis was put on books, where requirements for state accreditation—which the Foundation schools needed if they were to survive—were specific. By mid-August the library at Prince Edward Academy had received three thousand books and an unspecified amount of cash, much of it from outside the county.[35] Robert Crawford's laundry trucks were ferrying between Farmville and the United Daughters of the Confederacy headquarters in Richmond, which served as a kind of state collection point. Editor Kilpatrick in Richmond donated some eighty books. To a considerable extent through his efforts, in a concentrated drive, the library was brought up to accreditation. But Kilpatrick wanted more than that. He wrote of librarian Kate O'Brien in a letter to columnist John Temple Graves: "I wondered as I talked to her how many high school libraries in Manhattan exhibit the same dedication to the Miltonian ideal. How many in Philadelphia or Buffalo or Chicago or Detroit have my book, or yours, or Charlie Bloch's? My guess is that very few have even one book that reflects in any way 'the Southern side' of this controversy. Yet little Prince Edward will have in its library one of the most complete pro-integration shelves in the state. I am so proud of them I could bust." [36]

There is little evidence, however, that many of the donors were interested in building up the Foundation library's pro-integration shelf. One report indicated that some twelve thousand books had descended upon the Foundation by the end of the year and that they ranged from Nietzsche to Lorna Doone to Shakespeare.[37] The UDC and the Daughters of the American Revolution, however, were among donors who largely sympathized with the county's position in the school closing.

The extent to which financial contributions from outside the county helped the Foundation reach its goal is open to some question. J. B. Wall, Jr., the editor's attorney son, told a reporter after the first year of private school operation that of the $300,000 contributed, only between $10,000 and $20,000 came from outside the county.[38] If this were so, given Wall's own estimate of the availability of money inside the county, some of the wealthier county residents must have put up considerable amounts towards the first year of school operation. For whatever value it had, the old Defenders' mailing list was used to solicit funds around the state.[39] Senators Byrd and Robertson made public statements supporting the fund-raising effort and declaring that all contributions would be tax deductible.

Eventually the effort to raise the money and establish the means of education in the county on an emergency basis bore its final fruit. On September 10, the Foundation staged a formal opening in the largest auditorium available to it, Farmville's movie theater. Some fifteen hundred white children, all but a handful of the white school population, were enrolled. They would attend school in sixteen buildings scattered throughout the county, mostly churches but, in Farmville, including former homes, stores, and even a blacksmith shop.[40]

The job was done. It was hardly an unqualified success. The

equipment was catch-as-catch-can, the buildings were simply available, the teachers were the same as in the public schools, and the headmaster was R. C. Gilmer—the man who had told the Jarman Hall meeting in 1955 that he would teach without pay if necessary to educate the county's white youth; a former football coach and assistant principal at Farmville High School and, although a man of good will, hardly the choice for headmaster that would have been made by a private school with a reputation in education to uphold. The Foundation schools were makeshift at this point and deserved the appellation however much the Foundation officers resented it.

The astonishing thing is that they were able to open at all. As the speakers filed out on the stage of the theater to take their seats that overcast September morning, an air of unreality cloaked the proceedings. The theater marquee proclaimed the arrival of a Hollywood spectacular, and inside adults were instructing children on how to catch buses (surplus buses had been purchased) to get to their assigned churches where blackboards were set up for their instruction. This was the "unique experiment in American education" that the *Richmond Times-Dispatch* proclaimed with no apparent recognition of irony.[41]

The moderate people of Prince Edward who were simply trying to stave off educational disaster may have thought that the private school system was temporary. This is not the way the Foundation people saw that system. On the stage of the State Theater, Pearson, tired but pleased, alluded to the hoped for impact of the Prince Edward "experiment": "The spotlight will be on you and your accomplishments. If we have a successful year, the hopes of hundreds of thousands will be kindled."[42]

And Foundation President Blanton Hanbury, who had been saying how difficult it was to get across the idea that public schools were a thing of the past in the county as far into the future as one could see, was equally sure of the future of private schools: "Private schools are here to stay, there's no question about it."[43]

While the white participants in Prince Edward's "experiment in education"—its critics would later call it an "experiment in ignorance"—were engaged at the State Theater, the Negro participants were disengaged. That was another, and far sadder, story.

On the night of June 17, 1959, the Negro community of Prince Edward held a mass meeting in response to the action of the board of supervisors cutting off funds for public schools. For about three hours some two hundred Negroes at the New Hope Baptist Church near the Charlotte County line heard speakers whose purpose, according to W. Lester Banks, was to reassure them "that things were not as bad as they seemed." [44]

Yet there was little about the meeting that might conceivably have been reassuring to the Negro parents in attendance. Oliver Hill talked at length about the vote and the chance that Negroes had to unseat the offending supervisors. He hinted that further action in court might prevent the schools from closing—"they're not closed yet." Mr. Griffin delivered a lecture on the injustices suffered by Negroes and the necessity of standing up to them. The Reverend Wyatt T. Walker of Petersburg, later to become a leader in the southern "nonviolent resistance" movement, concentrated on this doctrine. [45] But in truth, things were every bit as bad as they seemed even though the Negro leaders were reluctant to believe it or, if they believed it, to discuss it. With only a few weeks remaining before an old and deep-rooted threat to close schools was to be carried out, no plans whatever had been made for the education of the Negro children. Not a word of this came out of the New Hope meeting, nor was there any sign that the absence of plans was noted by anyone in the audience.

The truth was that the Negroes by and large could not bring themselves to believe that the whites would go this far or that the courts would permit them to go this far. The Negro plaintiffs had, after all, won the case. They were used to seeing the federal courts enforce their civil rights victories. Besides, the county's action would go against the tide of state policy and against the advice of the governor. Dr. N. P. Miller, a good observer, summed up the feeling in the Negro community during this period: "I think that they were in full good hope that the schools would open." [46]

Mr. Griffin may have felt otherwise. He did not seem optimistic in talking to reporters in May, but neither was he calling for reinforcements to stave off disaster. In his public utterances he was much less guarded. The Reverend Dan Bowers, a white preacher then serving as executive director of the Virginia Council on Human Relations, remembers attending a meeting during this time at Mr. Griffin's church. "I remember that Griffin kept saying 'those buses are going to roll.' He figured that the county would back down, that it would not close its schools. Oddly enough, so did I." [47]

Mr. Griffin now says that he was merely fulfilling the age-old function of the Negro preacher, offering hope to people who could get it nowhere else. He had no doubt, he now says, that the whites would close the schools if they were allowed to do so. And he could see that the time to stop them was indeed short. [48]

At that, he waited late in the day before acting. A story in the *Herald* in August indicated that of the various neighboring counties only Lunenburg had reported Prince Edward Negro applicants for school—three in number. Other neighboring counties indicated that they would take only a nominal number of Negro students or none at all. It was obvious that if the children were to be educated the following year, they would have to be sent out of the county at some distance and in some organized way. Yet it was September before any public notice appeared that this would be done. The *Herald* reported that fifty Negro students were enrolled at Kittrell College near Henderson, North Carolina, an institution sponsored by the African Methodist Episcopal Church. [49]

Mr. Griffin recalls that his immediate concern was with the high school seniors. If the schools remained closed for a full year—and nobody in the Negro community thought that they would remain closed longer than this—the seniors would suffer most. They would probably get jobs, and in the normal course of events forego their opportunity to get a high school diploma when the schools reopened.

Mr. Griffin remembers talking over this problem with Reverend A. I. Dunlap, a Methodist minister then in Farmville. Mr. Dunlap got in touch with Bishop Frank Madison Reid and through him an arrangement was made with Kittrell, which offered high school as well as college courses. The school asked for half the normal tuition from each of the Prince Edward students, but stipulated that all who would go be sent even if the money could not be raised. Before the school year was up, some sixty-eight students took advantage of this opportunity and the school had to add a ninth grade. When the vanguard left for North Carolina in September, they were in a twenty-car motorcade, horns tooting, symbolic of an effort—however small—to keep the process of education turning for Prince Edward's Negro children.[50]

When the Negro teachers of the county began to disperse in search of other jobs shortly before the schools would have opened, it became apparent even to the most sanguine supporters of public schools in the Negro and white communities that their case was lost, at least for 1959–60. The NAACP continued to talk in terms of increased voter registrations, hardly a substitute for education. It appeared to some of the more conservative members of the Negro community that if their children were to be educated in the school year to come, it would be in private schools set up in collaboration with the whites.

This idea had been advanced publicly as far back as June, when the Foundation announced that it would help Negroes set up their own private schools if they were interested. Mr. Griffin at that time responded coolly that Negroes had no immediate plans other than waiting for the due process of the law.[51]

The Foundation people who were interested in the private-schools-for-Negroes idea were determined to pursue it further. In the intervening months before September, they were too busy with their own problems. Editor Wall recalls this period: "We were so busy taking care of ourselves and Griffin kept telling the Negroes, I am told, not to worry about the schools being opened in the fall, that they would be open—first on the fifteenth of September, then on the fifteenth of October, and then in November. I think it was in November that someone came up with the idea of Southside Schools." [52]

Whoever the someone was, Wall's son J. Barrye, Jr., is usually given credit for being the prime mover behind Southside Schools. He and other Foundation leaders asked Dr. Roy B. Hargrove, Jr., to serve as president. Dr. Hargrove, himself a firm segregationist, remembers that the group decided to communicate by telephone with certain members of the Negro community who might be sympathetic to the private school idea. As in the past, the real opinion leaders of the Negro community were ignored. Dr. Hargrove summarizes: "I can guarantee you that it would not have been with the Reverend Griffin because we knew how he felt." [53]

As a consequence, when the announcement of the charter for Southside Schools appeared in the *Herald* in December, the organization was under a double handicap.[54] It had not invited the participation of the Negro community—which alone was probably enough to doom it.[55] And it presented as its board of directors some of the most devout segregationists in all of Prince Edward County. Blithely, the Southside directors announced that letters would be sent to the parents of every Negro child in the county to determine who wanted education. The reaction from Mr. Griffin was bleakly negative: "How can segregated private schools meet the need when segregated public schools were not satisfactory?"[56]

Moderates in the county have felt all along that the Southside Schools proposal was nothing but bluff. The Foundation's segregationists had determined to their own satisfaction—this theory goes—that the Negroes would not accept private schooling. The Southside directors could look noble by making the offer without running the risk of having to deliver. Dr. Hargrove answers the charge in this fashion: "No question that we thought it was a wise thing for us to do because they ought to be in school. We felt that way not just out of love of education but because we knew that public opinion was going to be better with the Negroes in school than out. But my standard answer to this question is that any Negroes who thought that we were proposing this just for propaganda could have called our bluff by applying for the school."[57]

A sounder theory of the moderates is that the Southside people were interested, too, in getting Negroes to apply for and receive tuition grants for private schools under a program set up by the General Assembly. It was under this program that students attending private, segregated schools in Norfolk, Front Royal, and Charlottesville were receiving tuition. But those communities had public schools as well. It was feared that if only whites took tuition grants where Negroes had no schools, the grants would be unconstitutional.

Dr. Gordon Moss felt that there was another motive in the Southside Schools offer: "The ultimate evidence of the trickery of the offer and its hypocrisy is in connection with the Foundation's need for the use of the white school buildings. Two weeks after the Negroes had definitely turned the offer down the Foundation had to ask officially for the use of the school buildings. They would have gotten them had the Negroes preceded them in their request by asking for and getting use of the Negro school buildings for their private school system."[58]

Nonetheless Dr. Hargrove and other Southside supporters believe that a number of Negroes really were anxious to see their
children in school—any kind of school. One group, he says, went
to Richmond where he presumes the NAACP cast cold water on
the proposal.[59] After posting the letter to county Negro parents,
the Southside directors learned that the Negro ministerial alliance was actively working to discourage Negroes from signing
up for the private schools. Reports of threats and intimidations
upon Negroes who wished to sign up were received, Dr. Hargrove says.

Mr. Griffin and Banks scoff at this. Mr. Griffin says that in
spite of the circulation through the county of a small group of
Negroes who spoke out in favor of Southside Schools, interest
actually was low. His theory is that Negro suspicion of private
financing of schools dates back to when they were solicited for
improvements in the old public school system.[60] Dr. Moss, who
was meeting with Negroes a good bit this time, agrees with Mr.
Griffin's assessment.[61]

Shortly after the announcement that letters were being sent
to Negro parents on behalf of Southside Schools, a Christmas
party was held, nominally for the school-less Negro children of
the county. Actually the party, which Mr. Griffin says had a
casual beginning with some remarks he dropped in Washington
earlier, was turned into a forum for NAACP opposition to Southside Schools. The message came through in Oliver Hill's words:
"Some benighted individuals are trying to entice you away from
your rights by promising you a private school. . . . Christ made
the supreme sacrifice. All you will lose will be one or two years
of Jim Crow education. But at the same time, in your leisure,
you can gather more in basic education than you would get in
five years of Jim Crow schools. . . . A private school is being
organized for one of two reasons . . . either white schools are
failing, need bolstering, need money, or because the white
people are afraid of the pitiless spotlight of public opinion on
Prince Edward." [62]

Hill's call for "sacrifice" and his hint that the schools might
not open even the next year were taken no more seriously by the
Negro community than was his suggestion that Negroes would
educate themselves in their leisure time. In the perspective of
history, Hill's words have a chilling sound—the Negro children
of Prince Edward would have all too much leisure time at their

disposal in the years to come. But the speech had its intended effect.

The *Herald* tore into the Christmas party in print: "The NAACP offers speeches to the adults, candy and nuts for children they have rendered school-less, and the Southside Schools, Inc., directed by sincere white citizens, offers leadership in established education for the children. The NAACP is controlled in New York; the Southside Schools, Inc., is operated by Prince Edward people. A decision has to be made by the Negro people of Prince Edward." [63]

The decision was clear-cut. Southside Schools got exactly one application, from that stalwart Negro segregationist Bluitt Andrews for his granddaughter. In January, 1960, Southside Schools announced that it was postponing its efforts on behalf of the Negro children of Prince Edward.[64] With that announcement, for all practical purposes, the Southside Schools idea ceased to be a live option for the Negro children of Prince Edward.

The Bush League sprang from a series of events beginning with an effort by the Foundation to buy the public school buildings and culminating in the resignation of the school board.

School Board Chairman Lester Andrews, who had succeeded Calvin Bass, was dead set against the sale of these public buildings. At stake was the major difference of philosophy between the school board on the one hand and the supervisors and Foundation people on the other. To the school board the public schools were closed only temporarily. To the supervisors and the Foundation supporters, they were closed for keeps—unless the Supreme Court reversed its own desegration decision, an event they conceded was unlikely.

So the school board refused to exercise its privilege of selling Farmville High School as surplus. When the Foundation mapped plans to ask for sale of all of the public school buildings, Andrews, fearing a tie vote on the school board that would allow a tie-breaker sympathetic with the Foundation to approve the sale, led a walkout on the part of the board. Before the dust had cleared, five of the six members of the school board had walked out. The resigning members released a report that is a beacon of enlightenment in the murky controversy:

> In its decision the school board has been guided by the fundamental belief that education must be provided for all the school-age children of the entire county. Anything short of this we regard as contrary to the best interests of all of us in the long run. We know that educated citizens are absolutely essential to the very existence of democracy

in local affairs as well as in state and national ones. If a community leaves uneducated any large portion of its citizens, because they cannot afford its cost, or for any other reason, it inevitably creates for itself enormous problems in welfare, delinquency, crime, and unemployment. It means numbers of illiterate laborers which are difficult to absorb in the labor force. Today business and industry are demanding a higher level of training from employees than ever before.

Unless some new system of education for all can take over the whole job of the public schools and have its cost guaranteed in a reasonable manner, we fear the economic consequences to the county. This year, for example, when the people of the county have paid all of the cost of education in the county, we have seen at least a half million dollars not come into the economic life of the county which did come in earlier years. We refer specifically here to two items. In the past we have received approximately $400,000 from the state for operation of public schools. Also in the past the large taxpaying corporations in the county have paid approximately $100,-000 in local taxes. This year, this money did not come to the county in any form.[1]

This was April, 1960. The resignations shook the community as nothing before had done. Here were substantial men, highly regarded men, leaving civic service rather than do what the Foundation majority wanted done. The *Herald* treated the matter decorously, expressing sympathy for the resigning school board members. In the *Herald's* view the courts had put untoward pressure on the board members; differences with the supervisors were not mentioned. At all costs the *Herald* wished to preserve the myth of the monolithic community. But the paper did print the full text of the resigning members' report.[2]

The resignation of all but one member was the last independent act taken by the school board. The new school board was entirely consonant with the Foundation's position. No new efforts were made to buy the schools, however. The Foundation announced that it would launch a drive for $150,000 to build an academy with at least twenty-six classrooms, to be ready by

September. Here would be a permanent building, symbolic of the permanency of the private school system and drawing the patrons closer together in a bond of economic investment.

As for the old school board members, those who had doubts about the course of action the county was taking would have to act outside the official channels of civic power in the community. Such a person was Lester Andrews, a solid, unpretentious man highly respected in the community, who has said, "When I was growing up, I had patches on my pants. I went to high school, public high school, and then I went to Hampden-Sydney for a year and quit to go to work. If it hadn't been for public schools, I wouldn't be here." [3]

Andrews was born in Chesterfield County, one of a family of eight. His father was in the construction business in Prince Edward, and, after attending elementary schools in Chesterfield, Andrews went to Prince Edward High School. When he went to work for the firm in which his father was employed, Maurice Large was at the University of Virginia getting his law degree. When Large came out, in 1944, he went back to the firm, where he had worked for a year or so earlier, and he and Andrews took over its operation as partners.

The Farmville Manufacturing Company has been good to its operators, Andrews is quick to point out. The business has been good to Farmville, too; it is one of the city's economic assets. And Andrews, as well as Large, has served the community. He has the typical credentials—past president of the Rotary Club, director of the People's National Bank, member of the Farmville Baptist Church, head of the Community Chest drive, and chairman of the county savings bond committee for ten years—that fix him as a successful businessman in a small city.

But it was his appointment to the school board that offered him a real opportunity for service. To the surprise of some who thought they knew this big, genial man, he aligned himself with those who were more interested in public education than in segregation. Like virtually everyone else in the county's business community, he swore fealty to the principle of segregation and regretted the Supreme Court decision on schools. But he did not rush out and proclaim that the decision could not be enforced.

Almost as soon as the controversy over selling the schools arose, the pressure on the school board members began to pile up. Andrews, the popular man, with many friends who believed that the schools should be sold, felt this keenly. His phone rang quite a bit. A friend would want to know why he felt so strongly that schools ought to be left boarded up when his children and others needed buildings. Another would want to be reassured that Andrews really did believe that segregation was best for all. Bitterness began to show up in his daily relations with these people. He remembers several small incidents in this vein: "My wife and I were scheduled to take a trip with a couple. It so happened that these people went with someone else without even telling us about it. This was a direct result of our not selling the schools. I see this man now and I can talk to him but this is always between us. And we were close; I thought a lot of him.

"After the school board refused to sell the schools my oldest boy came to me and said 'Daddy, if you'll sell the schools I can go to a party. . . .' " [4]

Andrews has a stubborn streak. His resignation from the school board was a tactical measure, to avoid a school sale vote. He had no idea of quitting his efforts to get the public schools reopened. He found that even this modest step required that he think seriously about race relations for the first time: "I would say that my thinking has changed to the extent that I believe that there must be better communications, general relations between the races, that the Negroes must be taken into the processes of race relations. I would say that my contacts with Negroes prior to all this were individual. . . . No, I can't say I had any idea what the Negro community thought or wanted." [5]

With the Foundation people fully in charge and no sign of a crack in the front of unanimity, Lester Andrews found that there were others like him in the community—solid men, also— who had no sympathy with the idea of closed schools. It was from this group that the Bush League would be formed. The time was ripe.

As early as November, 1959, if Andrews' memory serves,[6] small groups of businessmen had been meeting in living rooms in Farmville to discuss regretfully the unique situation in which the county found itself. Their ideas about what should be done were disparate, but they all agreed on one thing: the public schools should be reopened as quickly as possible.

These Prince Edward citizens formed into a group as a result of the attempted school sale and school board resignations. These events drew the lines more sharply between those who had abandoned public schools and those who had not. Anyone who fell into the latter group was philosophically eligible to belong to the Bush League. The members were a mixed bag, including even one high official of the Foundation; but this was the group's strength.

The name, conceived in derision by Foundation critics, referred to the meeting places that eventually were chosen in the country, specifically to the Cumberland County cabin of Maurice Large, who had by now joined his partner, Andrews, in the effort to reopen the schools. One Bush Leaguer recalls: "They would call you a Bush Leaguer with a sort of sneer. 'Are you a Bush Leaguer?' Something like that. I always answered, 'Sure, aren't you?'" [7]

Behind the humor was a cutting edge. The meetings that grew from living room to cabin size came in for bitter criticism from those who wished to believe that the county was united in its intention to keep the public schools closed. The Bush Leaguers were called integrationists, although probably not one of a hundred of them was interested in integration. Large explains the motivation simply: "Frankly the whole thing was based on one idea. Get the schools open so that the Negroes can have schools." [8]

The Bush Leaguers saw the closed schools as an economic as well as a social disaster for the county. They were businessmen, by and large, not unlike similar groups that worked to reopen schools briefly closed by the Almond administration elsewhere in the state. Dr. Moss and colleagues, who were meeting with Negroes at the time, persuaded the group to hold an interracial meeting, at which a plan was presented calling for Negroes to accept a three-year moratorium on desegregation in the schools in return for acceptance by whites of the principle of the Supreme Court decision and the establishment of a bi-racial committee.

There is general agreement that nothing much was accomplished at this meeting. The fact that it was interracial may have fanned criticism of the league whose meetings, while private, were scarcely secret in spite of efforts made to find suitably concealed meeting places.

An all-white meeting was scheduled for June 3 at Large's cabin. Those responsible for calling it saw nothing remarkable about it. Some Bush Leaguers who had been present at earlier meetings were asked to invite friends to this meeting, a procedure by which the leaders of the movement hoped to increase its membership quickly. Unofficial estimates of the League's strength at this point were that from 350 to 500 people who wished to see the schools open were available for help and that, of these, some 150 had met at one point or another. The cabin could hold only so many at a time. Perhaps 40 or so showed up for the June 3 meeting. But by this time a great many more people in the county knew about the meeting.

Large was hopeful that sufficient support could be gained for opening the schools to persuade the supervisors to change their position. One purpose of the meeting on June 3 was to get those present to go to their respective supervisors with this proposal.[9]

Large recalls that there was discussion about inviting a reporter from the *Herald* to come out to this meeting. At least one of those present favored the idea, but the others shouted him down. One explained in confidence: "There was right much feeling against anyone who would take a stand against the Foundation."

Some of those present think that notice of the meeting had leaked as much as two days before it was held. One story is that a tape recording of the meeting was made secretly. Certainly, somebody in attendance at the meeting gave out a fairly accurate version of what had happened within hours after the meeting broke up.

Large noticed that the cars of two Foundation members were pulled over to the side of a school as he drove out of Cumberland County: "They pulled over and watched. They dashed up and down and watched."[10]

By the time Calvin Bass left the meeting a car was parked in a nearby public road, its lights shining on all the cars coming out.[11] Lester Andrews spotted a Foundation friend of his in a car taking notes on who was coming out of the meeting.[12] There are stories of persons attending the meeting being stopped and questioned about it as they drove up to their homes. There is even a story that one of those watching from a car made an effort to run down one who had attended the meeting. Probably there is as much myth surrounding these confrontations after the meeting as there is about the meeting itself. But there can be no doubt that a few people unsympathetic to the Bush League did their best to intimidate its members.

The shining lights and the screeching of automobiles were merely the initial weapons. On the next day a set of "minutes" of the meeting appeared in quantity. Passed about, they soon became the main topic of conversation along Farmville's public streets.

Those who were present generally agree that the purported "minutes" largely were accurate as far as they reported what happened. But the tone was patently hostile. For instance, one professor's brief remarks on the meetings with Negroes were reported in this fashion: "Mr. Bittinger reportedly stated that there had been meetings held with Negro leaders [NAACP officials] and that he felt that this was very enlightening and elevating and that he never felt better than when he left the table after this conference." [13]

But the authors of the "minutes" did not content themselves with reporting, however loaded. They lapsed into polemics in one long, eye-catching passage: "It has come to the attention of those of us who have worked and sacrificed for the preservation of segregated schools in Prince Edward County and who have been most vitally concerned by the unconstitutional rulings of the Supreme Court of the United States bearing directly upon the welfare of the white children of our county that an insedious [sic] movement instigated by certain business men in our town and county who are willing to sell their honor and the moral upbringing of our white children for a few dollars which they alledgedly [sic] lost by a business slump blamed by them on our school situation. It is a well-known fact that the business slump has been felt nation wide and those persons who are the enemies of your children and mine are using this economic weapon as a tool to force us into an integrate [sic] society. It must certainly be true that certain good men who have been duped into this movement have allowed greed to compromise them into an alliance with these socialist, intergrationalists [sic], do gooders' and educationalists who would sacrifice your children in order to further themselves economically and politically." [14]

This blotched, purple prose had the effect of condemning everyone who had attended the meeting, many of whom were named elsewhere in the "minutes" and virtually all of whom were known by name anyway. Where the document did not reach, word of mouth carried even more distorted versions of the meeting. One Bush Leaguer remembers one bootleg version of the cabin meeting: "The rumors about that meeting on the lake are something fierce. Now they have it that Oliver Hill was there and that we all were going to integrate the schools right then."

It is not easy to imagine how a meeting whose intent was so innocent could have aroused community passions as the June 3 meeting did. Yet I was in Prince Edward County for two visits immediately afterwards, and I can attest that hostility toward the Bush Leaguers in the town of Farmville, at any rate, was vivid. Most of them refused to discuss their attendance at the meetings at all, and those who would talk privately quickly revealed the depth of the schism in the community.

One man told of hearing that a lifelong friend had called him an integrationist—the ultimate term of reproach among the county's whites. He went to the friend's store and had a public confrontation with him. He remembers it as a terrible, hurtful scene.

Friends passed each other on the street without speaking. Others stopped doing business where they had been going all their lives. Nor did the economic effects of the hard feeling stop at this. One Bush Leaguer recalls: "Two men at that meeting had their jobs threatened as a result of their attending. In fact one of them, when his boss told him he didn't want him working for him and attending that kind of meeting, told him that he would quit. The boss apologized the next day but the man right now is working for another company." [15]

One of the Bush Leaguers reportedly was so upset by the things being said about him that he visited a lawyer in Richmond to investigate the possibility of a slander suit.

As the repercussions of the meeting broadened, the Bush Leaguers settled for whatever cover they could find. Some few simply disowned their part in the discussions. Some tried patiently to explain what actually had happened. Large and Andrews called their workers together and gave them a straight version of the meeting.[16] That quieted the rumors in one Farmville retail firm.

But most simply took their opinions underground and elected to wait out the storm. The intensity and irrationality of the criticism leveled at them had offended many people in the community and had raised doubts among some Foundation leaders.

Editor Wall told me that he thought the reaction to the meetings was regrettable.[17] Yet the *Herald* carried not a word about the meetings nor about the reaction: it all might just as well have been a figment of community imagination. The editor reasoned that the meetings were private and that they were reportable only if the participants invited the press. He agreed with some of the Bush League leaders that publicity might easily have heightened feeling against them and killed the movement.[18]

The movement died anyway, though, and it would be hard to make out a case that it could have died any sooner or have been buried any deeper. The more interesting question is whether the prompt publication of accurate accounts of the meetings would not have had quite the opposite effect of legitimizing the dissent movement and opening the door to the kind of full-scale county debate on the subject of the closed public schools that never did emerge.

As it happened, discussion was impossible. Lester Andrews told me two weeks after the meeting that he was through: "If the type of group we got together could meet with freedom— freedom of speech, freedom of assembly, all those other freedoms the Foundation people say they are trying to preserve—if I could walk down Main Street and feel like I was free to discuss this thing—then we might make some progress. But all the debate is through gossip channels. Any person questioning the idea that we are out of the public school business is subjected to economic and social boycott." [19]

In Andrews' case, the effects were quite tangible. He and Large had opened up a shopping center, Farmville's first, only a few months before. Andrews' part in blocking sale of the public school property and the roles he and Large played in the Bush League brought about a retaliatory boycott of the stores in the center. For a while, business was very slow indeed.

The depressing effect of the twin boycotts and the shambles in which the League was left in the wake of the massive criticism it had received persuaded Les Andrews to call it quits. He reasoned that no progress could be made in the present climate. It would be difficult now even to get together a group to meet much less to make the movement strong enough to exercise influence on the board of supervisors.

And Les Andrews' family had had just about all that he was willing for them to take. When he took them to a ball game, they noticed that a chilly cloud seemed to follow them about. Mrs. Andrews passed friends on the golf course who would not speak to her. The Andrews children had to put up with the kind of scorn that only other children can bring to bear.[20]

The Bush Leaguers were not men like Mr. Kennedy and Principal Bash—professionals who could regard themselves as merely passing through. They were lifetime residents. They had no plans to move, no place to go.

They agreed with Andrews and Large that the usefulness of the League was at an end. The more optimistic of them would add "temporarily," but no such qualifier could be justified. Too many of the League's members had had a conclusive dose of being the detested minority in a small town. One put it this way: "I have not lived in this town all my life to be an outcast at this late date."

So with the meeting of June 3 came the break-up of the Bush League. It never met again. With its passing went the only significant movement of dissent—as distinguished from individual dissenters—that the county was to experience. The only county in the country without public schools lapsed into an ersatz atmosphere of unanimity. Long years of stalemate lay ahead.

13.   THE ELEMENTS
OF STALEMATE

The public schools were closed, and they were to stay closed for five long years. How could this be? How could the county, the state, the nation sit by this long while hundreds of children went uneducated or half educated? Why did not a reaction set in at some time during these years sufficient to get the schools open again?

The answers to these questions are complex. A condition of stalemate very gradually did develop in which each of the opposing forces at work in the county came to feel that it had taken a position from which there was no retreat. In these circumstances it was easy for all sides to declare that the courts must settle the matter. Rarely have the mills of justice ground so slowly as they were to grind in the Prince Edward case.

Among the important elements of stalemate was the success of the private school effort in terms of its ability to stay afloat financially and to present at least the outward appearances of a successful educational operation. This success probably surprised the Foundation's most ardent supporters, who knew they had no lack of determination but who blanched at the idea of depending upon voluntary contributions over a period of years. As for the Negroes and the white moderates of the county—they simply did not believe that the Foundation would survive.[1]

For one thing, the Foundation's leaders proved adept at fund raising. They were energetic and, through their absolute control of the county's political and civic organs, they could take charge. They had sold the idea that private schools should be a matter of community pride. They went on to sell the idea that beneficiaries of the Foundation were getting more education (with fewer frills) than they had been getting under the public schools. Finally, they made of the county a symbol of resistance to what they called the encroachment of the federal government on states' rights all over the South. These achievements brought the problems involved in fund raising within range of solution.

The problems were considerable. For the first year of their operation the Foundation schools were financed entirely on a voluntary contribution basis, with taxes lowered proportionately. The state tuition grant law was amended in time for the second year's operation and was regarded as posing less risk to the private schools. The Foundation established tuitions of $240 for the lower school and $265 for the upper school to make up an operating budget of $348,500. The state tutition grants plus local grants approved by the board of supervisors enabled parents to come within $15 per child per year of being covered. For a time, the future looked rosy.

But the unexpected refusal of the school board to sell the white high school forced the Foundation to go to the public at large with what was advertised as a $300,000 fund drive to build the upper school of Prince Edward Academy. The school construction drew heavily upon local free labor and the completed building, while valued at $400,000, had an actual cost of only $240,000.[2] The Foundation proclaimed that 90 percent of the contributors were county people.[3] This is not to say that 90 per cent of the contributions came from within the county, however. A good source told me that one contribution of $50,000 to the building fund was received from New York.

In spite of outside help, there were rumblings of dissatisfaction within the county at the way the drive was conducted. A reporter for the *Lynchburg News*, which was one of the few papers in the state that was unfriendly to Prince Edward's school closing, discovered some townsmen boiling mad at the fund-raising tactics employed. "They assess you and you'd better pay," reporter Robin Gross quoted one unidentified informant. Another, she reported, referred to "Hitler-like" tactics employed by Foundation canvassers who regarded any opposition to the private schools as necessarily stemming from Communists and integrationists.[4] The story stung Editor Wall to a reply in a letter to the editor of the *News* in which he—as chairman of the Capital Fund Committee—denied that such tactics had been employed.[5] To this the *News* responded with an editor's note by Associate Editor

John A. Hamilton, who was to maintain a close interest through the years in the Prince Edward story. Hamilton backed Miss Gross and said that he had run into this resentment himself: "Special committees, we were told, paid calls on families not contributing a 'fair share' to the school operation costs." [6]

What is more remarkable than the resentment that did exist was that it was healed over, at least outwardly, and that the Foundation continued to make a success of its fund-raising. The major test came in August, 1961, when Federal Judge Oren R. Lewis ruled that the state and local tuition grants as applied in Prince Edward County were invalid. The public schools of Prince Edward were closed, Judge Lewis pointed out, so the state's "Freedom of Choice" program offering pupils either public schools or tax-paid grants to attend private schools was not operative in Prince Edward. Judge Lewis hinted that if the county reopened its public schools, it might well be eligible once again for the grants.

Most moderates in the county firmly expected that Judge Lewis's decision would spell the end of the Foundation's schools. Dr. Moss predicted that without the broad base of tax dollars, the private schools would not last more than a few months. [7]

These people reckoned without the political support the Foundation had always enjoyed. Senator Byrd and his lieutenants throughout the state were in complete sympathy with the Foundation's goals; in fact, with the very substance of the county's resistance to the Supreme Court. With the *Herald*'s announcement that a $200,000 fund drive would be launched to provide scholarships so that no white Prince Edward child would be denied a Foundation education, the political forces swung into action. State Senator William F. Stone of Martinsville wrote a letter to the editor published in the *Herald* calling on three thousand people in the state whose principles were worth a $100 contribution. [8] Wall followed this up with a letter to Defenders all over the state, calling for $100 contributions and setting forth the role that the Foundation people imagined they were playing: [9] "Prince Edward people man the defense ramparts with their backs to the wall while you are able to operate your schools, your county affairs, your community normally. If our defense is broken you will face immediate school integration." [10]

In October, after the Foundation had begun its third year of operation by breaking in its new upper school academy building (lower school pupils were still housed in churches and other buildings around the county), a group of Southside politicians met to speed the scholarship drive. Representative William M. Tuck of the Fifth Congressional District and Representative Watkins M. Abbitt of the Fourth presided at the meeting. Foundation President Hanbury touched the theme of the primacy of the Prince Edward case: "More and more people are beginning to realize that Prince Edward is the test case for Southside Virginia and the entire South, for that matter." [11]

The *Herald*, declaring that three-quarters of a million dollars already had been raised for private schools in the county since 1959, called on a renewed effort and praised the Tuck-Abbitt committee which quickly enlisted the aid of sixteen members of the General Assembly and a number of prominent businessmen around the state.[12] Despite the vigor of the drive, Hanbury announced in March that the Foundation was still $50,000 short of its goal.[13] No further indication was given of how the drive turned out, but in August, 1962, in an attempt to explain how the scholarship drive worked, Pearson revealed that requests for aid from white families who could not provide any or all of the tuition payments had come to $158,361, and that actual grants amounted to $136,725.[14]

The Foundation had gotten over this considerable hurdle by playing repeatedly on the theme of Prince Edward County as a beacon for segregationist sympathies in the South. This approach contributed incalculably to the stalemate.

The Foundation actively sought to persuade visiting delegations from other Southern states that they, too, could close their public schools, open private schools, and stem the tide of desegregation. These delegations came from all of the deep Southern states. In return, Pearson—who had become something of a zealot —visited Southern points. He visited Atlanta and spoke to the Georgia legislature at the height of that state's convulsion over school desegregation. He looked at sprawling, cosmopolitan Atlanta and adjudged that it would have no more trouble than Prince Edward in setting up private schools—except that it would need more of them.[15] He went to New Orleans and reached the same conclusion.[16] To meet the mounting demand for accounts of how Prince Edward had solved the multitudinous problems of shifting to a private school system, Pearson sat down and wrote a book, which the Foundation offered for sale to the curious and the speculative.

With all of this ferment and effort, not one single state or sub-division of a state elected to close its public schools. This fact did not seem to perturb the Foundation propagandizers who took the view that NAACP suits elsewhere in the "hard" South would have forced school closings if Prince Edward's "test case" had not already been in the mill.

The belief that Prince Edward represented the South in court lifted the dispute out of the racial arena, as far as the Foundation leaders were concerned. They imagined themselves not so much stemming the black tide—although that image lay behind their words and thoughts—but turning back the minions of the federal oligarchy. They were not white supremacists really, but states' righters. Their interest was not so much in society as in law. The central issue of the Prince Edward dispute then—in their view—was not whether Southern public schools should be desegregated, but whether the courts could force a county to appropriate money to operate public schools at all. If they could, Editor Wall warned solemnly again and again, Americans lived under true judicial tyranny.

Many outside newspapermen agreed with the Foundation's assessment of Prince Edward as the testing ground for private, segregated schools in the South; but few could carry the argument to the dry, remote ground of legalism where Editor Wall dwelled. His frequent editorials during the years of stalemate did more than anything else to depopulate and dehumanize the dispute and place it snugly between the covers of a legal brief. When a *Times-Dispatch* story suggested, for instance, that some lawyers thought the Prince Edward case would be stronger if the public schools were reopened, Wall reacted with horror: "It is inconceivable that any lawyer would suggest that the heart of the litigation be admitted in any court case." [17]

And what was that heart? "The fundamental legal question *raised by the NAACP* [italics mine] is: Can a federal court order the board of supervisors of Prince Edward County to assess taxes from the people of Prince Edward to pay for integrated public schools?"

Editor Wall celebrated this theme. It was Prince Edward County's duty, he argued, to test this question to the last so that other counties that might similarly be oppressed could learn what control they had over their own power of appropriation. When Attorney General Kennedy touched the communal nerve by noting that the only places on earth not providing free public education were Communist China, North Viet Nam, Sarawak, British Honduras, and Prince Edward County, Virginia, Wall responded by saying that for ten years Prince Edward had been fighting for the rights of *all* parents to educate their children as they saw fit and that while this issue was being litigated it was "impossible" to open the public schools.[18]

Here the argument reached its ultimate detachment from reality. The local power of appropriation could only be important to counties that wished to close schools. As the years went on and state after state, county after county, avoided this step, it was fair to ask if the legal issue the Foundation espoused so firmly would not produce an empty settlement. Wasn't the *Herald* "tilting at windmills"? in the phrase of a critic within the county.

Looking at the years of lost education for the Negro children and the turmoil and damage undergone by the entire community, one observer commented acidly that the Foundation's legal position could be summed up by a familiar jingle:

Here lies the body of John Hay,
Who died defending his right of way.

Behind Editor Wall's comfortable legalisms more practical considerations moved the Foundation's strategists. They could see only defeat in the reopening of the public schools. If they took this step—even if the tuition grants were once again made available to the private schools as Judge Lewis had hinted—some whites might attend the public schools, thereby officially integrating them. If the grants were declared illegal, Prince Edward would be caught with only public schools open and the prospect of massive integration. This was the social reality behind Wall's editorials and the courtroom heroics of J. Segar Gravatt, the supervisors' chief counsel, who talked of litigation to the bitter end.

But Wall spoke through his editorial page more to the skeptics of the world outside Prince Edward County than to the segregationists within. There had to be something for everyone, and if the *Herald*'s righteousness wore uncomfortably on Crawford's man in the tobacco patch, speakers could be found whose words were more direct. One such speaker was William J. Story, South Norfolk's superintendent of schools and a member of the State Board of Education, who told a Prince Edward Academy graduating class that the issue at stake was racial amalgamation. "The integrators and those who would destroy white civilization are one and the same. If you mix white and Negro blood in this county, the white race is lost irretrievably and forever and there's nothing you can ever do to get it back." [19]

The familiar theme of the Communist conspiracy was sounded by T. Coleman Andrews, the States' Rights candidate for President in 1956, whose dedication speech at the new Prince Edward Academy building in September, 1961, was printed in full in the *Herald.* Andrews, a regular columnist in the *Herald,* spoke of the conspiracy of the Fabian Socialists who had penetrated every aspect of American public life and who derived from George Bernard Shaw, "a Communist," and Sigmund Freud, "a medical man of sorts." Because the good people of Prince Edward County believed in segregation—"the only hope of compatible living among two races as different as night from day"—the Fabian Socialists were determined to smash it to an integrated pulp.[20]

The Andrews version of what had happened in the county was totally antiseptic, eliminating all discomfiting history in a stroke.

Whether one accepted Editor Wall's line or turned to Andrews for more spiritual edification, the ultimate message was the same: keep the schools closed. The white children were being educated, as far as one could see on a par with their former education in public schools. The Negro children were the recipients of frequent efforts to establish for them private schools—and what more could one who believed as T. Coleman Andrews believed, or even as Wall believed, be expected to do for them?

Even the efforts made by the Kennedy Administration to see the schools reopened contributed to the stalemate. The most notable of these efforts came in April, 1961, when the Administration attempted to intervene in the court case on behalf of the NAACP. Through Attorney General Robert Kennedy, the government asked the court to bar state support of any public school in the State of Virginia until Prince Edward County schools were reopened on a desegregated basis.

The timing of the move was unfortunate. It may be merely

wishful thinking on the part of moderates in the county that the board of supervisors was for the first time close to a decision to reopen the schools. Concrete evidence of a leaning in this direction is scarce. But Virginia was in the midst of a Democratic gubernatorial primary pitting Governor Almond's Attorney General, Albertis S. Harrison, against Lieutenant Governor A. E. S. Stephens. Harrison enjoyed the blessings of the Byrd administration, while Stephens, although an organization man, was considerably more liberal.

Comment on the action of the Justice Department fixed the lines of dispute firmly. The NAACP's Banks, in Richmond, was "delighted"[21] whereas firebrand Representative Abbitt called the action "totalitarian."[22] Senator Byrd typically seized upon the weakness of the Kennedy motion—its seemingly punitive nature. The government was seeking to close schools throughout the state to punish one county in the state, Senator Byrd said.[23] It did little good for the Justice Department to insist that its intention was to open the schools of Prince Edward, not to close the schools of Virginia.

Most observers agree that the Kennedy intervention worked against the cause of those who had asked for the schools to be reopened. Stephens and his running mate, who had taken a position that the schools should be reopened and who had supported President Kennedy, took a bad beating in Prince Edward County and lost in the state as well.

As Governor, Harrison showed that he had learned his political lessons well. He spoke out in favor of reopening the public schools of the county, but for almost half his term of office he took no action toward this end. More important, he contributed materially to the spread of the idea that no action on a state level was possible while the case was in the courts.

This, of course, was precisely what the Foundation people in Prince Edward County were saying. By agreeing with them, Governor Harrison accepted the stalemate. With the dissolution of the Bush League, no effective action to open the schools on a local level would arise. With the election of Governor Harrison, no action on a state level seemed possible. With the rejection by Judge Lewis of the Kennedy Administration effort to intervene in the suit, little apparently could be done by the federal government. Any solution that might emerge presumably would have to come from the courts.

A court solution was what the Foundation people wanted, of course, But, then, eventually it came to be what the NAACP wanted as well.

The Foundation thought that time was on its side. Gravatt, the powerful courtroom voice of the supervisors, stated publicly that if Prince Edward could get by for a year without integration, the NAACP would be completely discredited and the old status quo re-established.[24] For its part, the NAACP was sure that time was on its side.

This last calculation, however, was based not so much on the imagined strength of the NAACP's legal case, but on its belief in the weakness of the Foundation. Oliver Hill could talk seriously about the duty of Prince Edward County Negroes to get out the vote not because he imagined that this tactic would somehow open the schools (the supervisors were not even up for re-election until 1963), but because he and other NAACP leaders hoped that it would not be necessary for them to open the schools. If the Foundation failed, as they expected it to fail, the schools would reopen and the lesson would be so much the sharper for the rest of the South.

The expectation that the Foundation would wither away from economic malnutrition was by no means universal among Negro leaders. Griffin says that he believed it some days and doubted it just as heartily on other days.[25] A neutral observer concludes that proximity had something to do with this healthy skepticism: "The NAACP at a state and national level had a poor idea of what the strength of this little white community was. Griffin knew that he didn't know. They didn't even know that." [26]

What the NAACP leadership did know was that the legal route to reopening the schools was over previously uncharted territory and promised a rough journey. With the closing of the schools that otherwise would have been desegregated, the known phase of the litigation was finished. Some new strategy had to be devised to test the right of the county or the state to keep the public schools closed.

A combination of circumstances arose to bog down the NAACP's legal program. For one thing, Judge Hutcheson announced his retirement, and the NAACP preferred to wait for his successor, Judge Oren R. Lewis of Arlington, rather than proceed in state courts. The NAACP had an abiding suspicion of state courts and an almost pathological fear of being bottled up there, with issues the federal courts could not decide because the state courts would not decide. The fact that their first stop in state court would have been Judge Joel Flood, a relative of Senator Byrd who had once threatened to stow Mr. Griffin in jail for failure to produce NAACP records, further inhibited a move in this direction.

It was not until September, 1960, the first anniversary of the school closing, that the NAACP filed a supplemental complaint with the new district judge. The burden of the complaint was that the schools of Prince Edward were remaining closed in defiance of the state constitution which required the General Assembly to maintain a "system" of schools. The *Virginian-Pilot* in Norfolk put the question this way: "If Prince Edward doesn't have to maintain a public school system, doesn't the state have to do so in Prince Edward?" [27]

Nowhere in the years to come would the state of Virginia volunteer an answer to this question. In January, 1961, the NAACP filed a further supplemental complaint attacking the use of public funds—state and local tuition grants—in the Foundation's private schools.

While the NAACP struggled to organize its new legal attack, signs of strain were beginning to show up in Prince Edward's Negro community. At first, after the initial pep rallies in the fall and winter of 1959, enthusiasm for registration was high. Long lines forced the county registrar to keep his doors open a little longer, and frequent alarums in the *Herald* bearing on the increasing Negro registration brought about a retaliatory registration campaign by whites. If the purposes of democracy were so served, there is little evidence that the balance of power was significantly altered. Figures on registration vary, but the proportion of white to Negro voters registered hung somewhere between three and four to one despite the Negro drive. The Negroes might elect a justice of the peace, as they did in November, 1959, and they might look forward to using their vote to tip the scales against selling the schools in the referendum that never took place, but the idea of replacing members of the board of supervisors four years or even forty years hence did not seem practical.

Under the circumstances, it was easy for the Negroes of Prince Edward to conclude that the NAACP was doing nothing for them. The legal case languished, and the best the NAACP attorneys could do was to talk about the pie-in-the-sky Negro vote. To many Prince Edward Negroes the best hope of solving their dilemma lay with the moderate whites of the county, who were engaged in the Bush League meetings and were seemingly in a mood to compromise.

This mood is reflected in an interview Griffin gave to the *Herald*'s Ben Bowers in April, 1960.[28] Although Griffin made it clear that he could not support a compromise that would preserve segregation, he did call for appointment of a bi-racial committee to attempt to work out a satisfactory solution. Privately, he told Bowers that Negroes would be willing to trade moderation for acceptance of the principle of the Supreme Court decision. Privately, too, he expressed some doubts about the NAACP's handling of the Prince Edward case.

But the routing of the Bush League and the scattering of its members put an end to reasonable hope of compromise. Gradually, as the lines of opposition began to harden, the Negro community turned more to consideration of "direct" action.

One consideration prompting this change of attitude was NAACP policy towards the education of the Negro children of the county. After the Kittrell students had been bundled off, the Negro community had to decide what measures of education to take for the remaining children of school age. They would not accept the repeated blandishments of the nonexistent Southside Schools. At a meeting in Washington in January, 1960, under the sponsorship of the National Council of Negro Women, representatives of twenty-one organizations named Griffin chairman of a project to set up "training centers" for the Negro children. Churches, lodge halls, and other available private buildings would be used. Certain basic subjects such as reading and arithmetic would be taught, beginning in February. But the centers would not be real schools. They would be "morale builders" only. They would not offer genuine education. Some $16,500 was to be raised for the centers and tuition owed to Kittrell.[29]

The decision on what sort of educational system should be set up was basic and, as it turned out, irrevocable. It was not entirely unanimous. At various meetings educators present suggested that genuine education ought to be offered the Negro students. But the fact was that the fate of the Negro cause in Prince Edward County was not in the hands of educators, but of organizations interested primarily in racial integration. The NAACP, the National Council of Negro Women, the American Friends Service Committee—none of these organizations are structured to provide specific educational help.

A glance at the thinking that activated the civil rights groups with an early interest in Prince Edward is useful. In the fall of 1959, staff members of the Southern Regional Council, the NAACP, and the American Friends Service Committee were requested by the Southern Interagency Conference to consider the plight of the school-less Prince Edward children. At a consultation in Washington in December, the staff committee suggested certain criteria for projects. The projects were not to jeopardize the legal strategy for desegregation and they were not to be of a nature that could be interpreted as taking away from local or state authorities their responsibility for public education.

Plainly, these criteria ruled out any effort that might have been mounted to establish adequate substitute schooling for the Negro children. Such an effort would have had to overcome immense difficulties in any case and probably could have succeeded only if all the organizations involved had placed the education of the children at the head of the list of priorities.

They did not, partly because legal questions seemed of paramount importance at this time and also because it seemed likely that other school systems would be closed in the backlash of massive resistance. AFSC was interested, for instance, in Yancey County, North Carolina, where Negro parents had boycotted unsatisfactory educational facilities. Here, again, legal strategy seemed all important.

At the same time neither AFSC nor the other interested groups were thinking of long-term school closings. They believed the courts would move reasonably soon. Even if they accepted the NAACP's caution that the public schools might not reopen until 1961, they never dreamed that they would still be closed in 1964.

The decision to keep the centers below the level of schools and not to put on a drive for the best possible educational system was tactical and was agreed to both by the NAACP and local Prince Edward leaders. In an interview, Griffin offered something of an explanation. He was asked how hard the Prince Edward County Christian Association—an organization he had confected to give the Negro community a sense of solidarity—was working to get Negro children out of the county. "We are not trying to locate all of the children in Prince Edward. We are trying to give some of them an opportunity. At the same time we are not trying to lighten the burden of responsible authorities by relieving them of their obligation to give every child free public education." [30]

The NAACP decided against providing substitute education on a mass scale for the Negro children. Locally, responsible Negro leaders—Griffin included—feared that acceptance of private education would be equivalent to acceptance of the status quo. They feared that their own people would be satisfied with this half loaf. Some felt with Reverend Calvin Hill, one of the leaders of the Negro community, that no education should be provided below the level of high school juniors and seniors the first year the schools were closed. Hill reflected on this later: "This way, the pressure would have built up. The Bible says that a house divided against itself cannot stand. I don't think that they'd [the segregationists] have held out this long." [31]

The decision locally drew significant support from Negro leaders on a level below official NAACP status. More important, perhaps, the dissidents on this subject were identified readily as belonging to the "Uncle Tom" group that had opposed the school suit and its consequences from the beginning. If there was any significant and serious debate within the Negro community over the education issue, no record of it is available.

On a state and national level the NAACP saw distinct disadvantages to the establishment of a system of education for the Negro children within the county. These disadvantages were psychological rather than legal. The case could have been prosecuted in court as long as one lone plaintiff held out, but the NAACP was far from convinced that the quickest relief lay in this direction. Its appeal was as much to the conscience of the county, the state, and the federal government as to the courts. If the Negro children all were being safely educated, consciences everywhere would be relieved and the chances of public schools' being reopened by social pressure would be sharply reduced. The NAACP, as Lester Banks indicated, was thinking beyond the boundaries of Prince Edward County: "Had there been any wide acceptance of private schools, it would have had a disastrous effect on other Negro centers, in the Black Belt and elsewhere in the South. Even if the case was still prosecuted, the effect would have been disastrous." [32]

So the NAACP spurned its opportunity to educate the broad masses of Negro children of the county. In its behalf, it must be said that the full impact of the educational disaster that was building up did not come at once and could not be anticipated easily in advance. As the period of closed schools stretched from two to three to four years, the pressure on the NAACP not to compromise increased. To the new Negro militants who arose to challenge NAACP leadership Prince Edward was a cause. This fact made it even more a cause to the NAACP.

Again and again mass meetings in Prince Edward brought noted speakers to exhort the good, Negro citizens of the county to stand fast—just as the segregationist press was urging the good, white citizens to do. Martin Luther King urged Negroes to endure, not to trade their birthrights for "a mess of segregated pottage." [33] Roy Wilkins came to a crowded rally on the courthouse steps one hot May afternoon in 1961 to urge Prince Edward Negroes who had fought to end public segregated schools not to settle for private segregated schools.[34] Oliver Hill declared that the whole world was watching Prince Edward and cautioned his listeners that acceptance of segregation there would make integration more difficult elsewhere.[35] The Prince Edward case was prominently mentioned by speakers in the NAACP cause everywhere. The more NAACP prestige became committed to a just— that is, an integrated—conclusion to the case, the less inclined the organization was to reduce pressures by getting the Negro children back in school.

The Negro children of the county were not totally bereft of educational opportunity. The Kittrell program continued during the years in which the schools were closed and the American Friends Service Committee did a yeomanlike job in lining up homes for students whose parents would consent to send them to integrated Northern public schools. It was easy for those who wished to salve their consciences to forget that these programs reached only an infinitesimal fraction of the Negro children of the county and that the training centers sank further below acceptable levels as educational institutions each year. Something—it seemed—was being done for the children all the time.

Meanwhile the court case was winding its tortuous way through a legal labyrinth. The NAACP attack on the closed schools was two-pronged. An effort would be made to force the board of supervisors to appropriate money to run the schools. A second effort would be made to force the state to see to it that the schools were operated. The Virginia Constitution states specifically that the boards of supervisors of the various counties *may* appropriate money to this end. The logical place to test the issues then was in the state courts. But the NAACP, as previously noted, was not interested in this approach. Legal counsel felt that the case could best be won on the federal issue of denial of equal protection under the Fourteenth Amendment; children of other counties had public schools, children of Prince Edward, none.

Judge Lewis, however, felt very strongly that the issues should be raised in state courts. He resisted NAACP efforts to enter through federal courts and continued to urge in his utterances from the bench that state courts be utilized. In September, 1961, the NAACP in response asked the State Supreme Court of Appeals to compel the board of supervisors to appropriate funds for the schools. But in so doing the NAACP did not pose the question of whether the state was obligated to open the schools if the county did not.

The question of whether the supervisors could be forced to appropriate tax money for schools they did not want was one the segregationists welcomed. Their attorneys had contended from the beginning that no court could compel such an action. If they had to raise money, would a court tell them how much? If they refused to comply, what could the court do? Gravatt raised these questions with the conviction that they must be answered in his favor: "I mean to see these questions litigated to the very end. When we feel that supervisors cannot be fined or confronted with imprisonment by judicial order, we will be on the way to solutions. Until that is done, I don't see how any solutions can come." [36]

Again, this kind of talk may have been meaningless to the man in the tobacco patch. But it was all-important to the legalists of the states' rights cause, and they were in full control of the fate of the case.

In March, 1962, the State Supreme Court ruled that the supervisors could not be compelled to appropriate money to run the schools. The issue of the state's responsibility lay untouched. In July, Judge Lewis handed down his decision: the schools of Prince Edward could not remain closed while schools elsewhere in the state were open; the county could not use tuition grants of a state or local nature until this situation was corrected. Judge Lewis gave the county until September to present a workable plan for compliance. The county responded that it would follow state procedure under the pupil placement act. Judge Lewis decided to stay execution of his order pending the county's appeal.

This meant another long delay. The appellate Fourth Circuit Court of Appeals held the case until August, 1963, before finally reversing Judge Lewis. The court held that the judge should have waited for state determination of the meaning of the Virginia Constitution. Until such time as the Constitution was interpreted fully by the state courts, the Fourth Circuit concluded, it was impossible for federal courts to tell the state to operate schools or to forbid the county from using whatever tuition grants were available to it. After three years of effort in the federal courts, the NAACP was right back where it started—except that now it could appeal finally to the Supreme Court, where it hoped to get a friendlier response.

The route that the NAACP refused to take through the state courts was taken, finally, by the county. Did the State Constitution require Virginia to operate Prince Edward schools as part of its "system"? The county, itself, asked the question. In December, 1963, the State Supreme Court ruled that the state had no legal obligation to operate the Prince Edward Schools. In a blistering dissent, Chief Justice Eggleston labeled the decision "a clear invitation to the federal court to step in. . . ." It was the United States Supreme Court now, or nothing, for the Negro children of Prince Edward.

The stalemate in the courts reflected the growing conviction of the segregationists and the NAACP that nothing short of a legal answer would do. But to virtually everyone else in touch with the situation, as the years piled up, it was apparent that no court could provide an answer that would make up for the loss of education being suffered by the children. With this conviction new pressures began to build up that had little to do with the courts.

They built up and spilled over in this county that found itself a kind of national celebrity. Holding down the lid was Mr. Griffin.

On February 1, 1960, a group of North Carolina Agricultural and Technical College students in Greensboro, North Carolina, touched off a national wave of sit-ins when they attempted to be served at a downtown lunch counter. Overnight the focus of the civil rights effort moved from the courtroom to the street. The

NAACP, more comfortable in the courtroom, was slow to grasp the meaning of the change. Its man in Prince Edward, the Reverend L. Francis Griffin, was not so slow.

Griffin had no idea that the sit-in techniques ought to be applied to Prince Edward where, after all, the major preoccupation had to be schools. He was inclined to follow the sit-in movement where it did develop. When Negro college students and others in Petersburg, to the east, attempted to desegregate the library, Griffin was with them. Wherever leaders of the new movement went to discuss strategy, Griffin went along. He had status, as the leader in Prince Edward; he wanted a broader identity in the civil rights movement as a whole.

As the Prince Edward case became better known, Griffin as the central local figure representing the Negro became something of a celebrity. His friend, Francis Mitchell, wrote an article about him for *Jet* magazine in which he recounted the preacher's long struggle. Mitchell found Griffin in better spirits than he had been when Rowan visited five years before. He was suffering from an ulcer (which Mitchell commented was a strange ailment for the pastor of a two-hundred-member Negro church in a Southern town) that eventually had to be operated on, but his leadership in the county was secure, his reputation was growing, and his financial problems had cleared up with his joining the NAACP payroll as special consultant in the county.[37] His relative affluence prompted Bluitt Andrews, the preacher's harshest Negro critic, to write a bitter letter to the editor published in the *Herald* denouncing unnamed civil rights leaders who were driving new cars on the spoils of the Prince Edward case.[38]

The sit-in movement marked a kind of watershed in Prince Edward too. It brought to the forefront new organizations whose approach to racial problems was extra-legal. Dr. King's Southern Christian Leadership Conference, and the Student Non-Violent Coordinating Committee—each of these organizations visualized a role for itself in Prince Edward at one time or another. It became apparent that efforts would be made to break the stalemate outside the courtroom.

The idea of a boycott in Prince Edward actually was older than the sit-in movement. In June, 1959, at the mass meeting at Mercy Seat Baptist Church that followed the Board of Supervisors' fund cut-off action, Griffin had warned that the Negro might unbalance the equation by refusing to shop in downtown

Farmville. The comment was buried in the texts of the meeting and attracted no attention. But when Griffin made the threat formal in presenting petitions from Negroes to the supervisors calling for the reopening of public schools in December, 1960, reaction was immediate. Griffin called the closings "unethical, unChristian, and undemocratic." He said, "Our children are being penalized unnecessarily by the actions of this board and have been over a period of the past two years. We have exercised great restraint in the face of the tragic closing of the public schools. We appeal to your good faith and sane judgment in taking action in opening these schools soon. We hope that drastic actions on our part such as total boycott will not be necessary. If you refuse our petition, we are prepared to use any non-violent means to achieve our purposes." [39]

The language—"non-violent means"—was that of the new Negro militancy of the sit-ins. Griffin told the supervisors that he thought he could persuade the Negroes of Prince Edward and the five surrounding counties to stop buying in Farmville.

Editor Wall responded sharply in the *Herald* that the boycott idea, not the school closing, was "unAmerican and unChristian," [40] which tempted Professor Marvin Schlegel of Longwood, one of the few public critics of the school closings, to point out that boycott might be unchristian but that it was hardly unAmerican, as the British of pre-Revolutionary days could attest. [41] The threat did provoke letters of condemnation in the *Herald*, a rare instance of aroused public opinion in Prince Edward. Merchants commented that the boycott would put no one out of business. *Newsday*'s Bonnie Angelo Levy discovered a strong strain of Negro opposition to the boycott and attempted to analyze Griffin's quandary: "In a sense Mr. Griffin's task is thankless, for he must bear the brunt of the white community's anger and at the same time is aware that many of his own people have no heart for the fight. He knows that white people say that he doesn't care about the Negro children's education, what he really wants is integration. Some suggest that he is trying to be another Martin Luther King, and to achieve this bases his moves on publicity mileage." [42]

Griffin was torn between decisions. He had no compunctions against use of the boycott as a weapon in the fight. Yet he was a practical man. He was not interested in creating a brief sensation that would be productive of a few headlines and then go down in failure. He had to look to his own interests, protect his leadership. He realized that a boycott of bus service, such as Dr. King had staged in Montgomery, depended for its success on its own limitations. A six-county boycott of all shopping facilities in the only major shopping center at hand—nothing like that had been tried. It would require awesome preparation. The logistics alone were enormously complicated. Who would furnish the transportation corps necessary to take thousands of Negroes to Lynchburg, say, on some regular schedule, to do their shopping? [43] Indeed, as Miss Levy pointed out, Griffin could not count on the full support even of Prince Edward County Negroes, many of whom would be under severe economic pressures from their employers not to cooperate in a boycott.

In the end, Griffin dropped the boycott threat of 1960. He was tempted by the idea on more than one occasion after this, but his influence continued to go against the use of the boycott. As time went on, and as the civil rights movement picked up its full momentum, this influence became more important. From 1961 to 1963 Griffin would be called upon more often to restrain outside organizations from action than—his old role—to stir Negroes within the county to action. This was the period when Prince Edward became the target for civil rights activists.

Curiously, the first militant outside organization to become interested in Prince Edward County was the Black Muslims. Their interest antedated their public prominence by several years. Enticed perhaps by the steps the whites had taken in the county towards perpetuating the segregated society, a group of Black Muslims from Philadelphia established a small community in the Green Bay section of Prince Edward County. They began attempting to make converts and preaching the advantages of separate black and white societies. Had the whites closed the Negro schools? Fine, now the Negroes could establish their own.

One moderate in the county tells of how one of the Muslim leaders and a prominent segregationist conferred for some time without discovering any areas of disagreement between them. "But then," he adds, "The segregationist never got around to asking the Muslim *why* he wanted to be segregated." Griffin was hugely amused by the whole business: "One of them greeted me in Hebrew, and I answered him in Hebrew and this impressed him very much. They started calling me Brother Francis X, or I guess it was just Brother Francis, really; they save the X for those who are really with them. . . . I told them I couldn't accept their religion or their politics or their views about the white race being a race of devils, but I had to agree with their economics. I mean about Negroes building up their own businesses and banding together to help each other economically. I think they are right about that." [44]

The Muslim community in Green Bay did not thrive, in spite of the industry of its founders. Members could be counted readily by their mailboxes, one of which bore what must be a classic name in the annals of Muslim infiltration into the South—Willy Lee X. After a time, the Muslims moved on without having given the merchants of Farmville a sample of what total segregation really could do to the economy of a town built by white men to serve white men and Negroes.

Griffin's real problems were with organizations that were trying to be helpful. Much of this was plainly his own fault. His leadership qualities were exhortative; he was not the best man imaginable to organize a sustained effort of the kind that built up in Prince Edward County. There was too much in him of the boy who ran away from home, the bright boy who had to be coaxed back to school. Newspapermen from afar hit him again and again for his failure to show up for interviews. The harshest criticism leveled at him in print came from the Saturday Evening Post's Irv Goodman: "Griffin is forty-three years old, heavy-set and slightly disorganized. He accepts speaking dates outside the county and often fails to appear. He says it costs $2,650 a month to run the centers but is unable to produce an accounting of the funds. He claims he is too busy to visit the centers and he knows little of what goes on there. Stories in two Northern newspapers produced a shipment of donated desks and chairs and books for the centers. The material was piled up in a Farmville garage and Griffin asked the center leaders to come down and help themselves. His organization, PECCA, is little more than a weekly prayer meeting in his church, with perhaps seventy-five people gathered for some hymn singing, a sermon, and the passing of the collection plate. Griffin skips a few of the meetings himself. Last year he moved his wife and five children to New Jersey, where the children are going to public schools. Not even the NAACP lawyers, who were planning to use one of his children as a plaintiff in their court case, knew that the youngsters were no longer in Prince Edward.[45]

Griffin claims that Goodman was the only major reporter to come to the county and depart without talking with him. Goodman did not perceive that the value of PECCA was precisely that it was a small organization of community leaders that became, in Griffin's hands, the instrument of opinion in the county Negro community. Goodman could not know how much of the materials sent into the county by well-meaning people from distant locations proved worthless and partook of the fate of the desks and chairs in the garage. Nor could he share entirely Griffin's anguished decision to send his children to public school in New Jersey, after having kept them out of school altogether the first two years so that he could not be accused of avoiding the full personal impact of the school closing. (They were back in the county shortly after Goodman's article appeared, and the eldest was used as a plaintiff in the case.) Still, there was substance to Goodman's criticism. A more knowledgeable critic, and a friend of Griffin's, the Reverend Dan Bowers, executive director of the Virginia Council on Human Relations, summed it up this way in a report: "Reverend Griffin is a good speaker and money raiser. He is the central image of resistance both in the white and the Negro community. The best answer to what is PECCA is simply that it is Griffin. He has serious limitations about keeping books, accounting for money, and keeping records straight. However he is the central figure—no one can go into Prince Edward and work unilaterally. Griffin cannot be bypassed."

For every reporter who noted Griffin's tendency to miss connections—often simply a matter of his having overextended himself—there was one who found that he would go out of his way to be helpful. Ben Bowers of the *Herald,* who maintained a close working relationship with Griffin for some years, praised him for his fairness and co-operation. My experience with him over a period of five years was similarly rewarding.

The truth is that Griffin was being spread thin during these years. He was trying to be the official "martyr" that one NAACP spokesman made of him—the "giant" that Dr. King saw—and still transact the business of the resistance movement in the community. He was away on speaking engagements as much as at home, and if he devoted more time and effort to the work he enjoyed —the speaking and counseling—than to the bare-bones organization work, he merely reflected the NAACP view that the county must be kept a national issue.

Much of Griffin's time, too, was consumed in wrestling with the more militant groups who, with the burgeoning of the demonstration protests around the country, began to take an interest in Prince Edward. Some of these groups were well-intentioned; others, as Griffin noted, could not even be credited this far: "You know, these are not always people who want to help; more often they are guys in the fringes who want to be projected into something." [46]

One of the more persistent of the activist groups that attempted to exert influence in Prince Edward was Dr. King's Southern Christian Leadership Conference, headed, in Virginia, by Dr. Milton A. Reid. This group's self-appointed role may be illustrated by an incident that occurred in August, 1962. Reid and two other Negro clergymen returning from the Albany, Georgia, demonstrations announced that they planned to attack racial segregation from top to bottom throughout Southside Virginia, including, of course, Farmville and Prince Edward County. A mass meeting was called by the state SCLC organization at Stony Creek, near Farmville, and the organization announced that it anticipated an attendance of one thousand Negroes. At the meeting goals amounting to nothing short of immediate, total desegregation were announced. There was talk of negotiations already under way with community leaders in the area. If these negotiations did not prove fruitful, the release issued at the meeting stated, Negroes stood ready to disconnect their telephones, turn off their lights, and conduct freedom walks in Petersburg and Hopewell until the telephone, electric, and transportation companies involved began hiring Negroes on the same basis as whites. [47]

The trouble with this account was that it was nonsense, from top to bottom. The meeting at Stony Creek was sparsely attended, and little was heard again of the negotiations that were supposed to be going on or of the demonstrations that never took place. Griffin commented wryly: "The whites around here ought to know just how conservative the NAACP really is." [48]

It was true. The NAACP's role settled into firm conservatism with the advent of the new push for civil rights. Most of the NAACP figures familiar to the Prince Edward scene—Griffin, Oliver Hill, Lester Banks, Roy Wilkins—were of the middle generation. They could not always adapt to the methods proposed by the young, hot-eyed Negroes who began to take to the streets in earnest in 1963. Yet accommodations had to be made, for this movement, unlike the earlier posing of the SCLC group, was the real thing.

Griffin and the NAACP took due note of this. When Roy Wilkins began joining marches and getting arrested, it was time to ride with the new tide. When some of the young preachers of the Negro community asked if they could stage some sit-in and closed school demonstrations in Farmville in the spring of 1963, Griffin gave the idea his blessings.[49] He even saw his way clear to bring in a youthful organizer for the Student Non-Violent Co-ordinating Committee—one of the more militant civil rights organizations. All that summer, as teachers from New York and Philadelphia and other Northern points labored to repair the damage done by four years of closed schools, their pupils marched in the streets of Farmville, carrying placards. Some of them were arrested.

They vowed to boycott the Farmville stores. It was not a widely successful boycott, but the teachers imported from outside the county and the hard core of resistance inside the county did observe it. Griffin preferred not to think of it as a boycott and did not seek publicity.

He was sure that the public schools of the county would not be opened by a boycott, and this was the fight that he was interested in primarily. Griffin was by now president of the state NAACP. His personal prestige was at stake in the school battle in the county. Furthermore, he had come to believe across the years that only a court settlement of the Prince Edward case could be entirely satisfactory. It would not be enough to get the schools open again. He has said: "We might secure the opening of the public schools of Prince Edward by boycott or by some other 'social action' method. But everyone else in the South who desires the same thing would have to do the same to get it. My feeling is that we must exact something in this county that will apply all over the South. Let our children grow up in ignorance so that the law might speak." [50]

Although they would not have put it the same way, the ardent white segregationists of Prince Edward scarcely would have disagreed with this thesis. They, too, thought that only the courts had the answer.

The pressures that worked on Prince Edward from the outside to reopen the public schools found across the years only a weak answering echo from within the county. With the dissolution of the Bush League, organized dissent was done; nobody arose, as in other Virginia localities, to fight for public education. Public sorrowing over the Negro children who were out of school was fashionable even for Defenders—who inevitably explained that the NAACP's preference for integration over education was responsible—but no amount of grief, spurious and genuine, fashioned another movement within the county to return to public education.

This attitude has been explained in several ways. Critics of the school closings have argued that the county's commitment to public education was insubstantial, even for the South, which, as we have seen, came to public education late and under distasteful circumstances. Dr. C. D. Gordon Moss, the Longwood professor who had been named dean of women, went far beyond this speculation in arguing, in a widely publicized speech in Charlottesville, that the race issue was merely a shield for the true purpose of the school-closers: "But that primary purpose is to destroy public education for both, yes, the Negro children of the county but also the white children of the county in order that they might maintain an unlimited cheap labor supply for the few, for the industries of the county." [1]

If there is any substance to Dr. Moss's theory, it clearly applies only to the philosophers of the Defender-Foundation movement. To the rank and file the issue of public versus private schooling probably was secondary to constitutional or frankly racial issues.

To the average Prince Edward County resident, the real lack may have been a commitment, not to public education itself, but to the central theory of public education, that philosophy which holds that the state has an obligation to educate all in spite of parental indifference, believing that the purpose of education is precisely to overcome the mass ignorance of which this indifference is one aspect. Prince Edward people had little interest in compulsory education; but neither did other communities in the state during this period, most of them accepting the state's repeal of a compulsory education law with equanimity.

The county's failure to mount a back-to-public-school movement can be explained more satisfactorily in other ways. Dissent itself was at a minimum. With few exceptions the college communities lay silent; the pulpits for the most part ignored the problem; civic organizations busied themselves with other matters. It is probably safe to say that the average resident of the county either agreed with the Foundation position during most of the time the schools were closed or could see no satisfactory path between the courses steered by the Foundation and the NAACP. But this assumption alone does not account for the lack of dissent.

Institutional reasons are advanced for the failure of a dissent movement to flower in the college communities. One graduate of Hampden-Sydney offered in partial explanation of that institution's quiescence that it had discovered sociology only recently and was not certain of its validity yet. Hampden-Sydney was and is a classics college, academically conservative. Along with this kind of conservatism goes a political conservatism that issues from a well-heeled, largely native alumni which produces fifty thousand dollars a year in donations. Another observer commented that the faculty at Hampden-Sydney is severely "inbred." This tendency of graduates to consider acceptance on the faculty as the main goal in life tends—he feels—to make the faculty think more like the town than like a college.[2]

Public financial support does not exempt Longwood from money fears. The State Legislature's grip on the purse strings is in the care of men like W. C. "Dan" Daniel, who represents at once Prince Edward and the Foundation viewpoint. Longwood, too, had the example of Dr. Moss, who represented public dissent to the point where others of like mind were content to let him speak for all. When his statements seemed extreme, as they often did even to those who generally agreed with him, this was all the more reason for the liberal-minded not to identify themselves with his cause. Many felt with the president of the college, Dr. Lankford, that they would achieve more by avoiding identification with any single viewpoint, so as to be in a position later on "to pick up the pieces." [3]

Others who might have dissented felt their ties to the community were not sufficiently strong to demand this action of them. In spite of the dispersal of housing for faculty through the county, the academic community tends to keep pretty much to itself. The dissent that did emerge from the representatives of the "gown" made their alienation from the "town" just that much more complete. One observer noted that Farmville was composed of three groups of people: the old townsfolk, the college professors, and the group of "transients" that included most of the Longwood students. Only the first group, by far the most conservative, effectively employed its community voice.[4]

Most of all, there was fear of reprisals. The way in which these reprisals worked has been widely misunderstood. It is not merely a semantic distinction that Mr. Kennedy was not driven from the county as more than one account in the press indicated. Mr. Kennedy was merely made unwelcome: this was the treatment that was used on outsiders like him, in the hope that they would leave, and insiders like Lester Andrews, in the hope that they would either reform or choose silence in preference to acute discomfort.

The treatment was fully repressive enough; there was little need for the harsher means, as most residents of the county recognized and most outsiders did not. Reporter Josephine Ripley of the *Christian Science Monitor* infuriated segregationist leaders, for instance, with a series of stories that offered a theme of barely muted violence and widespread fear.[5] Hostility, so the stories indicated, might be near. Open hostility is always a possibility in such cases, but evidence that it was near in Prince Edward County was pitifully weak—really nonexistent beyond an undocumented account of a rock thrown at the automobile of a Friends representative. The more interesting reality was the absence of this kind of hostility; the potential dissenters were disarmed by looks and words and silence, the arsenal of social coercion.

The clergy had the Kennedy case as a frame of reference,

and most found the example sufficient. The colleges could look to Dr. Moss's case for guidance on what to expect in return for public disagreement. Another professor at Longwood who chose to ignore this example found himself soon estranged from his community and religious life and, in the opinion of some observers, overlooked for promotion. A Farmville town councilman was defeated for office largely because his enthusiasm for the Foundation's fund-raising campaign was insufficient. A civic club member lost the presidency of her club when she wrote a letter to the *Herald* agreeing with Attorney General Kennedy that Prince Edward was, educationally, on a par with North Vietnam. In religion, politics, social, and civic life, it simply did not pay to express views openly hostile to the course the county had chosen to take.

Some of the reprisals may have been organized through the channels available to the pro-Foundation majority, but very little organization really was needed. The acceptable position in the county was widely advertised in the *Herald,* and newcomers were not long in learning what could be said and what could not. One young couple attached to one of the institutions of higher learning remember how shocked the Town Councilmen were when they attended a council meeting, an act which they considered a simple exercise of civic interest but which was regarded with deep suspicion until they explained that they had not come with unfriendly questions. The wife likes to tell of the bridge game they participated in the first night in town, when their views on the county's situation as "outsiders" were solicited by their new neighbors. They pleaded insufficient knowledge and a few days later were briefed by their landlady on the authorized, accepted version of the county's dilemma. The husband remembers that "after that, people began to wave at us as they passed." [6]

It would be a mistake to assume that all dissent was treated alike. No dissent was accepted casually, certainly, but it was possible for certain kinds of individuals to criticize within sharply circumscribed bounds. Dr. Moss might have gone quite far with his criticism if he had muted it, as he owned a special status in the community. But he allowed himself the luxury of extraordinarily frank talk and delivered himself of views that were considered extreme by most of his neighbors—both he and Mr. Kennedy branded the school closings with that unforgivable epithet "unchristian." Those who kept their criticism discreet were allowed more leeway. It was only when criticism became celebrated outside the county that the full weight of communal wrath was leveled at the critic. Editor James Jackson Kilpatrick of the *Richmond News-Leader,* an old friend, was not cast out utterly for his eventual advocacy of school reopening—partly, no doubt, because he knew where to place the blame for the school closings. A professor at Hampden-Sydney, D. M. Allan, was able to write several highly intelligent letters to the *Herald* raising serious questions about the county's course of action without unduly exciting neighborly ire. The tone of Professor Allan's pleas for school reopening was gentle and modestly persuasive: "The question that is being raised most insistently by thoughtful people is this. Will the legal determination of our responsibility tell us any more than we know now? Suppose the verdict of the courts is that the white people of the county have been technically within their rights and that neither the federal or state authority can take over operation of the schools. Will not this only intensify our moral responsibility! . . . As Pollack said in his 'Jurisprudence,' 'Legal justice aims at realizing moral issues.' The seventh President of the United States once said in this regard: 'The law is what is right between us.'" [7]

Professor Allan talked about the county's moral responsibility, but he couched his message in the language of the lawyer. Above all, he did not scold. He might have had in mind the example of Dr. Moss, who spoke and wrote with evangelical fervor, damned about on all sides and who, consequently, had to be made to pay and pay.

When the Reverend Dan Bowers, executive director of the Virginia Council on Human Relations, was preparing a memo early in 1960 telling of Dr. Moss's opposition to the school closings, he appended this observation: "He is also a rather definite segregationist, and was somewhat disappointed that the Negro community did not accept the offers of the Southside Schools, Inc."

The assessment was generous compared to Dr. Moss's own. He styled himself in the 1940's "ignorant, unconcerned, and indifferent" to matters of race abroad and in Prince Edward County. [8] He remembers the tar paper shacks, but he also remembers that he had no realization that the Negro high school was seriously overcrowded until a colleague, there to make a talk, returned with a description of the chaos caused by students having to track through the auditorium to classes. Even then, Dr. Moss was not stirred to action. In 1959, he opposed the school closings on humanitarian grounds primarily. If he was not the definite segregationist that Mr. Bowers thought, he was surely no integrationist.

Had he chosen to act as the mild conscience of the county, criticizing gently from within, he might have been tolerated. He was immensely popular with the students at Longwood and was well-liked in the town, too. Beyond this general popularity, he had had—townsfolk would tell you—a tragic life and deserved credit for bearing up. One townswoman's comment is typical: "Dr. Moss has had such a hard life that he wouldn't get mixed up in something like this unless he really believed in it."

Dr. Moss's beginnings were in Lynchburg where he grew up the son of a life insurance agent, a devout Baptist who set a religious environment for his son. Dr. Moss's first impulse was to foreign missionary work, probably the result of having had so many missionaries stay at his house. At Washington and Lee he was president of the Young Men's Christian Association and by his third year had decided to do educational missionary work in China. In these years at the end of World War I, he attended interdenominational student Y.M.C.A. conferences at Black Mountain, North Carolina. It was only afterwards, while teaching in high school for three years, that he developed intellectual doubts about religious missionary work and concluded that he would prefer college teaching in this country. His Master's essay at Yale (1924-26) proved, to his own satisfaction anyway, that American missionaries in the Far East were too often the tools of diplomatic interests. He had lost the taste for missionary work, but not the zeal that such a taste inculcates. He puts it this way: "I have always assumed—I reckon that I am as much a preacher as I am a teacher—that you ought to train young people's minds and hearts so that they would live as decent and sensible lives as possible. My main concern in teaching American history is to teach succeeding generations the mistakes and errors the past generations have made and to get them to make decency their goal in life." [9]

The thing that friends of his early life remember most clearly about Dr. Moss is his personal courage. Philip Lightfoot Scruggs, editor of the *Lynchburg News* and a boyhood pal, remembers that the young Moss worked a great deal of mileage out of a minimal athletic ability. "It was guts: Gordon would smack on through. . . . A large part of Gordon was character. He had a feeling for the underdog and hated bullies." [10]

Scruggs remembers that while at Washington and Lee, Moss was a non-drinker in an age of alcoholic heroics. Moss describes himself as one of the "angels" in a liquor drinking fraternity, and Scruggs falls back on an expression of the day—"He was what we called a Yale Christer." [11]

The years afterwards brought the temptation of alcohol within range. His wife suffered spells of illness and was institutionalized periodically. Moss, bringing up a family of three, began "experimenting" with alcohol. Scruggs remembers the shock he received when his friend showed up for a visit with an odor of alcohol on his breath. Dr. Dabney S. Lancaster recalls that it was while he was president of Longwood that Dr. Moss became seriously involved with drinking. On one occasion, he recalls, Dr. Moss tendered his resignation, saying that he feared that his drinking was impairing his ability to discharge his faculty responsibilities. Dr. Lancaster says, "I told him I wouldn't accept his resignation but that if any reports came to me that he had been drinking when it might interfere with his duties he would have to get out." [12]

Characteristically, Dr. Moss met the problem head on. He joined Alcoholics Anonymous. He never attempted to hide the fact that he belonged to AA, and he has never since had a problem with alcohol.

In the way of small towns—perhaps particularly small Southern towns—Farmville accepted Dr. Moss's problem and his solution of it with a certain grace. The beloved but eccentric professor was a familiar and not displeasing social cliché, and Dr. Moss was of Farmville, having married a Farmville girl, and having taught at Longwood all in all almost twenty years. His conquest of alcohol gained him respect, and insofar as it was possible for an academic man to be in a position to speak his mind independently when the school closings occurred in 1959, Dr. Moss was that man.

When he and Professor Bittinger spoke out in the board of supervisors' meeting in 1959 against closing schools, both were regarded as safely segregationist. Mr. Bowers' assessment of Dr.

Moss was supported by Mr. Griffin: "He told me some of his history. He said, 'I was born only about fifty miles from here, and I have the same attitude that Southern whites have that the races should be segregated.' He said he had never so much as eaten with Negroes. He thought it was in the best interests of both races that they be segregated. . . . But he was ready to have a modicum of integration to save public schools." [13]

Given the distemper of the community opinion makers at this time, no criticism would have been accepted gracefully. Dr. Moss, again characteristically, spoke bluntly. The supervisors' action in cutting off funds for public schools was "unchristian," he said. [14] His stinging charge was repeated at least once in print. He put his son in private school in Richmond, ignoring the Foundation school. Then he and his colleagues began meeting with the Negroes, and that got around.

Somewhere during this period some prominent townsmen approached Longwood President Francis G. Lankford, who had succeeded the retiring Dr. Lancaster, and spoke with him about Dr. Moss. The theme that was to be repeated so often in the following years was first stated here—Dr. Moss's utterances were bound to be accepted as the official position of Longwood; because of his position, he should remain silent. Dr. Lankford offered no agreement with this idea, but he did mention the visit to Dr. Moss. [15] It was clear that Dr. Moss had to make a decision to take the calculated risk of continuing to criticize.

It was not a simple decision. Stocky, white-haired Dr. Moss had been an exceedingly popular dean. His students were extremely fond of him, possibly, as one female observer has noted, "because he is susceptible to tears," but also for his gentleness and bubbling good humor. When he smiled he showed tobacco-stained teeth and a thousand wrinkles of mirth. His manners were courtly. His voice was cracked but soft and sibilant. He looked and sounded a little like a ruined saint. The faculty respected him for his ability.

Should he jeopardize all this in order to fight a battle that seemed destined for a losing cause? His instincts were evangelical, but a man who could speak out confidently about the values of segregation would not choose the Prince Edward situation for a crusade. Dr. Moss was changing. The bi-racial meetings he had initiated survived the successful effort to block sale of the public schools and the unsuccessful Bush League. If the meetings had no other visible effect, contact with Griffin and other Negro leaders like Dr. Miller, whom he admired, was broadening Dr. Moss's views.

So he elected to continue to speak out. He went beyond that; he sought out opportunities to become more deeply involved in the civil rights movement. In the fall of 1960 he attended a meeting of the Episcopal Society for Cultural and Racial Unity in Richmond and accepted an invitation to join this unofficial organization of church clergy and laymen pledged to oppose segregation in all forms. When the group met in Williamsburg during the following January, Dr. Moss was present.

Stories given wide distribution in the Virginia press quoted Dr. Moss as having said that he was ashamed of being a Virginian. In some cases they left the impression that he was party to a resolution favoring racial intermarriage. He explains it all this way: "I went down there to see whether I thought that this organization could do any good. At the first meeting two buck niggers from New York got up and howled that they had already been refused service at one restaurant and, turning the other cheek, had crossed the street and were refused service at a second restaurant. They urged the organization to picket these places and some of these bleeding hearts got up and said 'Let's do it,' and it looked to me as though the whole convention would be destroyed before it even got started. . . . I got up and to get the attention of these hysterical people I said it made me ashamed to be a Virginian with such things going on. When I finally got their attention, I said that what had happened was that two private restaurants had refused service to two Negroes and that, at this very time, Negroes and whites were sitting together in Williamsburg's oldest church—Bruton Parish— and that a Negro was preaching there and that that was more the true story of what was happening in Virginia than this other thing. . . . A UPI man got the first part of what I said entirely accurately but he passed up the second part altogether. Since there was also something about racial intermarriage, I was stuck with that too. . . ." [16]

A storm of criticism of Dr. Moss blew up. His telephone rang. Angry letters arrived denouncing him. Angrier letters were sent to the State Board of Education, the superintendent of instruction, and the governor. Most of these eventually landed on the desk of Dr. Lankford, who answered them individually, defending Dr. Moss's right to speak his mind. Dr. Moss, himself, felt called upon to write the *Richmond Times-Dispatch*, explaining what he had actually said and what his intent had been.

Finally, a petition was circulated in Prince Edward County calling for the dismissal of Dr. Moss and Dr. Marvin Schlegel, who had written a letter to the editor of a Richmond newspaper questioning whether white children were good enough to go to school with Negroes. Prince Edward segregationists began signing the petition in number.

Dr. Moss was in deep trouble. The minister of his Episcopal church in Farmville publicly read a statement by the vestry denouncing Moss's participation in the ESCRU meeting. Dr. Moss offered to resign from the vestry and as treasurer of the church: "They accepted my resignation from the vestry—a position requiring little work—but they allowed me to continue to collect the church's money." [17]

His troubles at home were minor as compared to the troubles building up on a state level. Leonard G. Muse of Roanoke, chairman of the state board of education, was concerned about the existence of the petition, which he felt could produce the kind of publicity that would heat up the already explosive situation in Farmville and at Longwood College. He asked a board member who knew the segregationist leaders of the county to go to Prince Edward to persuade them not to make a public display out of delivering the petition to the board. He wanted to keep the story out of the papers.[18]

Dr. Lankford was present at the February 3, 1961, meeting at which the petition was discussed. The public portion of the meeting was routine enough. Then, he recalls, the board went into executive session. Dr. Lankford left with the press and waited in an anteroom to be called back. It was some time later before he was called back, and when he expressed his unhappiness with this procedure, the board informed him that it had not intended to exclude him.[19] The subject of Dr. Moss and Dr. Schlegel was before the board, and Dr. Lankford read a statement he had drafted:

> We recognize the right of every American citizen to freedom of expression. We do not believe that a person should have to forgo this right in order to serve on the faculty of a Virginia institution of higher learning.

In the case of Dr. Moss, we commend him for the statement he made following the meeting in Williamsburg and for his decision to withdraw from membership in ESCRU, for we believe this organization will not contribute to improved relations between the races. On the other hand, we think he should have investigated this organization more carefully before deciding to affiliate with it.

In the case of Dr. Schlegel, we feel that the statement he made in the *Times-Dispatch* on January 18, 1961, represented very poor judgment. It contributed nothing to the solution of the school problem in Prince Edward, or elsewhere. We recognize his attempt made in later statements to explain his first statement, but we are certain that it did not quiet the animosity created needlessly by his first statement.

These activities of Dr. Moss and Dr. Schlegel have brought considerable criticism of themselves and of Longwood College. We remind them that the college must always get credit or blame from the activities of its faculty and administration. Accordingly, we urge them to apply these criteria to their public statements and activities in the future:

1. Will they reflect favorably on the college they serve?
2. Will they contribute to the solution of the problem toward which they are directed? [20]

Dr. Lankford asked for and was shown a copy of the petition. The board itself took no action, and Dr. Lankford considered himself free to handle the matter administratively. Upon returning to Farmville, he called Dr. Moss and Dr. Schlegel to inform them that things had gone pretty well.[21]

That evening, Dr. Moss recalls, a Richmond television station had a broadcast saying that he had been discussed by the State Board of Education. Whether through the friendly member of the board or in some other manner, the people interested in the petition to fire the two professors had the story abroad that the two men had been effectively silenced.

Dr. Lankford says this rumor simply was not so. He read to the two men the statement he had read to the board. He felt that the message of the board was that both had to use "discretion" in what they said. He recalls telling Dr. Moss: "I don't know what the reaction of the board would be if this happened again. I don't know if I could successfully support you." [22]

Dr. Moss felt as though he had received "the word." Everything had been done so antiseptically that the story never reached print. Yet Dr. Moss was left with a difficult judgment to make. If he continued to speak out, would his words be judged as "reflecting favorably on the college" or "contributing to the solution of the problem?" Who would make the final decision on whether what he said met these standards. Would it be Dr. Lankford? Or would it be the State Board of Education with which he had no contact and which clearly would have preferred that he not stir the waters?

Some question exists of how much actual danger Dr. Moss was in. He could have been removed as a faculty member only on charges of moral turpitude or malfeasance, and then the charge would be subject to investigation by the American Association of University Professors. He was more vulnerable as dean, subject presumably to removal by the president or the state board. His past was not invulnerable. He weighed the risks and worried. A friend recalls: "He was definitely concerned about everything that happened in this period. If a man thinks he is under pressure, he is." [23]

Scruggs remembers that Dr. Moss came to visit one day during this period: "He was pretty much on edge. He came up here to ask me what I thought about his position with relation to his family. . . . He was pretty high strung and nervous about it. . . . We sat and talked for most of the afternoon. I think he was more emotionally involved than at any time since. . . . He was more concerned with the ultimate responsibility of a person. Am I hurting things rather than helping things by taking a stand?" [24]

Central to the issue was whether or not he was free to speak out publicly as an individual, with or without discretion, and not be understood as speaking for the college. He felt that he had not only the right but the duty to speak out. If he could not speak out because of the position he held, then men of responsibility were systematically robbing themselves of a public voice as they rose in their profession. Besides, in Dr. Moss's view, silence by the college implied assent with the school closings. He felt that quite probably the college *should* take an official stand against the school closings. However, when he spoke, he was careful to identify his opinions as individual.

For the first time in his life, Dr. Moss did not feel free. But if he could not speak out, he could work. Helen Baker, the Friends representative in the county at this time, described him as emotionally overwrought in this period. She quoted him as telling her as she left the county: "If at anytime you need me for anything—anything—call me, and I will come and do what I can at any cost. I have made up my mind."

He did not really think that the State Board would move against him, but he could not be sure. He determined to seek an audience with Colgate W. Darden of Norfolk, former governor and former president of the University of Virginia. Darden also was a member of the State Board. If he could get Darden's word that he was not threatened, he would feel free to continue to express himself.

While he waited for his appointment, the *Saturday Evening Post* article by Irv Goodman hit the streets. Goodman had visited Prince Edward before Dr. Moss had been discussed by the State Board. Dr. Moss had talked with Goodman with his customary candor. After the State Board meeting, Dr. Moss told Dr. Lankford what he had done and asked if he should write Goodman removing permission for attribution. Dr. Lankford had said that he thought that that would be wise. When the article appeared, considerable space was devoted to the dissenting activities of an unnamed professor who was quite plainly Dr. Moss:

> The professor was pressured because of his open opinions. Letters were sent to the governor and state superintendent of schools condemning his public statements. In town he was called "nigger lover" and "integrationist." Delegations went to the college president complaining about him. While I was in the county, a petition was circulating demanding his dismissal. Then, a week after I left Prince Edward, I received what I think is the saddest letter I have ever read, in part: "I was told yesterday by the president of my college that should I open myself to renewed attack, he believed that the state board of education would find it necessary to be relieved of so controversial a person as I seem to have become. Since I have three children wholly dependent upon me for support, I have no recourse but to submit to withdrawing from the battle. . . . There is nothing else that I can do." [25]

Newsmen were unable to get the State Board to comment on the *Saturday Evening Post* story. Dr. Lankford also refused comment, although he was unhappy with what he believed was Dr. Moss's public misrepresentation of his private interpretation of the State Board's mood. He and Dr. Moss had their appointment with Darden, who saw nothing in Dr. Lankford's statement to the board to prevent Dr. Moss from speaking his mind as an individual.[26] Dr. Moss remains convinced that the *Saturday Evening Post* story, with its revelation of the pressures on him, had made it possible for him to speak out safely.

He did continue to speak out and, on occasions, ventilated the issues with provocative letters to the editor of the *Herald* and the Richmond papers. By far the most strenuous exercise of Dr. Moss's views became a subject of public debate in Prince Edward through the good offices of the *Herald*, which elected to print in full a tape recorded talk he had made in Charlottesville in October, 1962.

The speech was a rouser. Dr. Moss explained later that he had been asked to address the local council on human relations and had expected to find only a handful of people. When he arrived and found between 150 and 200 people present in a Negro church, he decided it was time to put on the full treatment. A radio station had asked for permission to tape the talk, and Dr. Moss had granted permission. He had every reason to believe that the speech would be made available to those interested elsewhere. He says that he assumed that J. Barrye Wall, Sr., would obtain a copy.[27]

The editor of the *Herald* was the main object of attack in Dr. Moss's long, extemporaneous speech. The college dean accused Wall of typifying the county's paternalistic attitude toward Negroes and of having said once in one of the current events discussion group meetings both men attended—and that broke off in the post-school closing atmosphere—that it would be a good idea for public schools in the county to be abolished entirely, at least for a while.

It was in amplification of this urge to close schools that Dr. Moss set forth the theory that the ruling class of the county wished to maintain a supply of cheap, unorganized labor: "I grant you that this is one of the most cruel, heartless things I have ever seen in my lifetime for 1,700 or 2,000 children regardless of the color of their skins to be denied education." [28]

Moss also charged that Southside Schools was a bogus offer of education to Negro students and that the white drop-out problem in the private Foundation schools was severe. He brought out in public the attempt he and a colleague had made at a compromise in 1959 and Wall's rejection of it.

Printed in the *Herald*, the speech took up more than four columns. Wall contented himself with brief editorial notice of it in which he did not offer comment on the charges except to say that his record of support of public education "under conditions conducive to the learning process"—by which he clearly meant segregation—was beyond reproach. He did not intend to deal in personalities. That was all.[29]

The speech drew even more comment than was usual with Dr. Moss's utterances. Bob Crawford wrote to say that Editor Wall was in favor of public schools. Letters came in supporting the Foundation's scholarship policy and attacking Dr. Moss's theory of planned economic deprivation. One letter came from Dr. Allan, the Hampden-Sydney professor and lifelong Prince Edward resident. He called for conciliation and lamented the failure in the 1930's to follow up a long-forgotten bi-racial meeting in the Farmville Methodist Church in which ways of improving race relations were discussed: "The meeting was amicable, the discussion candid, and the spirit constructive. Unfortunately, it was not followed up. If it had been we might have been spared the present distressing situation."[30]

Nobody saw fit publicly to join in the regrets for opportunity long lost. Dr. Moss refrained from commenting on the current interracial talks, which continued sporadically, with different personnel on the Negro side more often than not. These meetings never had been acknowledged publicly; their purpose, as they went on, could only be to keep open lines of communication, however weak, between the races.

For his part, Dr. Moss pushed ahead. He had changed. He knew it. He joined the Virginia Council on Human Relations and became interested in the work of the Southern Regional Council. He even thought about joining the NAACP, electing finally not to wave that particular red flag in the faces of his critics. Mr. Griffin was a little in awe of the changes he perceived in Dr. Moss: "It was an amazing transformation. I think it was as much the way the white community reacted to criticism as what he [Dr. Moss] got from the group. I think this started him to thinking about the viciousness of the pattern of segregation. I think he would even support social action today." [31]

Dr. Moss offered his own explanation: "I have learned how much larger the racial issue really is, how it affects the life of the Negro, and I have come to see that not only should they have the right to integrated schools and the right to vote, but the removal of all things that brand them as second class citizens." [32]

The vigor of Dr. Moss's assault on race barriers alienated some in the community who counted themselves in agreement with him on the school issue. His theory of economic deprivation was ridiculed widely in the county. His Charlottesville account of the compromise that he had tried to work out put Mr. Griffin in the position of having to contradict him where he had said that he had the assent of the Negro leadership to the proposed plan. But he did not think of himself as a leader in danger of overreaching his leadership. He thought of himself as a man with an obligation to speak his mind. Characteristically, he hoped with the Charlottesville speech to shock the state into some action; the idea that local action might occur was secondary to him. The issue had gone far beyond the local level. Dr. Moss was taking this fact into account. Some of his friends even found strategic grounds for his shakier statements. One assessed him coolly: "He thinks of himself as a crusader. He is capable of saying hasty things and just plain incorrect things. But he is not always as wrong as you may think. His idea, for instance, in talking about the theory of the few holding the many in economic servitude was to plant the germ of doubt in the minds of some that the few are really with them." [33]

Dr. Moss went about his business, bustling about his office during school hours, gently and humorously tending to the multitude of problems that beset young ladies off to teachers' college. "It's only at night," one observer commented with a smile, "that he turns into Mr. Hyde."

When the demonstrations came to Prince Edward County finally in the summer of 1963, and Negroes planned to try to sit in some white churches in Farmville, Dr. Moss was ready. He asked for and got a ruling from the bishop that any Negroes who appeared should be seated. When it developed that they would be put in the first row—a procedure that struck him as a kind of reverse Jim Crow—he decided to act. He stopped the church official who was escorting them into the church and asked that they be seated in his pew. Afterwards he sat smiling blandly at the members passing by, including one lady who swept his pew with a glance of sheer disbelief.[34]

Mr. Griffin had been right. Dean Moss was ready to support social action. In commemoration of his advance to a new posture of social awareness, the church stripped him of his post as treasurer—the job with the work attached to it.

Willie Redd once paid fifteen dollars in an effort to show that he had never belonged to the NAACP, but he thinks the whole misunderstanding cost him a lot more than that. He reckons his losses as a result of the rumor that he was an NAACP member in six figures, as befits the county's most prosperous Negro contractor. But if not being understood by the white power structure of the county has cost him deep in his pocket, not being understood by his fellow Negroes has cost him dearly in embarrassment, pain, and humiliation.

Willie Redd is a roly-poly figure of a man, quite dark; a vigorous, disputatious talker, a man given to speaking his mind. He does not look the part of the Uncle Tom many in the Negro community take him to be, but then he does not look the part, either, of the spokesman of Negro leadership that for so long the white community took him to be.

It was the failure of white segregationist leaders such as Barrye Wall and Bob Crawford to recognize that he no longer could speak for the Negro community that led Willie Redd's trouble with the bogus NAACP membership. This situation occurred in 1951, after the school strike and the resultant suit by the NAACP. Unwilling to believe that Redd had exerted himself fully enough to turn the local Negro leaders away from the school desegregation suit, some of the white leadership began to blame him for what had happened. Griffin, the upstart preacher, had staked his pastorship on the suit issue and had won. Willie Redd had staked his reputation in the white community on his ability to forestall it. He was caught in the backlash when Mr. Griffin dramatized his hold on the congregation by offering to resign to a show of opposition. The rumor began to circulate in some white circles that Willie Redd secretly supported the preacher and was even more secretly a member of the NAACP. Had not he been thick with the preacher's father?

Willie Redd heard about the rumor from his friend, Bob Crawford, who was simply relaying something his wife had picked up: "I told him Mrs. Crawford had never been more wrong in her life." [35]

He thought about offering publicly a thousand dollar reward for anyone who could show that he ever belonged to the NAACP. Finally he dropped this idea and settled instead for an advertisement in his good friend Mr. Wall's paper, the *Herald*. It was printed duly as follows:

> As a citizen of Farmville and Prince Edward County, I wish to clarify once and for all my position in the current integration law suit filed against the Prince Edward County school board. I frankly state that no person connected with the NAACP suit has approached me in any way to solicit my support in the matter. I have not, as erroneously stated, given financial aid to this cause. Those persons with whom I have had the pleasure to work, both on the school board and in civic matters, know my view very clearly. Over a period of years I have been called upon to support many movements. I have unstintingly given my support, both morally and financially, to movements which I considered progressively sound. Oftentimes I have made sacrifices far beyond my ability simply because I believed such to be for the best interests of Farmville and Prince Edward County. I believe personally that our goals can be reached satisfactorily only through mutually frank discussions and a working out together of our common problems on local issues. I have maintained previously and I maintain now that every citizen of Farmville irregardless [sic] of race, should actively work together without being forced by pressure from without to make Farmville a better and more progressive place in which to live.[36]

Whether or not the white leadership was entirely satisfied by this disclaimer is not known. But the Negro leadership was elated. "Ol' Willie Redd," chuckled preacher Griffin. "Ol' Golden Crown Willie Redd."

It would be difficult to find a more admirable example than Willie Redd of what sheer determination, hard work, and what is often referred to as old-fashioned American business know-how can do. Willie Redd's great-grandfather bought his freedom from slavery after learning the blacksmith trade, which he passed on to his son. He also established Redd's Shop which still stands on the border of Prince Edward and Charlotte counties. The Redds, then, have land that has been in the family over two hundred years. Willie, one of eight children, did not take to the family trade of blacksmithing. When he was ten years old, he had his first job, in a brickyard, and by the time he was twelve he was a permanent employee, carrying water for twenty-five cents a day. He finally went into the construction business as a brick-layer's helper, and he has struggled upward ever since. Now he had a fine brick house in a desirable part of Farmville, and he is worth some money.

Like many other Negroes who succeeded financially despite a minimal education (he got some high school by attending night school for a number of years while he was working), he regards education as the godhead, the salvation of his race. It is his greatest source of pride that all six of his children are graduates of colleges like Fiske, Tuskegee, and Howard.

It is hardly surprising that Willie Redd came to believe that integration was not worth the price of possible lost education. Take care of the education and you take care of the segregation too, describes his attitude at the time of the school strike. He did not favor the strike as an instrument, regarding it as a piece of insubordination by minors. He said later that he would have supported adult action to remedy inequalities in the Negro schools, but he did not favor the suit for desegregation. Having taken this position and having inserted in the *Herald* his NAACP disclaimer, Redd found himself effectively cut off from the Negro community. He recalls, "I was catching it from both sides. One side told some falsehoods about me and some people believed them. I was called an integrationist, and I've been called just about everything else." [37]

Possibly because he was closer to the white leadership in Farmville than were the real Negro leaders like Mr. Griffin—who was as ignorant of their means and goals as they were of his—he had no illusions about whether the whites would close the schools as they threatened to do. One of his daughters was teaching school in Prince Edward the year before the schools closed. He went to her: "Certainly I saw what was coming. Mr. Wall and Mr. Taylor and all of them told me that the schools would be closed if integration was ordered. The colored people didn't believe it. I told them don't you fool yourself, they'll do it. I told her you better get out while the getting is good." [38]

His daughter got out and went to Petersburg to teach. This kind of prophecy, though, hardly was calculated to make Redd's position in the Negro community any more secure. It merely added fuel to the conviction that he was a white man's toady.

It seemed to me when I talked with Willie Redd in the summer of 1962 that he had come a considerable distance back towards the prevailing course of the Negro community. He was clearly out of touch with the white leadership that once bulwarked his position in the community. He spoke in terms of general agreement with Mr. Griffin—"We just have different approaches." He waxed enthusiastic about the Kennedy Administration's appointment of Negroes like Robert Weaver and Carl Rowan to high position: "You've got to be for someone when they are working for your race. . . Things I never dreamed of are happening. . . ." [39]

But it was clear that there were limitations on his ability to follow with enthusiasm the new Negroes' efforts to break down the old order. He told me, for instance, that he would like to see all Jim Crow signs ("White Only") removed: "What they should do is they should take down the signs. Then they could put it simply that they do not serve out of a private policy." [40]

Somewhat astounded, I asked if such a practice really would satisfy him. Would he be satisfied if a waitress simply came out and said that she was sorry, that the management didn't serve Negroes? He said he would prefer that some other reason be given.

His attitude seemed to me at the time a wonderfully profound elaboration of the position of the Negro establishment in the South. These are men like Redd, men of substance, dignity, and meaning in their community. They are not so much interested in changing the actuality of things as the appearance of things. The rudeness of Jim Crow bothers them far more than the effect of it. The eagerness of the young Negroes to rip down the fabric of segregation bothers them too. They wish to defend their position against both threats: Take down the signs.

Obviously Willie Redd was unprepared for the wave of protests that broke in the summer of 1963. When they reached Prince Edward County, he let it be known that he was not in sympathy with them. The eager, young militants who flocked the streets of

Farmville on those hot days seized upon Willie Redd as the symbol of all they found backward and degrading in the old Negro.

One day a group of the youngsters caught Willie Redd on one of Farmville's streets, surrounded him, and followed him along through town chanting "Uncle Tom" as they went. On another occasion they rocked his automobile as he sat in it. His old antagonist, Mr. Griffin, who himself had to step lively to keep his position modern enough for the youngbloods, warned them not to do that again.[41] Willie Redd looked at what had happened in Prince Edward County and uttered a pessimistic judgment: "Now so much has been said on both sides it has given the town a bad name. I wouldn't have invested a nickel in the town if I had known this was going to happen. Now that describes how I feel about all this. . . . It's not a healthy town. I don't mean economically. I mean like in a family when there's been a big fight. . . . I've laid awake nights but I don't know how to make it come out right." [42]

Violence was not done Willie Redd. Yet for the heresy of his views he was punished no less severely than any of the white dissenters. In his case, the ironies are especially sharp, because he was learning to accept change. Like many another American he had simply been unable to accept it fast enough; he was living proof of how fast events were moving and how far the nation had to go to catch up with the Negro vanguard. Willie Redd's white friends would still speak to him, but they were more distant than in the past. And his Negro friends?

He says, "I don't think I ever had any colored friends." [43]

Prince Edward County drew visitors from afar. A Rockville Centre, New York, dental surgeon and his wife, Dr. and Mrs. Lee Roth, visited the county in a station wagon crammed with school supplies on Christmas, 1960. The Roths had been aroused at the plight of the school-less Negro children by Bonnie Angelo Levy's stories in *Newsday*. They set about to collect supplies with *Newsday*'s help.

On Christmas morning they were ready to set out. Dr. Roth later wrote an essay describing portions of the trip and its aftermath: "Early Christmas morning we loaded our station wagon with some of the materials from our now half-filled garage, those which in my wife's professional opinion would be most needed. Our three children, Susan, Gail, and Merrill, were crowded in with supplies all around them. Then off we went to Farmville, the seat of Prince Edward County.

"Our station wagon was so overloaded that before we had gone thirty miles we developed a flat tire. This cost us a new tube and two hours' delay. They were spent pacing a cold New York City street, waiting and worrying. What would we find in Farmville?

"Even after the repair, our troubles weren't over. On the Thruway our car swayed dangerously. What could it be? We slowed down; we had over-inflated our tires. Fatigue took the place of the last several days' excitement. Crowded in, the children complained, and we had lots of time to reflect: Was this trip necessary?

At last our modern-day Conestoga wagon reached the outskirts of Farmville, 350 weary miles from home. It was late. Rather than start our search, we sought lodging, hoping that *Newsday*'s re-

port of our trip had not reached this community and aroused the
ire of its segregationist element.

"The next morning we set about looking for someone to receive
our offerings. All we had were the names of a church, its minister,
and an American Friends Service Committee worker. The church
was closed, its surroundings lazy-quiet. I stopped several Negro
passers-by. 'Where can I find the Reverend Francis Griffin?' Finally I was directed to a Negro dentist who was also an elder of
the church [Dr. N. P. Miller.].

"The dentist and his wife heard our story. They were overcome
with emotion that people so far away were interested in helping
them. They graciously helped us store the materials in a room in
his office. I also left with him the money some of our friends and
neighbors had insisted we take in lieu of supplies which they did
not have. The dentist and his wife made no complaints about the
school situation—they told us only what the Negroes in the community were doing to alleviate it. My Southern colleague then
phoned one of the three Negro public school teachers who still
resided in the vicinity to come and show us around. She accompanied us on a tour of some of the sixteen centers where 450
children of all ages met three days a week for a few hours in
place of formal school. . . .

"We left in silence, wondering how we could help. Our guide
rode beside my wife and me as we slowly bumped our way along
a backcountry dirt road, looking for another center, a school
which had been abandoned years before because it had been
declared a hazard. At this moment a group of white men carrying
rifles suddenly appeared from the brush. They were coming towards us. My throat became parched. A swallow stuck halfway
through it. I got that sinking feeling of blood draining out of my
arms and legs. I could feel my wife tense then tremble slightly
beside me. Would they shoot? However, they waved to us and
smiled genially as they passed by. Merrill summed it up for all
of us, 'Wow. .eeee, I sure thought we were goners until I saw
that they were only out hunting.'

"No, they didn't care. None but a few in this quiet town seemed
to care. Maybe if they had cared, the problem would have been
resolved long ago. . . ." [1]

But, of course, some of them did care, some of the people of
Prince Edward County cared and did not know what to do;
some, like Dr. Moss, spoke out; and some, like the school strikers
of old, acted. Months before Dr. Roth and his family paid their

sojourn to Prince Edward County, one of the strikers of 1951—a reluctant rebel then, much under his mother's influence—was at Shaw University, having been a soldier, aircraft plant worker, and janitor, and, at last, having turned toward the ministry in the footsteps of Mr. Griffin. James Samuel Williams scarcely could have been at a more opportune place when the sit-in movement of 1960 broke out. At Shaw, the ministerial students had been ready for action for a year. The NAACP chapter on campus was more interested in social than legal action and when the college students in Greensboro began the month of February with wildcat sit-ins downtown, Shaw students were not very surprised. Everybody was planning—it was just that there was no co-ordination of plans.

Williams became chairman of the group movement with the responsibility of getting demonstrators to the right place at the right time. Lunch counters were the primary targets these early days of street protest; soon they were closed by management, and the students had to resort to picketing.

Williams' main interest remained the problem in Prince Edward County. On weekends he drove to the county to assist Mr. Griffin in preaching. Mr. Griffin was counting on Williams to take over a considerable responsibility upon graduation. On several occasions he told me that "Sammy," who had gotten married, could not seem to take hold. The older man tried unsuccessfully to fit him into the operation. He did not even do well as a "guide" around the county to help groups that came in either to teach or to do research work. Williams himself says, "Mainly, I was concerned with my academic life. The only time I had to come home was holidays, and I had to preach for Reverend Griffin on Sundays. I stayed out of the county more than in. I was eager to help, but, yes, I guess you could say I was pessimistic. I couldn't see what we could do." [2]

There were sufficient grounds for pessimism. In 1961 and 1962 one disappointment followed another in the county. Williams talked to the county leaders and the people who came and went through the county and concluded that only the courts could solve the problem. He was no lawyer; he could find no useful role for himself. It was all right for Mr. Griffin who, after all, was the symbol of the resistance itself. But what of a newcomer to the fight who could find nothing effective to do?

The turning point came in 1962 when Williams was made chairman of the Voters Registration League of Prince Edward County.

At first, he was afraid that the job would be either a bad joke, which nobody would take seriously, or an impossibility. Then he made a discovery: "As I journeyed through the county I discovered there was more determination among the people than I thought. I began to see things in a different light." [3]

His own church in Green Bay, starting with a handful of registered voters, soon showed 100 per cent registration. Williams had found that he was effective. He went to Griffin in the spring of 1963 and talked about bringing in some demonstrations for the summer. The movement had gathered its full momentum by this time, and Griffin saw plainly in which direction the future lay. He approved the idea, reactivated the NAACP Youth Council, and put Williams and the Reverend Goodwin Douglas, a bright West Indian up from Methodist Kittrell, in charge. [4]

The first action took place in April, when Negro students from Hampton Institute and Virginia Union paused long enough from their labors of surveying the county's uneducated to attempt sit-ins at the theater and two lunch counters. They failed to gain entrance on this occasion and on another occasion in July. It was late in July that the demonstrations took the permanent form of picketing, with placards calling for open public schools and equal job opportunities in Farmville's business establishments. The weekend of July 27 saw a total of thirty-three persons arrested in demonstrations, some of them for parading without a permit on Saturday (the town granted marching permits for the demonstrators every day but Saturday), and the rest for singing in front of the white Baptist Church on Main Street during services on Sunday. This latter group, led by Williams, had been denied entrance on the same day that Dean Moss ushered Negroes into his church. Williams said later that the singing was spontaneous and that there was no desire on the part of the demonstrators to be arrested. Mr. Griffin was displeased with the provocation to arrest, and Williams admitted that the demonstrators should have avoided singing.

When the police closed in and arrested the twenty-two Negroes in front of the church, only one failed to heed the signal to go limp. That was Williams. Along with Griffin, he shares an aversion to this nonviolent technique that has lined the corridors of Southern police stations with stretchers: "I'd rather walk where I'm going, to jail just like anyplace else." [5]

Williams says that he was treated well in jail, although police

officials tricked him into coming downstairs to take his picture—
which they had forgotten to do when he was booked—by telling
him that Mr. Griffin was waiting to see him. Later he was not told
he was being released until he was on his way out the door: "I
guess they were afraid I would have refused to leave. But I
wouldn't; I'm not as recalcitrant as some of the others." [6]

In August, James Samuel Williams, who once had doubts about
joining his fellow students in a school strike, was sentenced to
twelve months in prison—six months suspended on good behavior
for three years—for interrupting and disturbing an assembly met
for the worship of God, "one of the oldest statutes on the nation's
penal books." The sentence was, in Mr. Griffin's view, an "out-
rage." [7] But of course it would be appealed. Nobody expected
Williams to serve it.

A big, square-set man who looks a little like Mr. Griffin minus
the sleepy eyes, Williams has made up his mind now what he
wants to do: "I plan to remain here in the South, whether in
Farmville or somewhere else I don't know. But I'm not planning
to go North. I'm interested in the social events that are going
forth in the South. I think I'll stick around."

Williams is of the "strike" generation that such a short time
ago was scandalously ahead of its elders in its demands for civil
rights. But the movement was producing new "generations" with
every few years. While Williams was at Shaw and Barbara Johns
Powell was a Philadelphia housewife, remote from any scene of
racial conflict, young Carlton Terry was out of Prince Edward
trying to get his schooling. His parents had not thought that the
schools really would close in 1959 and had been taken by surprise.
He missed the first year of school and then got in the Friends
program for three years, schooling in Holyoke and in New York
City, and New Bedford, Massachusetts. In New Bedford, in 1962,
he stayed for a time with a white family, attended white church,
and participated in interracial debate. He stayed also with a Negro NAACP official and his wife during which time he got the
idea of demonstrating in Prince Edward in the summer. An essay
he wrote for the school newspaper was warmly applauded:

> While the federal court of the United States ordered
> the University of Mississippi to open its doors to James
> Meredith, it has not done so in the case of Prince Edward
> County, Virginia, where schools have been closed com-

pletely for four years [since 1959]. There have been an estimated number of one thousand seven hundred Negro children out of school. Reason: integration against segregation.

Prince Edward County is located in the southeastern part of Virginia. Its county seat is Farmville, population four thousand. The county has two colleges, Hampden-Sydney for boys and Longwood College for girls. As you can read, it is quite educational as far as the two institutions for higher learning are concerned, but yet ignorant in the denial of public education.

We are cognizant of the fact that this problem is a disaster to the Negro children of Prince Edward and not to the white. Many of the children that have been without formal education for four years are very unlikely to return back to school when and if ever they open again. They will feel as if they are too old to be in.

I am Carlton Terry, now a freshman at Keith Junior High School. I have come to this school because I have been denied a public school education within my own county.

We, the Negro, think that the cause of this is because in 1953 [sic] when my two sisters were in high school, we boycotted for a new school rather than the old 'tar top' high school that we did have. The decision was taking so long to be ratified, that we asked for integration instead. We quickly got a response to our order. Our new school would be completed in 1955.

The name that I have given this essay, 'The Crippled Generation,' is an excellent title in my opinion because it is a good description of the situation as it happened. A generation left lame, and to be cured must take a great deal of money, effort, time, sweat, and a few tears to do the job accurately.[8]

That summer the author of "The Crippled Generation" made good his pledge to do something about the situation in Prince Edward. He offered his services to the young man who had gone to old Moton with his sisters and who was so like a big brother to him that he answered to the word "brother"—James Samuel Williams. The latter put young Terry to work with placards and

mimeographed boycott notices. On the Sunday when his big
"Brother" was arrested, young Terry was across the street, kneel-
ing on the sidewalk in prayer. On the following Saturday, though,
he won his badge of honor, a few hours of arrest at the county
courthouse.

Young Terry belongs to the generation at the halfway point
beyond that of the Moton class of '51. His advisors were members
of that class; his companions on the streets were youngsters like
Leslie Griffin, the preacher's eldest son. His eyes flashed when he
talked about the injustice of the closed schools: "I think the
people here are very ignorant. It simply cannot be explained. This
is the crippled generation. . . . Why do they keep the schools
closed anyway? Can anyone explain this to me?" [9]

He is slight and intense looking, and it is difficult to believe
that he is only fourteen.

16. THE CRIPPLED
GENERATION

The effort to get the federal government to help to open the schools of Prince Edward began shortly after the school closings. At first it was thought that Washington should intervene on behalf of the NAACP in court. The Eisenhower Administration, which was largely anti-intervention, was urged in vain to lend its prestige to the reopening. The Kennedy Administration, however, caught the full brunt of the Negroes' demands. The abortive court intervention of 1961 was followed by more persistent demands that the government interest itself directly in the situation.

Direct intercession also had been suggested before. The American Friends Service Committee was active on behalf of the Prince Edward children in Washington from the winter of 1959-60 on. But as long as it appeared that a court decision would come along soon to end the dispute, it was difficult for the various governmental agencies to envisage for themselves a role in Prince Edward. And the idea of the federal government's stepping into a state with its financial resources arraigned for social action was not politically appealing in the face of southern sentiment for states' rights. It was not until the wave of civil rights demonstrations through the South touched off by the Birmingham demonstrations of the summer of 1963 that pressure to do something about Prince Edward became irresistible.

Negroes were staging demonstrations on the streets of Farmville that summer, and Mr. Griffin believed that the schools could not be permitted to remain closed another year. He sensed that inside the county, in the Negro community, and outside the county, among those sympathetic to the cause of civil rights, the time of decision was at hand. The case in court seemed hopelessly snarled; the school closings that hopefully were to last only one year had stretched out across four years. "We had stayed out of schools long enough to let the world know that this was a nasty and unique situation. I thought that public sentiment was sufficiently aroused." [1]

In the early months of 1963, Griffin circulated a petition around the county, obtaining on it signatures of some 650 heads of families. It called on President Kennedy to sponsor a survey of the size of the educational problem in the county and to back a program designed to help the children prepare for the reopening of the schools.

Through its Washington sources the NAACP had been exploring ways in which the federal government might help. In May it was announced that a United States Office of Education grant of $75,000 would finance a Michigan State University study of the effect of the closed schools. Dr. Robert Lee Green, a Negro educator, was placed in charge of this study. [2] In June the Institute of Educational Research announced that it had been provided a grant of more than two million dollars for a reading skill development program and mental health study of as many as five hundred of the county children and other children from Indian reservations, slum areas, and migrant labor camps. [3] Some Southern congressmen objected to the idea of appropriating money for "mental health" and using it to teach Prince Edward children how to read. When their objections were made known to the appropriating committee, the project died. [4]

By the end of June, Dr. Green's preliminary report had been filed, and the Kennedy Administration had explored and rejected several other avenues of aid to the county. In meetings in the office of Burke Marshall, the Justice Department's civil rights specialist, Griffin remembers discussing the possibility of getting Manpower Retraining Act money to operate the schools. [5]

It had been decided that the federal government could not actually operate schools in Prince Edward, and it was decided next that the federal government could not finance such schools. It could, however, furnish the organizational zeal and the fundraising machinery. To this end William J. Vanden Heuvel, a young New York attorney who was president of the International Rescue Committee, was appointed a special assistant to Attorney General Kennedy and assigned to work out the solution to the Prince Edward school problem.

Vanden Heuvel found that, after recovering from its initial surprise that the Kennedy Administration would try to open schools in so direct a manner, the state government in Richmond was entirely co-operative.[6] Governor Harrison set about to assist in bringing the project to fruition.

In mid-July Brooks Hays, speaking for the Administration in Washington, had set about to land the one man in Virginia whose prestige was sufficient to make a success of the project. He called on his old friend former Governor and former President of the University of Virginia, Colgate W. Darden, Jr., of Norfolk, and asked him to take on the job of chairman of the board of trustees of the new schools.[7]

Darden felt that he had to turn down Hays's offer. He was firmly convinced that the children had to get back to school, but he was not sure that the method selected was the correct one and he was not eager, in any event, to commit this much time to a project in which the state of Virginia seemed to have only a marginal role. His health had not been of the best, and he had vowed to serve his native state in a highly selective way.[8]

On August 9, in Richmond for a bank trustee meeting, he heard from Governor Harrison. The Governor called him out of the meeting by phone and asked him if he would drop by later on in the day. He had a "little thing" he wanted Darden to do. When he arrived at the Governor's office, Harrison told him that he wanted him to head the board of trustees of the Free School Association, for which he had already found five members. Darden remembers his initial response: "I asked him, 'Albertis, is there any other little thing you'd like me to do?' "[9]

Turning down a representative of the federal government was one thing and turning down the Governor of Virginia was something else. Darden had been governor, and he knew how much help the job required. He had always felt that citizens owed their state a certain amount of sacrifice when it called upon them for duty of this kind. Harrison's concern that the demonstrations taking place at that time in Farmville would get out of control also impressed the former governor. He agreed to take the job on certain conditions, the first of which was that both races support the project wholeheartedly.

Vanden Heuvel had found a spirit of co-operation all around in the county upon his earlier visit.[10] Darden's experience was no

different. On August 10 he drove to Blackstone, met J. Segar
Gravatt, the board of supervisors' attorney, and drove with him
to Farmville where they talked with Foundation leaders. Darden
was encouraged.[11]

On August 13 he was called to Richmond to meet with Gravatt,
school board attorney Collins Denny, Vanden Heuvel, and Negro
leaders. Griffin and Lester Banks represented the Negroes, and
Darden asked them to agree on two conditions. First, he wanted
assurance that the Negro leaders would get the children to attend
the schools and keep them in the schools. On this point, full
assurance was given. Secondly, Darden asked that the Negro
leaders promise that there would be no more demonstrations.

Darden emphasized in imposing this last condition that he did
not oppose the demonstrations on ideological grounds. He simply
did not think that they were conducive to the educational process.
He did not want to see students who should be studying parading
about the streets.

Griffin thought that the Negroes had made a number of con-
cessions since the school reopening plan had been adopted. In
the beginning they had insisted that no Prince Edward people
or heads of state organizations be involved. The position the
Negroes took on this point gave a clue as to the real depth of
the Negro community's resentment: "I told them [the school or-
ganizers] I had no reason to believe that the whites would do
the right thing by the Negro people, as evidenced by the closed
schools." [12]

But heads of state bodies were placed on the board of trustees,
and School Superintendent McIlwaine and other local men were
to play a role in establishing the new school system. Griffin and
Banks were not in a mood to compromise about the demonstrations. They said that they had no intention of disrupting school
hours with demonstrations, but neither would they discourage
demonstrations by the youngsters conducted properly and at a
proper time.[13]

Darden left the old Senate Chamber where they had been
meeting and went up to the third floor of the capitol building
to see Governor Harrison. His intention was to bow out of the
picture since his conditions had not been met, but the Governor,
Vanden Heuvel, and Gravatt talked him out of this. Vanden
Heuvel expressed the belief that the NAACP leaders had right

on their side and he supported them, but he did not think that there would be more demonstrations once the schools opened. Darden finally agreed to serve.[14]

The job of raising the approximately one million dollars that was estimated as needed to keep the schools operating for a full calendar year devolved largely upon Darden. This was a difficult and time-consuming task, but it was not the immediate task: that was the assembling of a staff to be ready for the opening of the first free schools in Prince Edward County in four years—scarcely a month away. Darden scouted the field and finally hit upon a man to handle the superintendent's job. He was Dr. Neil V. Sullivan, a New Hampshireman who had pioneered in non-graded teaching and who had experience teaching various kinds of deprived students. Sullivan, in charge of a Long Island, New York, school system, agreed to serve in Prince Edward for a year and set about putting together a staff that would answer the broad and various needs of the deprived Negro children of Prince Edward County.

The job was done in time for opening ceremonies on September 16. Four public school buildings—including formerly white Worsham High School—were utilized for the approximately seventeen hundred Negro students who took up their public schooling during that first week. The teaching staff was made up, first, of those old Negro teachers in the county who wanted their jobs back; specialists carefully chosen from school systems around the country; and idealistic young teachers eager to throw themselves into this unique educational experiment.

Dr. Sullivan established a non-graded teaching system. Working with the results of tests conducted by the Michigan State team, his people placed the individual students where their capacities would allow them to progress. It was a mixed picture. There were eleven-year-olds who had had enough reading at home to be at their proper reading level, but who could not do the simplest arithmetic. There were fourteen-year-olds who belonged in classes with seven-year-olds. In order to handle the multitude of problems sufficient teachers were hired to give the school system a high pupil-teacher ratio. On a high school level in some instances this amounted virtually to a tutoring system.[15]

Community reaction was largely good. Three white students were attending the Free School Association with the Negroes— one of them seventeen-year-old Richard Moss, Dean Moss's son—

but this token integration did not disturb segregationists who drew a clear distinction between a few whites attending school with Negroes and Negroes attending schools with whites. Griffin was criticized at an NAACP rally for allowing a white Farmville man to be named business manager of the school association,[16] but Negro reaction generally reflected pleasure that the schools were open again.

Dr. Sullivan considered the educational problems in the county sufficiently grim: "Four years' loss will never be made up entirely. All I've said is that we'll narrow the gap." [17]

The older teen-age Negro youths constituted the special problem that most troubled the New England educator. Efforts to bring them back to school largely failed. Many had only a year to go to get their high school degrees, but many of these had established themselves as wage earners and were either unwilling or unable to make the adjustment back as students.

Below this age level, virtually all of the Negro youngsters of the county went back to school. On that first day they poured out of buses, clean and gleaming, and eager; it seemed that the buses would never stop coming. A Negro mother had come out of a nearby white home, where she was employed as a domestic. Her little boy hurled himself out of a bus and, acknowledging her wave with a serious tilt of his head, dashed for the schoolroom door. She raised a hand to the back of her head in a gesture half sad and half amused: "Well, he's gone back sure 'nuff. I'm glad to get him out of my hair. I'm glad he's gone back. I hope to God he learns something."

The free schools of Prince Edward County were closed for four years. During that time many people who did not speak out against the closed schools—indeed, some who favored the school closings—came to believe that the losses suffered by the community during that time never would be recovered. Discussions between people of this mind invariably turned on the educational loss suffered by the Negro children of the county, since this was the most obvious bitter fruit of the school closings.

But the subject that came in for the warmest debate was the extent and scope of the economic loss to the county. Had the closed schools left this rural community shackled to the past, economically stunted? Or had the harm been only minimal and temporary?

Certain social and economic changes were taking place in Prince Edward County in the decade of the 1950's that were reasonably typical of the experience of similarly situated rural Southern counties. Prince Edward lost population, after a century of relative stability. It is intriguing that this fact seemed to come as a surprise to many in the county. The *Farmville Herald,* which had been expressing the hope that the 1960 census would reflect some population growth in the county, quoted Mayor William F. Watkins, Jr., that the county's loss (from 15,398 in 1950 to 14,121 in 1960) was part of a national trend away from rural areas, as it was.[18] Neighboring counties by and large lost population too. Clearly, however, *some* of Prince Edward's loss had to be related to the school closings. How much, it was difficult to say.

The population loss was reflected most heavily in the Negro communities of the county. The white population declined slightly but increased in percentage of the whole from 55.4 per cent to 60 per cent in the decade.[19] Again, the school closings certainly had some effect on these figures. Again, it is difficult to say how much.

The population decline in the county was accompanied by an internal population shift from the rural to the urban parts of the county, again part of a national trend. In the decade of the 1950's Prince Edward's population went from 28.4 per cent urban to 30.4 per cent. Not surprisingly, the county lost farms at a fearsome clip, one-fourth of its 1,179 total in the last half of the decade. At the same time the size of the remaining farms increased; plainly the loss was of marginal small farmers, heavily Negro. Finally, the percentage of older people in the county increased sufficiently during this period to put Prince Edward above both the national and the South Atlantic state average.[20]

The over-all picture that emerges from these figures is of a county experiencing the typical pull away from small-farm agriculture and not developing its urban resources quickly enough to keep its people—particularly its Negroes, more particularly its young people, white and Negro.

Certain of these losses can be attributed positively to the school closings. More than seventy Negro teachers in the top economic echelon of their race were forced to find employment elsewhere during the years the schools were closed. Some continued to live in the county, commuting to their new teaching jobs in adjacent counties. Others left the county outright. Thousands of dollars of purchasing power which would have been spent in Farmville went with them. Then there were the Negro children who went to Kittrell and took part in the Friends program. The partial boycott of Farmville stores in the summer of 1963 is another example of an economic loss that simply cannot be calculated. Lastly there was the loss of Negro and white adults whose jobs were not affected but who left the county as a proximate result of the school closing. In this category, for instance, was one of Farmville's two Negro doctors—Dr. Lorraine Jones who left because she had school-age children—and an indeterminate number of college professors and other white professionals.

Dr. Jones bought a set of second- and fourth-grade books and attempted to maintain strict classroom discipline for her children during the first year of the school closings. She told AP reporter G. K. Hodenfield: "I couldn't continue this. I'm about to go mad now." [21]

By the next year, she had moved her family out of the county.

The story was much the same with some members of the college community. Professor Russell MacDonald of the English Department at Longwood tutored his son at home during the first year of school closings, leaving only when a second child was born. "We knew it was not possible for my wife to continue. . . . I would not have left under any circumstances if it were not for the school situation. I was predisposed to make a change strictly because of the county situation." [22]

Reliable sources at Longwood and Hampden-Sydney told me that at least three professors from each school left specifically because of the school closings. Undoubtedly there were others who considered the closed schools among their reasons for leaving.

The effects of the school closings on the colleges extended beyond the simple departure of staff members. Many good teaching prospects who might otherwise have joined the staffs of the colleges decided not to come because of the closed schools. A high official of Hampden-Sydney told a reporter: "There have been men I wanted very much and the reason that they gave for not coming, when one was given, was the lack of public schools. Some individuals withdrew immediately upon discovering the problem. . . . I don't think there's any question that this has hurt us, but it hasn't damaged us too much as witnessed by the fact that we have an excellent faculty." [23]

Dean Moss estimated that between twenty and forty prospects had turned down employment at the two colleges because of the school closings. Since others eventually were hired to fill the available jobs, the loss was an academic one sustained by the colleges rather than an economic one sustained by the community at large.

But the community's economic losses cannot be limited simply to the purchasing power that left the county with the departing Negro teachers and children. There was a broader question of whether the normal anticipated growth of the community was realized. The years of closed schools were years of prosperity generally in America, and this prosperity was shared even by the depopulating rural counties of Virginia. A look at bank savings and retail sales during this period indicates that Prince Edward County, too, partook of these economic gains. Businesses in Farmville shared or failed to share in the prosperity in some part in relation to their dependence upon Negro business; but no major bankruptcies were reported. The question was not whether established businesses failed on account of the school closings but whether they would have succeeded more without them.

Beyond this was the question of industry. During this period Virginia communities, rural and urban, were putting out heavy efforts to attract industry. Something of this nature clearly was needed to check the population exodus from the rural areas; urban Virginia pictured itself as combining the economic best of the North with the social best of the South. In this respect Prince Edward County and Farmville were no different from the rest of the state.

Prince Edward's history, as we have noted, was a chronicle of economic failures. The Reverend Dan Bowers, who as executive director of the Virginia Council on Human Relations had used the "industry" argument against the school closings, admitted that he had had little faith in it: "We were saying that no new industries had come to Prince Edward in the last two years. Heck, they hadn't had any new industry to speak of for fifty years." [24]

With only minor exceptions this was true, but it did not reflect the full picture. For it was only in recent years that a nucleus of progressive businessmen in Farmville had begun trying actively to attract industry. Ironically, their purchase of a twenty-acre site west of town (with an option on additional property near the airport to bring the potential total of two hundred acres) almost coincided with the closing of schools in 1959. For the first time adequate real estate with sewerage and water was available to industry—any industry that would be interested in coming into a community that had abandoned public schooling. The newly formed Farmville Area Development Corporation found itself blanked out entirely in its effort in 1960, although a furniture manufacturing plant went to Lunenburg County and a tobacco processing plant went to Mecklenburg County, both nearby. Nor did the corporation have any better success in years to come. S. Waverly Putney, Jr., who was president of the corporation during this time and a member of the board of directors from its inception in 1950, relates that the closed schools definitely discouraged one industry and probably affected the decision of others. "We had one prospect who said that he didn't think he could sell the move to his board. No matter what their sympathies, he didn't think that they would move to an area where they would have—they employed both white and Negro—uneducated whites and Negroes after a few years." [25]

You could get up a debate over this point, too, but Putney is one of those who believes that the bad effect of the closed schools did not end with the reopening of the schools: "Sure it will last. You heard plenty about the after effects in Little Rock, didn't you?" [26]

What of relations between the races in this half-white, half-black community in which race was a burning issue for more than a decade? If the economic loss is difficult to assess, the loss in terms of good will between the two racial communities is incalculable.

It is necessary to make a distinction between what I call "good will" between the two races and what is commonly meant by race relations. In the broad sense of the word, there never have been race relations in Prince Edward. As in most, if not all, Southern rural communities in these years no organizations existed with the purpose of bringing the races closer together. It is commonly said that the racial crisis brought down the "lines of communication" between the races; but, in the most important sense, no lines of communication ever existed.

What did exist was a loose, informal system of personal contact whereby the white leadership made known its wishes and passed on any requests made by the Negro community through Negro leaders considered suitable. As we have seen, these Negro leaders were largely discredited in the school strike of 1951 and failed to perform their old functions after that—although the white leadership chose to ignore this fact.

What happened, then, was that the old system of communication between the races, however one-sided, was dismantled and no new system was constructed in its place. The only effort in this direction has been the talks held among Moss, Griffin, and others; and these, while they continue to furnish the one link between the two races in the county, are less than effective because they do not include the real white leadership of the county.

This situation must be taken into account in assessing the frequently heard evaluation that race relations have been surprisingly amicable during the long struggle over the schools. In Southside Virginia courtesy is the common denominator among people of both races. Mr. Griffin once styled the school business as a "dispute among gentlemen." [27] Visitors, particularly from the North, have expressed their surprise at the surface cordiality between the races. Helen Baker, the Friends field worker, was quoted as being surprised at what she found when she came to the county. "I came expecting all sorts of strife and tension and I have found instead a great restraint and unfailing courtesy. These people are not gun-toting bums; they are gentlemen." [28]

Others reflected the same line of thought, more or less. One of the teachers I interviewed during the crash program period when out-of-town teachers flooded the county told me that she was most surprised at the way she could park her car wherever she felt like stopping and leave it unlocked without being in danger of having her possessions stolen. "If I did that in New York . . ." she commented, "it would be goodbye." [29]

But what was on the surface—however useful in keeping the peace—was not necessarily what was in the hearts of the people of the county, white and black. The Negro in America has had a long history of silence. Mrs. Miller, a persuasive and highly respected Negro leader, regarded the old relations between the races as having seriously deteriorated: "We don't say everything we think. I don't say everything I believe. Because we are silent doesn't mean that we like it." [30]

And Helen Baker did not take long to see behind the curtain of cordiality: "We daily exchange all of the pleasant courtesies as we meet in the stores, post office, or on the street. These pleasant greetings and our menial contacts in services are our only points of contact, so that there is absolutely no communication between the races about any of the problems which have thoroughly upset our lives here. We laugh in passing about the weather as if we are each unaware of the loads on our hearts because of the children's absence. We buy and sell and bargain together forever pushing back the truth—pushing back the bridge that might untie us—the bridge; the suffering, the yearning in the hearts of all of the people in this county to find a real solution to this crisis." [31]

None of this is to say that genuine friendships did not exist between members of the two races before the crisis. Some of these friendships may have survived, but it is here that much of the lasting damage was done. One keen observer of the local scene noted that the attendance of whites at Negro funerals—a pretty good index of personal race relations in a Southern rural community—was down.

In some respects the closed schools themselves reduced contact between the races. The public schools had been an occasional point of interracial communion. White leaders often were invited to speak at Negro schools, and whites were in attendance at formal functions there—graduations, dramatic and vocal presentations, and the like. With the closing of the schools the Negro community shrank visibly. Negroes had had no access to movies, gymnasiums, bowling alleys, pools, skating rinks, or Y.M.C.A.'s. Their civic and social life had used as its focus the church and, more and more, the school. The disorganization within the Negro community caused by the closing of the schools had an effect on the Negroes of the county and their old relationships with whites.

In some cases Negro organizations simply ceased to exist with the closing of the schools. Mrs. Mada McKnight, one of the county's leading Negro women, tells of the passing of the Noblesse Oblige, a limited membership organization of Negro women with a high status rating. The Noblesse Oblige women were right off the top of Negro social and intellectual order and, as one would expect, most of them were school teachers. With the closing of the schools the membership scattered, searching for new jobs, and the organization collapsed. Another point of contact between the races disappeared. [32]

Quite apart from their economic effects, the demonstrations and boycott of 1963 had deleterious effects on whatever store of good will remained between the businessmen of Farmville and their Negro customers. Even those businessmen who did not favor continuing to keep the schools closed were not prepared to accept all of the blame for this condition. They were embittered by a mimeographed sheet handed out by Negro demonstrators (and reproduced in the *Herald*) during August, when efforts were in the making to reopen the schools:

MAKE YOUR $$$$$$$ WORK FOR FREEDOM

Our Negro Children of Prince Edward County have been: segregated . . . discriminated against . . . locked out of schools . . . denied the right to worship God . . . and jailed. The above acts have been condoned if not supported directly by the merchants of Farmville.

NEGROES CAN STOP THIS! ! !

Buy where you and your children will be treated with dignity and respect ! !

MAKE FARMVILLE A GHOST TOWN! ! !

Farmville must be as empty as a desert every day until we have public schools for all children in Prince Edward County.

Negroes of Amelia, Nottoway, Charlotte, Appomattox, Buckingham, Cumberland, and Lunenburg Counties support the BOYCOTT against the Prince Edward merchants. DON'T BUY IN FARMVILLE! ! BOYCOTT FOR FREEDOM! !

Sponsored by the Prince Edward Branch NAACP [33]

An observation of visiting educators on the effect of all the demonstrations and what had preceded them may be in order: "By the end of the summer it was noted that almost no casual conversation between Negroes and whites in downtown Farmville occurred." [34]

It would be too much to expect that with the reopening of the schools the bitterness generated across the years between the races would dissipate. It is not enough to hope that in time the old relationships will reassert themselves; it is too late in the day for many of the old relationships. The best result would be a frank admission on the part of both communities that no machinery exists for the mutual discussion of the problems that cross racial lines. The bi-racial committee that has become so popular in the urban South—and so convenient a dumping ground for insoluble problems in the South—may be the first necessity of Prince Edward County. Such a committee would be the skeleton upon which genuine race relations could be grafted.

The most hopeful sign in 1963 and 1964 was the attention being paid by Farmville merchants to efforts led by Mr. Griffin to improve job opportunities for Negroes. That this sort of thing could be discussed and that some satisfactory progress could be made is an index of the progress of the Negro social revolution in the South and the survival of a certain amount of reason in the wreckage in Prince Edward County.

Perhaps a county like Prince Edward, with its lessons learned at great cost, actually could exercise leadership in the direction of establishing contemporary grounds for race relations in the rural South. First, though, this county's whites and Negroes will have to learn to live with their memories, and that is a hard task in itself.

When Dean Moss coined the expression, "The Crippled Generation," on NBC television's Chet Huntley Reports show in August, 1962, he was referring to the Negro children of Prince Edward County. They had been out of school for four years and were the obvious casualties. The assumption was general that the white children fared just about as well in their private schools as they would have fared in the old public schools.

Very likely this is so. After the completion of the new campus variety of upper school building in the second year of operation, the only distinct disadvantages the Prince Edward Foundation had were in the area of facilities for the elementary grades. Teachers, as we have noted, were largely the same as in the old public schools. The curriculum was little different, although some Foundation leaders made a big stir about "cutting out the frills" from public education, by which they meant certain kinds of aesthetically oriented courses and extra-curricular activities.

Out with the frills went lunch. In order to avoid setting up a cafeteria system, the Foundation scheduled classes from 8:30 A.M. until 1:30 P.M. and dropped the noon meal. No doubt the children enjoyed the long, free afternoons, however, and there is no good basis for thinking that the schedule hampered academic achievement.

Finally, such evidence as did exist seemed to place the new schools on a plane of equality with the old. They were promptly accredited by the State Board of Education. A respectable 57 per cent of the Academy's graduates went on to college in the years in which the schools were closed. In the absence of a specific educational study, it is probably fair to say that the private school system raised more of a social than an educational handicap for the white children.

A more acute question, however, is whether a good many white children did not leave the county in part or in the whole because the public schools were closed. This issue was originally raised by Dean Moss in a letter to the editor of the *Herald*, in which he charged that as many as 180 white families had children out of school and that the number would increase as the Foundation ran into more difficulty raising money.[35]

There was talk around the county that the Foundation would not educate children who could not pay. Pearson released figures showing that, of the children in the Foundation schools at that time, 376 had paid full tuition, 371 had paid partial tuition, and 32 had paid no tuition. He insisted that no children were denied enrollment because they could not pay tuition. The Foundation executive committee would hear any appeal from a decision on whether the family could afford to pay.[36] Later that fall a story by *Lynchburg News* Associate Editor John A. Hamilton detailed the case of a soldier who complained bitterly of having to pay money he did not have to send his children to the Foundation schools.[37] Hamilton concluded that many children of poor white families were being denied education by the Foundation, and his story was mailed anonymously around the county by the Human Relations Council in Richmond. The Foundation contended that the soldier could pay a portion of the tuition and had done so finally. B. Blanton Hanbury, the Foundation president, denied that any children had been turned down for enrollment because their parents were too poor to pay.[38]

Whatever the actual case, there was no general outcry against the Foundation's methods. If poor white parents' children were being denied admission in any number, they were strangely silent about it. Yet there was tangible evidence that enrollment in the Foundation schools was down. The last public school enrollment in the county, in 1958–59, included 1,562 white students.[39] When Foundation schools opened in September, 1959, they enrolled 1,475 white students. By 1962 enrollment was down to 1,251 students.[40] Over four years' time the county had lost 311 students —almost 20 per cent of the original total. The figures were made even more dramatic by the evidence of a report made up by Dr. George V. Zehmer at the request of the school board, that showed an 18 per cent increase in white enrollment in the county public schools between 1949–50 and 1957–58.[41]

What was happening to the white students? One popular theory in the county was that many were attending public school in adjoining counties in order to avoid paying the tuition to the private schools. Yet an informal survey I took of the school system of nearby counties in 1963 indicated that almost as many students (48) were coming in to the county from adjoining counties as were going out (55). This interchange of students was an old story and was ruled by geography rather than any preference for public or private schools.

Another possibility is that the closed schools speeded along the departure of white families more swiftly than was generally realized. The 1960 census figures had showed only a slight decline in white population from 1950—but what happened after 1960? The Foundation schools never reported a drop-out figure of more that 5 per cent during the years of closed schools. Unless a great many white children were staying out of school altogether (and there is no evidence of this) some other explanation is needed. Time will tell whether a significant white population loss was sustained and whether it will be permanent.

The losses to the Negro children of the county were incomparably more acute. If the private schools were reasonably adequate educational substitutes for the white children, the centers were utterly inadequate substitutes for the Negro children. According to the best information available—the records of Mr. Griffin's Prince Edward County Christian Association—over six hundred Negro children attended the training centers from time to time when they were open, which was during the first three years of the school closing.

In May, 1962, I paid a visit to a reasonably typical training center located in the Loving Sisters of Charity Hall, a white frame building near Hampden-Sydney. Children romped about the grounds during lunch break (classes were from 9:30 A.M. until

1:30 P.M., including a half-hour break) skipping rope, playing ring games, baseball, and romping through the yellow bolts of scotch broom. Inside, later, two classes were going simultaneously in the same classroom with a total of forty-five students present. On one side of the room the little ones were noisily learning their alphabet while on the other side the third, fourth, fifth, sixth, and seventh graders were learning the rudiments of letter writing. With the younger children singing out their "A's" and "B's" and the older ones calling out instructions to a teacher writing a letter at the blackboard, bedlam ruled. Neither of the two teachers had any professional experience (the better educated one had finished eleven grades of school). They were patient, tolerant of the noise, making out as best they could. The walls of the classroom were filled with pictures of well-known American Negroes—from Jackie Robinson to Ralph Bunche—scattered among cut-out letters spelling "Follow in the Footsteps of Great Americans."

By this time the training center program had deteriorated badly. There had been ten centers in 1959–60 and fifteen in 1960–61, but there were only five in 1961–62 and the total enrollment had dropped to about 350 children. Mr. Griffin theorized that more children had left the county and that others had become disillusioned with the centers by then.

From the beginning, the centers had been under severe handicap. It was hoped that they would perform some of the functions of schools—keep the children together, busy, and advance their learning processes. Yet they could not *be* schools. No serious effort was made to put them on a professional basis.

Some of the centers were decidedly inferior both in physical plant and in quality of instructors. Near the Loving Sisters of Charity Hall was a smaller building that served for a time as a training center and was much photographed by a press eager to emphasize the difference between the centers and real schools. Mr. Griffin described the building, tongue in cheek, as "our exhibit No. 1." Ben Bowers of the *Herald*, a reporter not given to coloring his descriptions, wrote about it in March, 1961: "It is . . . a two-by-four sized hut, which is so overcrowded it appears to be a health hazard and a fire trap. Twenty-nine youngsters of an enrollment of forty-one were jammed like sardines into the building. . . . Mrs. Margaret Hill at best could only give a good course in human endurance." [42]

This was the "worst worst" of the centers as contrasted with the "best worst" in the phrase of one of the instructors. Physical plant inadequacies were not the major handicap of the centers, however; the major handicaps were the shortage of professional teachers and the lack of a capable administrator. Both of these unfilled needs stemmed from the conscious decision made by the Negro leadership to keep the centers from becoming real schools and thus relieving the white leadership of any obligation to re-open the public schools. This is not to say that it would have been easy to convert the centers—or something like the centers—into real schools and to impose the kinds of discipline necessary to give them educational stewardship for the entire Negro community. Difficult or not, it was never seriously considered.

Much more professional, although lasting a shorter time, were the "crash" educational programs operated in the county during the summers. In the summer of 1961 the Virginia Teachers Association carried out a strong program, using teaching machines and concentrating on remedial work in reading particularly. This program attracted 425 students. The following year the VTA and a group of northern graduate students put on programs attracting 560 students. In the summer of 1963, Queens College graduate students and teachers rounded up from the ranks of the American Federation of Teachers (largely from New York) put on a third crash program. The programs ran in length around a month each, but they undoubtedly exposed more of the Negro children to professional education than did any other program.

The most comprehensive program was the one that aided the fewest Negro students. This was the American Friends Service Committee's program, through which sixty-seven children were sent to ten communities in eight states during the years of the closed schools. They boarded out with Northern families, both white and Negro. The educational advantage to these children was considerable. Problems of adjustment were less serious than might have been expected, for the Friends were careful to pick children who could profit from experience. They were careful, too, to choose integrated Northern situations for the children in keeping with their own goals.

If the Friends program was restricted by its very nature to a few children, it did not end with the children. Actually the Friends were the only organization that attempted to work with the total Negro community. It might be added here that the Friends got to

Prince Edward long before it was a glamorous place to be and that they stayed as long as they could be useful and won the respect of the white as well as the Negro community of the county. A Friends Club was established to keep the parents of children being educated out of the county in touch with each other and aware of the problems and privileges of their young. A Leadership Institute was established to help the instructors at the centers— where the level of education was regarded as alarmingly low— improve themselves. The Friends set themselves up as a kind of clearing house for information and for the stream of contributions and goods that flowed into the county from liberals elsewhere in the country. They encouraged the county's dissident white leadership without notable achievement and bearded the segregationist leadership without discernible success. More than the visiting "rescue" teams of teachers—most of whom lived in virtual isolation from and under the suspicion of the white community—the Friends were absorbed by Prince Edward County.

But if the Friends program and the various crash programs and the Kittrell program all were small, and if the training centers were an educational loss, is it true that most of the Negro children of the county got no education at all during the four years of closed schools? It is hard to say. The school board's figures on Negro children out of the county in school are based on requests for transcripts, and elementary grade children did not need transcripts. An NAACP survey in 1962 set the number of Negro children in school out of the county at 492. The Michigan State survey the next year put the figure at 413.

Both figures probably are low. A practice impossible to take into account statistically was the "bootlegging" of children out of the county to various schools in adjacent counties. Negro teachers who continued to live in Prince Edward while teaching in nearby counties would fill up their cars with Prince Edward children and carry them to the out-county schools where they would enter classrooms and take up the work. The teachers, and in some cases the principals, winked at this practice.

So it is not easy to be sure how many Negro children actually got some education elsewhere during the years of the schools' closing. The best source remains the preliminary report of Dr. Green of Michigan State, who found that of the seventeen hundred children of school age, approximately eleven hundred had practically no formal and very little informal education during the

years of the closed schools. Only twenty-five Negro children in the
entire county had attended formal school all four years.

In the complete study released in 1964, Dr. Green and his
Michigan State cohorts concluded that the short-term remedial
programs had "minor effects." The study concluded that academic achievement for the Negro children was "severely retarded
by the lack of formal education" and warned: "Early school deprivation may, however, have irreversible effects. If this is the
case, then the rate of subsequent development should be substan-
tially different for children who have experienced severe early
deprivation. Terminal skill development of these children would
never attain a normal level." [43]

It is impossible also to measure the loss in terms of human
suffering, both for the children and the parents. Helen Baker of
the Friends recounted one of the many stories illustrating this
kind of circumstance: "Carol is eight years old. Last year she
attended no school, but this year her parents have made arrange-
ments for her to attend school in Petersburg, Virginia, which is
sixty-five miles away. Carol lives with a great-aunt; leaves home
each Sunday afternoon and returns to Farmville on Friday evening. Today, while unpacking Carol's laundry bag, her mother
found tucked in a dress pocket this carefully drawn note: 'I want
to go home now. Mother I love you so much I want to go home. I
want to go home now.' Carol is one of about four hundred Negro
children of all ages who must leave their home in Prince Edward
County for a week—a month—a semester—a year in order to
attend school. They may be as many white children who do the
same: I do not know." [44]

There were many like Carol; many less lucky, children whose
parents had insufficient resources to send them out of the county,
who watched helplessly as their children slipped far behind in
their studies.

There were some enriching experiences, too. Slight, well-spoken
Barbara Ann Botts, an eighteen-year-old with a quick, intelligent
manner, will tell you that she was one of the lucky ones. She was a
sixth grader at Moton when the schools closed and, like so many
others, she accepted the closings as a necessary, if bitter, incon-
venience, for the first year.

Then Barbara was thirteen. Her mother, a divorcée who
works as a domestic, did not have the funds to send Barbara away.
Here was a bright girl, though, who fitted well into the Friends

program. She was younger than most who were accepted for the unsettling task of transplanting to a strange town and a strange home, but the Friends took a chance on Barbara. Her first year, in Moorestown, New Jersey, where she was the only Negro child in her particular class, proved to be rough: "It was such a complete feeling of having to leave home. It all seemed so unnecessary, and I couldn't see the real reason for having to go. . . . In a way, too, I thought about it as accepting charity and I have a big thing about that. After I stayed out one year, I would have done anything to get back to school, though. . . .

"I never really felt that I belonged with the group in Moorestown. Most of the people there had lived there all their lives and I felt that I was intruding. No, I'm not talking about the whites now, I was living with Negroes and while I was the only Negro in my class, I had social contact largely with other Negroes." [45]

After a second year at Moorestown, Barbara went the third year to Newton, Massachusetts, to live with a white family there. Her class of twenty-eight students included six Negroes. Life in school and at home were freely integrated. Perhaps more important, Barbara made lasting friendships. She was a little stunned, although very grateful, at the way she was accepted: "Mr. H. has three daughters. From the time I came there, though, he talked about his four girls. It helped me not to feel like an outsider. I went to football games and took part in social activities just like anyone else." [46]

The experience committed Barbara to the idea of integration at the same time that it made it impossible for her to continue to live in the South. To this extent, it changed the entire course of her life. She is glad for her own experience but deeply regretful of the educational carnage she sees about her in her home county: "I will say that I feel that nothing much has been accomplished while the schools were closed. It seems to me that the adults could have had their little debate in court while the children continued to attend schools of some kind. . . ." [47]

Barbara has in mind the luckless ones, the children at the other end of the educational spectrum, who may have suffered what amounted in many cases to fatal blows to their educational hopes. The worst hit were those in the middle grades of high school, too old to wait for the schools to reopen and old enough to go to work. Such a person is John Smith, who is twenty-one now, and when I talked with him in 1963 had attended no schools since 1959 and had no prospects of going back. He was working on a Farmville garbage truck, making $49.50 a week, and "saving up" to get married.

The job of rehabilitation attempted by the Free Schools, which operated for one year, could not reach the John Smiths, but it could and did reach just about every other kind of educational casualty—and they were a plentiful and varied lot.

The tendency of colorful newspaper stories may have been to exaggerate the over-all educational damage—certainly they made no distinction between losses suffered in the old public schools and those sustained during the years of closed schools. Still, educators who came to the county from other places were shocked at what they saw. Richard Parrish, a public school teacher in the Bronx and organizer of the American Federation of Teachers' project in the county in the summer of 1963, was one of these: "It is obvious that there are gross needs. The most serious needs are in the county areas as distinguished from the Farmville metropolis. In the hinterlands you can run into a sixteen-year-old girl who can't read a first-grade book and children ten, eleven, twelve, and thirteen operating on a second grade level. . . . What we are doing now is trying to help those that can be saved. At least a third of them are gone, down the drain. . . . We've worked with about six hundred students, and we've had to drop out the four- and five-year-olds because we didn't have the people to teach them. These of course have not been damaged by the closed schools. . . . It is the kids who were ten to twelve in 1959 when the schools closed who are lost. . . . They're the lost generation. The only thing that would save them would be a massive federal program that would take them virtually case by case." [48]

Parrish spoke, of course, before the Free School idea had come into being. In its final form, it was close to "massive" in its effort. It employed team teaching, the equivalent of tutoring, the most modern devices for cramming a lot of education into a short teaching span. Able, vigorous Dr. Sullivan drove his willing staff and the equally willing children about as hard as they could go for a full year. If the schools were a disappointment from the standpoint of integration—only eight white students attended them— they were a godsend educationally.

It was popular for reporters to write, upon the closing of the Free Schools in August, 1964, that the students who had moved through the public school buildings utilized by the system had crammed three or four or five years of education into a single year's effort. Some did, perhaps. But the final judgment on the residue of damage to the children of four years of closed school will have to await more thorough study and the passage of time. Dr. Sullivan, in an article published at the conclusion of his year's work in Prince Edward, seemed optimistic, although not hazarding an opinion on how much lost ground had been made up. "Progress made by a vast majority of our children," he wrote, "substantiated the confidence I placed in the team arrangement and in the nongraded organization. These innovations had worked well in the sophisticated suburbs of the North. They worked equally well in the destitute tobacco country of southside Virginia." [49]

The Free Schools closed in August, and in September virtually the same student body moved into the re-established public school system in Prince Edward County, Virginia. After five years of closed public schools, the Supreme Court had ruled that public schools must be reopened in September. Justice Black went so far as to say that the courts had the power to force the supervisors to appropriate "adequate" funds to maintain a school system in the county similar to those operated in other counties. So, in the end, the question that the Defenders had made the cornerstone of their defense—could the courts make a county legislative body appropriate money for a specific purpose?—was decided against them.

And in the end, the public schools reopened, integrated. Only a handful of whites—mostly the same ones who attended the otherwise all-Negro Free Schools—enrolled in the public schools. The remainder of whites continued to attend the Foundation schools. With the public schools opened again, the patrons could draw tuition grants like other patrons of private schools—segregation-inspired and otherwise—around the state. The Supreme Court had not ruled on whether the grants were permissible where public schools were open.

In the end, the integration that came to Prince Edward was the reverse of the integration that had come to the rest of the South, where a handful of Negroes at last were permitted to attend schools with whites. In Prince Edward a handful of whites attended schools with Negroes.

The Foundation supporters pointed out that the difference was that no whites *had* to go to school with Negroes in Prince Edward.

But what if the tuition grants, recently invalidated again, should finally fail? The result almost certainly would be a massive rush back to the public schools and something like massive and immediate integration, the very kind that the South has dreaded as educationally disruptive.

Actually, when and if that day comes, the Prince Edward system, which already has an integrated teaching staff as one remnant of the Free Schools, may be the most integrated system in the South.

EPILOGUE

Everybody lost something in Prince Edward County between the years 1959 and 1964. I have tried to present this story in such a way that the reader will be able to judge for himself what was lost and whether the gains justified the losses.

I cannot leave the story, however, without setting down my own view, both taking the risk of writing too close to the events and at the same time fully understanding that readers with different viewpoints will not necessarily agree with my conclusions. I am eager to do this not just because I think that what was won is pitifully inadequate payment for what was lost, but because I think that there is a lesson in the Prince Edward County story that applies across this nation as I write in the winter of 1964.

It is tempting to second-guess history. Suppose, for instance, that the segregationists of Prince Edward County had said that they would accept Judge Hutcheson's decision calling for desegregation ten years from the Supreme Court's decree of 1955. And suppose that the NAACP had decided that in view of this willingness, it would not appeal the decision. The public schools of Prince Edward County would have remained open. The white leadership of the county could have applied one of two approaches: they could have opened a dialogue with the real Negro leadership of the county to assure a minimum of integration in the public schools in 1965—a few Negro students moving to formerly all-white public schools; or they could have set about establishing a private school system to open in 1965 with tuition grants. Assuming that most white parents in Prince Edward would choose the private system, the result would have been a few white students remaining in a public school system essentially Negro.

In other words the segregationists could have had in 1965 precisely what they got in 1964—without the tremendous cost in terms of money, suffering, and effort and without ever closing any schools.

The NAACP could have had in 1965 precisely what it got in 1964 without the staggering loss of education to the Negro children of the county and without the misery undergone by the entire Negro community.

I set down this all-too-pat accounting only to illustrate how little real difference the long and agonizing struggle has made in Prince Edward County, not because I imagine that the options I have posed are historically realistic.

In the Virginia of 1959, in the first backlash of state-wide massive resistance, the segregationists of Prince Edward began with the assumption that it was possible in the South to halt integration in its tracks altogether. All that was needed, these men thought, was sufficient firmness of purpose. They conceived of Prince Edward merely as the first link in what was to be a chain of resistance forged in every Southern community chafing at the Supreme Court's dislocation of Southern custom. Why could not twenty or two hundred Southern communities follow Prince Edward's example and substitute private segregated education for public integrated education? In their minds was the idea that if the Supreme Court could be made to realize that its decision was unenforceable, it would eventually reverse that decision.

On their behalf, it must be said that the mistake sprang from the thinking of the Southern leaders of that era. It was in the spirit of the so-called Southern Manifesto. It was made by the architects of massive resistance. It was made by the man in the South who is usually given credit for having coined the phrase "massive resistance" and who certainly made it his property by the strength of his exhortation—Senator Harry Flood Byrd.

Given this spirit of rebellion, the decision in Prince Edward is understandable, if not inevitable.

And given the segregationists' determination to balk the Supreme Court decision, the decision by the NAACP to appeal surely was the only one that could have been made. Not to appeal it would have been to invite the courts to put off desegregation for a decade wherever opposition was sufficiently fierce.

The segregationists' decision to close schools was one that history will likely treat harshly. It cut deeply against the grain of

the American educational tradition, and it represented a willingness to make reckless sacrifices in the name of a dying institution.
Yet even this decision, as we have seen, had precedent in the
actions of the state and status in the plans of the white community. Needless to say, the NAACP had to oppose this with all
of its might.

Once accomplished, the school closings tended to perpetuate
themselves. The necessity of setting up a private school system
brought the white community together, and the relative success
of the venture made it seem reasonable to carry on.

It also made it easy to lose sight of the notion that Prince
Edward would lead the South in successful refutation of the
court. As time went on, it became apparent that Prince Edward's
way—the way of closed public schools—would not be the way of
the future for the South. There was and perhaps still is the possibility that some other county or counties in the South will elect to
close public schools, but even this prospect is unlikely, other
communities having asked themselves where the money and political and moral support would come from now. As for the chance of
a Southern movement of closed schools—that has been out of the
questions for years, at least since the cracking of the color line in
the schools of the deep South: probably, ironically enough, since
the failure of massive resistance, which happened in Virginia prior
to the Prince Edward school closings.

In place of the real issue, which was dead, the Prince Edward
segregationists raised a bogus issue. Editor Wall began writing
about the necessity of finding out whether the supervisors could
be made to appropriate money for schools. He wrote about it
incessantly, as though by simple repetition to elevate the point to
importance.

What did this argument of Wall's mean? He called it a test of
the validity of the Constitution, a test of whether representative
government would survive or fall to a judicial oligarchy. The test
could only be made in Prince Edward, where these issues were
raised, he told his Prince Edward readers. It was necessary to let
the schools remain closed until the courts had decided the question.

Only rarely did an observer locally ask publicly what good
could possibly come of the question propounded of the courts.
Obviously, if they decided it against the county, the public
schools would have to open it again. If the courts decided with

the county, there would have been no rush at this late date to emulate the closed school example. Nothing would happen, except that the county leaders would have justified their position to themselves.

Few in America could subscribe to the goals of Prince Edward's segregationist leaders. But is not the greater tragedy that even after they had failed by their own lights, they continued to keep the schools closed? Even when the field of combat they had chosen was deserted, they clung to it and raised futile flags.

As the years passed, and it became clear that there would be no general school closing, the civil rights leaders had to change their position too. If Prince Edward were not the first link in a chain of resistance as had been thought, it was at least the ground upon which a significant constitutional test had been raised. By settling it in the courts, the NAACP could assure itself that this particular threat to integration and to public schools would never be posed again.

If it were essential for the segregationists to convince themselves of the rightness of their case in court, it was even more essential for the NAACP. The segregationists, after all, had put the white children back in school and could say that they had offered to help the Negro children continue in their education. The NAACP had advised Prince Edward Negroes against this offer and, moreover, had made no serious effort on its own to educate the Negro children. The decision to leave the children out of school was one made in real personal agony by the community: It could be justified only in terms of great potential gain.

So it was that the segregationists and the civil rights advocates came to agree on one thing: large constitutional issues of importance were at stake. As late as 1963, Editor Wall could write that Prince Edward had closed its schools so that all Americans could enjoy the freedom of education,[1] and a visiting NAACP official a few weeks later could counter by saying that the Negro children had stayed out of school so that all children could be educated.[2] Each man called upon the United States Constitution as his witness.

The process of adjustment to the closed schools was not so easy for Negroes at the county level. Even Griffin, the NAACP's voice in the county, found himself torn between his desire to see the children back in school and what he believed was the necessity of winning the case in court. Privately, he questioned whether the losses being sustained were too high a price for this victory; privately, he raged at the interfering, power-grasping methods some civil rights groups used to try to enter the county. But even privately he concluded that the ends sought justified the means employed; and publicly he supported the NAACP every time.

To a considerable extent Negroes conditioned to hardship and endurance accepted the prolonged closing of the schools as just another hard fact of being a Negro to be endured: at least now a greater goal could be seen. Dr. Miller, who was after all one of the few Negroes to get an education and return to the county, put it this way: "Although quite a few have been deprived of education, some few have gone on elsewhere and gotten an education they wouldn't have gotten here. Among these few there may be found a Moses for the children of Israel." [3]

The civil rights advocates who had devoted much time and effort to the Prince Edward situation but who had no immediate personal stake in the matter—men like Oliver Hill and women like Dorothy Height of the National Council of Negro Women— found it possible to take the long view. As Mrs. Height put it: "Look at the years of non-education but also look at the community—low income, negligible facilities. If it took one person going to jail, one person losing his life, one having his schooling lost outright to bring us to the point of saying that this kind of thing cannot be allowed to happen, maybe this is not too great a price to pay. . . ." [4]

Many would agree with this proposition as stated. But was the sacrifice of the wasted years of education necessary? Was it necessary to dramatize the losses in Prince Edward—and at the same time to increase them—in order to prevent a similar tragedy from occurring elsewhere?

The reader will answer these questions according to his own background and his idea of the proper means and goals in the matter of civil rights. For my own part, I think that there is at least a considerable measure of doubt that they can be answered positively.

It seems to me that these observations suggest two principal lessons that may be useful in the present and as the civil rights struggle unfolds in the future.

The first is that reliance on the courts to settle any and all problems within the framework of the continuing dialogue over civil rights can be as dangerous as the flouting of the courts in the nation's streets. In the Prince Edward case, absolute reliance upon the courts on both sides produced a long, deadening stalemate. The stalemate itself actually fed on the court case, for it appeared to the litigants that the longer the case continued, the greater their stake in a satisfactory conclusion.

With such a furor's being made over the legal aspects of the case, few seemed interested in setting forth the simple proposition that the Prince Edward case was of limited legal interest but of genuine moral interest. It posed the moral question of whether it is right and just in twentieth-century America for a county to close its public schools, for whatever reason. The civil rights advocates surely were right when they argued that the real responsibility for educating all of the children rested upon the county and the state. Virginia's constitution called for the maintenance of a system of public schools. If Virginia could win a ruling in court that the closing of one county's schools did not undo the system, where could it go for a ruling that said that the state had no responsibility—no moral responsibility—for the education of all of its children who wished to be educated? No courts could answer that question. No question in all of the Prince Edward case was so abjectly side-stepped as this one, to the everlasting shame of the state of Virginia.

The second lesson is suggested by the first: there is a positive danger that the hard and fast alignments that arise in the clash of viewpoints over civil rights will make it progressively harder to remember that human wants are complex and that human beings, after all, are the ultimate stakes. Total segregation in the schools was not essential to the health and welfare of the white people of Prince Edward County nor even to their right to believe that the Supreme Court was wrong, to say so, and to urge the court to reverse itself. Some measure of integration in the schools was not essential to the health and welfare of the Negroes, nor even to their right to work for integration in the schools while educating their children as best they could. Only a questionable understanding of human needs could lead a county in the United States of America in the mid-twentieth century to close its public schools and the victims to shun education for four years.

Prince Edward ended finally as a special case; but the thinking that led it into the quagmire was not special but general, and it is still general. It is a mistake for the segregationists to draw the line and say that this position, at least, will be defended to the last. The segregationists are losing, and the set-piece battle they welcome only attracts an equally determined and ruthless commitment from the civil rights forces. In the end, in my opinion, the civil rights forces will win the battles they must win because the tide of national opinion and the strength of national resources are with them.

I have no sympathy with segregation personally, but I do not find the notion of victory over it at any cost, at any time, and at any place hospitable. I think that it is also a mistake for the civil rights advocates to concentrate the full energies of their movement against a single state or area or county or—who knows?—individual. It makes no sense to me for civil rights leaders to declare that Birmingham, for instance, is the number one target of the movement. It seems to me that such talk is militaristic rather than civil, punitive rather than corrective. Are the people of Birmingham, black and white, any less deserving of understanding and human sympathy for the dark truths of Birmingham's immediate past?

If we are to continue to approach the complex issues of segregation and integration as though they are merely clashes of abstract ideology, we may find ourselves repeating Prince Edward's harsh lesson again and again. Perhaps it is even more important that the civil rights leaders understand this because they are winning. It is not always necessary to win everything. It is not always wise when the costs are considered. Such a strategy can produce the kind of empty victory won in Prince Edward, to be measured for the future not by its gains but by its losses. Civil rights leaders should remember, too, that their movement gains the support it needs as its goals seem relevant to individual human needs; it loses that support as its goals seem relevant only to doctrines or mass prescription.

Finally, if we forget in the years ahead that we are human beings after all, of whatever color, and that our color is not necessarily the most important distinguishing mark between us, a major lesson of the Prince Edward story will have been wasted. To waste that lesson would be a tragedy for the entire country.

NOTES

PART ONE   STRIKE

Chapter 1

1. "Economic Data," Prince Edward County, Virginia, 1960, Division of Industrial Development, State of Virginia, p. 1.

2. *Ibid.*

3. Herbert Clarence Bradshaw, *History of Prince Edward County, Virginia* (Dietz, 1955), pp. 539–40.

4. *Ibid,* pp. 538–54.

5. "Economic Data," p. 5.

6. The Reverend L. Francis Griffin, interview in Farmville, Virginia, August 17, 1961.

7. *Ibid.*

8. Mrs. Vernon Johns, Sr., interview in Petersburg, Virginia, August 2, 1961.

9. *Ibid.*

10. *Ibid.*

11. Mrs. C. H. D. Griffin, interview in Norfolk, Virginia, September 12, 1961.

12. The Reverend L. Francis Griffin, interview, August 17, 1961.

13. *Ibid.*

14. Mrs. Griffin, interview, September 12, 1961.

15. The Reverend L. Francis Griffin, interview, August 17, 1961.

16. The Reverend C. E. Griffin, interview in Norfolk, Virginia, September 12, 1961.

17. The Reverend L. Francis Griffin, interview in Farmville, Virginia, November 20, 1959.

18. Francis Mitchell, article in *Jet* magazine (May 18, 1961).

19. The Reverend L. Francis Griffin, interview, August 17, 1961.

20. *Ibid.*, interview in Farmville, July 5, 1961.

21. *Ibid.*, interview, August 17, 1961.

22. Bradshaw, *History,* p. 498.

23. *Ibid.* p. 486

24. Dr. N. P. Miller, interview in Farmville, Virginia, July 6, 1961.

25. T. J. McIlwaine, undated notes prepared for testimony in court, 1951.

26. W. I. Dixon, interview in Richmond, Virginia, October 4, 1961.

27. Records of Superintendent of Schools, Prince Edward County, Virginia.

28. M. Boyd Jones, interview in Lawrenceville, Virginia, August 9, 1961.

29. John Lancaster, interview in Prince Edward County, Virginia, August 19, 1961.

30. Report of the Committee Appointed by the State Superintendent of Public

Instruction to Survey the School Buildings and Recommend a Long-Range Building Program to the School Officials of Prince Edward County, December, 1947.

31. Maurice Large, interview in Farmville, Virginia, November 20, 1959.

32. Maurice Large, testimony before a three-judge federal court in the case of *Dorothy E. Davis et al.* v. *County School Board of Prince Edward County, Virginia*, February 25, 1952.

33. Minutes of the School Board of Prince Edward County, Virginia, June 24, 1948.

34. Large, testimony, February 25, 1952.

35. Bradshaw, *History*, p. 498.

36. Dixon, interview, October 4, 1961.

37. The Reverend L. Francis Griffin, interview, August 17, 1961.

38. Large, testimony, February 25, 1952.

39. Maurice Large, interview in Farmville, Virginia, August 19, 1961.

40. Minutes of the School Board, August 8, 1950.

41. Large, interview, August 19, 1961.

42. The Reverend L. Francis Griffin, interview in Farmville, Virginia, May, 1959.

43. Large, testimony, February 25, 1952.

44. Otis Scott, interview in Prince Edward County, Virginia, November 20, 1959; George Morton, interview in Prince Edward County, Virginia, June 21, 1960.

45. The Reverend L. Francis Griffin, interview, May, 1959.

46. Large, interview, August 19, 1961.

47. J. B. Wall, Sr., interview in Farmville, Virginia, July 6, 1961.

48. Large, interview, August 19, 1961.

49. *Ibid.*

50. Dowell J. Howard, State Superintendent of Public Instruction, Note introduced in court testimony, February 25, 1952.

51. Minutes of the School Board, December 12, 1950.

52. *Ibid.*, February 6, 1951.

53. *Ibid.*, April 12, 1951.

Chapter 2

1. Mrs. Barbara Johns Powell, interview in Philadelphia, Pennsylvania, January 26, 1961.

2. Mrs. Robert Croner, interview in Prince Edward County, Virginia, September 8, 1960.

3. Mrs. Powell, interview, January 26, 1961.

4. Mrs. Robert Johns, interview in Washington, D.C., November 2, 1961.

5. *Ibid.*

6. Mrs. Powell, interview, January 26, 1961.

7. Mrs. Barbara Johns Powell, letter to the author, February 12, 1961.

8. Mrs. Croner, interview, September 8, 1960.

9. Mrs. Vernon Johns, Sr., interview in Petersburg, Virginia, August 2, 1961.

10. Mrs. Johns, interview, November 2, 1961.

11. Mrs. Powell, letter of February 12, 1961.

12. Mrs. Barbara Johns Powell, letter to the author, May 11, 1960.

13. *Ibid.*

14. *Farmville Herald*, September 15, 1950.

15. John Stokes, interview in Portsmouth, Virginia, February 8, 1960.

16. John Stokes, interview in Portsmouth, Virginia, January 25, 1960.

17. *Ibid.*

18. *Ibid.*

19. Stokes, interview, February 8, 1960.
20. *Ibid.*
21. *Richmond Afro-American,* April 28, 1951.

Chapter 3

1. M. Boyd Jones, interview at Lawrenceville, Virginia, January 14, 1960.
2. Mrs. Barbara Johns Powell, letter to the author, May 11, 1960.
3. *Ibid.*
4. John Stokes, interview in Portsmouth, Virginia, January 25, 1960.
5. Mrs. Powell, letter of May 11, 1960.
6. Mrs. Robert Croner, interview in Prince Edward County, Virginia, September 8, 1960.
7. Stokes, interview, January 25, 1960.
8. James Samuel Williams, interview in Farmville, Virginia, June 3, 1960.
9. Mrs. Luther Stokes, interview in Prince Edward County, Virginia, August 19, 1961.
10. John Stokes, interview in Portsmouth, Virginia, February 8, 1960.
11. *Ibid.*
12. *Ibid.*
13. Mrs. Powell, letter, May 11, 1960.
14. Stokes, Interview, February 8, 1960.
15. Mrs. Barbara Johns Powell, interview in Prince Edward County, Virginia, August 18, 1959.
16. The Reverend L. Francis Griffin, interview in Farmville, Virginia, July 5, 1961.
17. M. Boyd Jones, interview in Norfolk, Virginia, December, 1963.
18. T. J. McIlwaine, interview in Farmville, Virginia, June 20, 1960.
19. Stokes, interview, February 8, 1960.
20. Maurice Large, interview in Farmville, Virginia, November 20, 1959.
21. Stokes, interview, February 8, 1960.
22. John Stokes, interview at Virginia Beach, Virginia, March 20, 1960.
23. Mrs. Powell, letter, May 11, 1960.
24. McIlwaine, interview, June 20, 1960.
25. T. J. McIlwaine, interview in Farmville, Virginia, August 18, 1961.
26. Stokes, interview, March 20, 1960.
27. Mrs. Powell, letter of May 11, 1960.
28. Oliver Hill, testimony before a three-judge federal court in the cases of *NAACP* v. *J. Lindsay Almond et al.* and *NAACP Legal Fund and Educational Fund* v. *J. Lindsay Almond et al.,* September 16, 1957.
29. Oliver Hill, interview in Richmond, Virginia, September 4, 1960.
30. Hill, testimony, September 16, 1957.
31. *Ibid.*
32. Hill, interview, September 4, 1960.
33. Oliver Hill, interview in Washington, D.C., November 1, 1961.
34. Spottswood Robinson III, interview in Washington, D.C., November 2, 1961.
35. Hill, interview, September 4, 1960.
36. *Farmville Herald,* May 16, 1950; "Memorandum" in the *Herald files*; and several interviews.
37. *Sweatt* v. *Painter.*
38. *New York Times,* September 3, 1950.
39. *The Crisis* (Official Publication of the National Association for the Advancement of Colored People), October, 1950.
40. W. Lester Banks, interview in Richmond, Virginia, October 4, 1961.
41. Robinson, interview, November 2, 1961.

270 THEY CLOSED THEIR SCHOOLS

43. Hill, testimony, September 16, 1957.

44. Stokes, interview, March 20, 1960.

45. George Morton, interview in Prince Edward County, Virginia, June 21, 1960.

46. Mrs. George Morton, interview in Prince Edward County, Virginia, August 19, 1961.

48. John Lancaster, interview in Prince Edward County, Virginia, August 19, 1961.

49. The Reverend L. Francis Griffin, interview in Farmville, Virginia, August 17, 1961.

50. Herbert Clarence Bradshaw, *History of Prince Edward County, Virginia* (Dietz, 1955), p. 669.

51. U.S. Department of Commerce, Bureau of the Census, *Census of Agriculture,* 1954.

52. Mrs. P. H. Shepperson, interview in Prince Edward County, Virginia, August 18, 1961.

53. Mrs. Powell, letter of May 11, 1960.

54. Mrs. Croner, interview, September 8, 1960.

55. *Ibid.*

56. Stokes, interview, March 20, 1960.

57. Willie Redd, interview in Prince Edward County, Virginia, September 5, 1960.

58. Joseph Pervall, interview in Nottoway County, Virginia, September 7, 1960.

59. *Richmond Times-Dispatch,* April 27, 1951; *Richmond News Leader,* April 27, 1951.

60. Banks, interview, October 4, 1961.

61. Fred Reid, letter to the editor of the *Farmville Herald,* July 20, 1956.

62. *Richmond Times-Dispatch,* September 13, 1953.

63. Mimeographed letter signed by M. Boyd Jones, principal, and faculty members of Moton High School, April 30, 1951.

64. Mrs. Shepperson, interview, August 18, 1961.

65. The Reverend L. Francis Griffin, interviews in Farmville and Prince Edward County, March 2 and 3, 1960.

66. Lancaster, interview, August 19, 1961.

67. Mimeographed letter signed by the Reverend L. Francis Griffin, co-ordinator for the NAACP in Prince Edward County, undated.

68. Pervall, Interview, September 7, 1960.

69. *Richmond News Leader,* May 3, 1951.

70. *Richmond Times-Dispatch,* May 4, 1951.

71. *Richmond Afro-American,* May 12, 1951.

72. *Ibid.*

73. Stokes, interview, March 20, 1960.

74. *Richmond Afro-American,* May 12, 1951.

75. Mrs. Croner, interview, September 8, 1960.

76. Griffin, interviews, March 2 and 3, 1960.

77. M. Boyd Jones, testimony before a three-judge court, in the case of *Dorothy E. Davis et al.* v. *County School Board of Prince Edward County, Virginia,* February 25, 1952.

78. T. J. McIlwaine, testimony before a three-judge court, in the case of *Dorothy E. Davis et al.* v. *County School Board of Prince Edward County, Virginia,* February 25, 1952.

79. Jones, testimony, February 25, 1952.

80. M. Boyd Jones, interview in Lawrenceville, Virginia, August 9, 1961.

81. Jones, testimony, February 25, 1952.
82. The Reverend L. Francis Griffin, interview in Farmville, Virginia, November 20, 1959.
83. Jones, interview, January 14, 1960.
84. *Ibid.*, December, 1963.
85. M. Boyd Jones, interview in Lawrenceville, Virginia, January 14, 1960.
86. Mrs. Powell, letter of May 11, 1960.
87. Jones, testimony, February 25, 1952.
88. McIlwaine, interview, August 18, 1961.
89. Jones, interview, August 9, 1961.
90. Large, interview, November 20, 1959.
91. *Richmond Times-Dispatch*, May 3, 1951.
92. J. B. Wall, Sr., interview in Farmville, Virginia, August 20, 1961.
93. *Ibid.*
94. *Farmville Herald*, April 27, 1951.
95. *Ibid.*
96. *Richmond News Leader*, April 28, 1951.
97. *Richmond Times-Dispatch*, April 28, 1951.
98. Stokes, interview, March 20, 1960.
99. *Farmville Herald*, May 1, 1951.
100. *Richmond Afro-American*, May 8, 1951.
101. *Richmond Times-Dispatch*, May 6, 1951.
102. Stokes, interview, March 20, 1960.
103. *Richmond Afro-American*, May 8, 1951.
104. James Samuel Williams, interview in Farmville, June 3, 1960.
105. *Farmville Herald*, May 8, 1951.
106. *Ibid.*, May 11, 1951.
107. *Ibid.*, May 15, 1951.
108. Robinson, interview, November 2, 1961.
109. *Farmville Herald*, June 1, 1951.
110. *Richmond Times-Dispatch*, May 11, 1951.
111. *Ibid.*, May 25, 1951.
112. *Ibid.*
113. Griffin, interview, August 17, 1961.
114. Wall, interview, August 20, 1961.
115. Griffin, interview, August 17, 1961.
116. *Farmville Herald*, June 26, 1951.
117. Interview of M. Boyd Jones by School Board, June 29, 1951, document on file in the office of the superintendent of schools.
118. *Farmville Herald*, July 5, 1951.
119. Large, interview, November 20, 1959.
120. T. J. McIlwaine, interview in Farmville, Virginia, July 5, 1961.
121. *Richmond Afro-American*, July 28, 1951, and sermon of the Reverend L. Francis Griffin, undated.
122. The Reverend L. Francis Griffin, interview in Farmville, Virginia, July 24, 1962.

Chapter 4
1. John Lancaster, interview in Prince Edward County, Virginia, August 19, 1961.
2. Mrs. Barbara Johns Powell, interview in Philadelphia, Pennsylvania, January 26, 1961.
3. M. Boyd Jones, interview in Lawrenceville, Virginia, June 26, 1960.
4. Mrs. Barbara Johns Powell, letter to the author, May 11, 1960.
5. *Minneapolis Morning Tribune* (Minnesota), December 5, 1953.

6. The Reverend L. Francis Griffin, interview in Farmville, Virginia, November 20, 1959.

7. The Reverend Vernon L. Johns, Sr., interview in Petersburg, Virginia, January 9, 1962.

8. *Ibid.*

9. Mrs. Vernon L. Johns, Sr., interview in Petersburg, Virginia, August 2, 1961.

10. The Reverend Vernon L. Johns, Sr., interview, January 9, 1962.

11. T. J. McIlwaine, interview in Farmville, Virginia, August 18, 1961.

12. Minutes of the Prince Edward County School Board, October 5, 1944.

13. The Reverend Vernon L. Johns, Sr., interview, January 9, 1962.

14. *Ibid.*

15. Jones, interview, June 26, 1960.

PART TWO   MASSIVE RESISTANCE

Chapter 5

1. *Southern School News,* September 3, 1954.

2. *Ibid.*

3. *Ibid.*

4. *Ibid.*

5. *Richmond Times-Dispatch,* May 18, 1954.

6. *Ibid.*

7. *Richmond Times-Dispatch,* May 19, 1954.

8. *Ibid.*

9. *Richmond Times-Dispatch,* May 20, 1954.

10. *Ibid.*

11. *Richmond Times-Dispatch,* May 21, 1954.

12. Benjamin Muse, *Virginia's Massive Ressistance* (Indiana, 1961), p. 7.

13. *Ibid.*

Chapter 6

1. Robert B. Crawford, interview in Richmond, Virginia, March 14, 1962.

2. *Ibid.*

3. *Farmville Herald,* May 21, 1954.

4. J. B. Wall, Sr., interview in Farmville, Virginia, April 5, 1962.

5. *Ibid.,* February 6, 1962.

6. Muse, *Massive Resistance,* p. 7.

7. *Farmville Herald,* June 4, 1954.

8. *Ibid.,* June 25, 1954.

9. *Ibid.,* July 9, 1954.

10. Crawford, interview, March 14, 1962.

11. Wall, notes from a speech to Farmville Chapter of the Defenders of State Sovereignty and Individual Liberties, November 3, 1954.

12. Crawford, interview, March 14, 1962.

13. Wall, interview, February 6, 1962.

14. *Richmond Times-Dispatch,* October 9, 1954.

15. Crawford, interview, March 14, 1962.

16. Robert B. Crawford, interview in Richmond, Virginia, May 21, 1962.

17. *Ibid.*

18. *Ibid.*

19. *Ibid.*

20. *Ibid.*

21. *Ibid.*
22. Haldore Hanson, "No Surrender in Farmville, Virginia," *The New Republic* (October 10, 1955).
23. Crawford, interview, March 14, 1962.
24. *Ibid.*
25. *Ibid.*
26. The Reverend L. Francis Griffin, interview in Farmville, Virginia, July 9, 1962.
27. Crawford, interview, March 14, 1962.
28. *Ibid.*
29. Crawford, interview, June 10, 1962.
30. Wall, notes, November 3, 1954.
31. Muse, *Massive Resistance*, p. 8.
32. Hanson, "No Surrender," *The New Republic.*
33. Muse, *Massive Resistance*, p. 10.
34. Crawford, interview, June 10, 1962.
35. *Richmond Times-Dispatch*, June 1, 1955.
36. Crawford, interview, June 10, 1962.
37. *Ibid.*
38. John Steck, "The Prince Edward Story," pamphlet published by the *Farmville Herald*, 1960.
39. *Richmond News Leader*, June 1, 1955.
40. John G. Bruce, interview in Richmond, Virginia, February 20, 1962.
41. *Richmond News Leader*, June 1, 1955.
42. Muse, *Massive Resistance*, p. 12
43. *Richmond Times-Dispatch*, June 3, 1955.
44. *Southern School News*, July 6, 1955.
45. B. Calvin Bass, interview in Prince Edward County, Virginia, May 9, 1962.
46. B. Blanton Hanbury, interview in Farmville, Virginia, February 7, 1962.
47. *Richmond News Leader*, June 4, 1955.
48. *Richmond Times-Dispatch*, June 5, 1955.
49. Hanbury, interview, February 7, 1962.
50. Wall, interview, February 6, 1962.
51. *Ibid.*
52. *Ibid.*
53. Herbert Clarence Bradshaw, *History of Prince Edward County, Virginia* (Dietz, 1955), p. 647.
54. Crawford, interview, March 14, 1962.
55. Bradshaw, *History*, p. 409.
56. *Ibid.*, p. 34.
57. *Ibid.*, pp. 107-27.
58. *Ibid.*, p. 34.
59. *Ibid.*, pp. 191-94.
60. *Ibid.*, p. 372.
61. *Ibid.*, p. 380.
62. *Ibid.*, p. 418.
63. *Ibid.*, p. 435.
64. C. Vann Woodward, *The Strange Career of Jim Crow* (rev. ed.; Galaxy, 1958), pp. 66-67.
65. Bradshaw, *History*, p. 445.
66. *Plessy* v. *Ferguson.*
67. Bradshaw, *History*, p. 588.
68. *Ibid.*, p. 587.
69. *Ibid.*, p. 647.

Chapter 7

1. The Reverend James R. Kennedy, interview in Front Royal, Virginia, August 12, 1960.
2. *Ibid.*
3. *Ibid.*
4. The Reverend James R. Kennedy, letter to the author, August 23, 1962.
5. *Ibid.*, interview, August 12, 1960.
6. B. Calvin Bass, interview in Prince Edward County, Virginia, May 9, 1962.
7. *Ibid.*
8. Maurice Large, copy of speech delivered at Jarman Hall, June 7, 1955.
9. Dr. Dabney Lancaster, interview in Richmond, Virginia, April 16, 1962.
10. *Ibid.*
11. *Richmond Times-Dispatch*, June 8, 1955.
12. Robert Crawford, interview in Richmond, Virginia, March 14, 1962.
13. The Reverend James R. Kennedy, interview, August 12, 1960.
14. J. B. Wall, Sr., interview in Farmville, Virginia, February 6, 1962.
15. *Richmond Times-Dispatch*, June 8, 1955.
16. Bass, interview, May 9, 1962.
17. The Reverend James R. Kennedy, interview in Richmond, Virginia, May 20, 1962.
18. *Richmond Times-Dispatch*, June 8, 1955.
19. *Ibid.*
20. *Ibid.*
21. *Ibid.*
22. T. J. McIlwaine, interview in Farmville, Virginia, February 7, 1962.
23. Wall, interview, February 6, 1962.
24. *Richmond News Leader*, June 8, 1955.
25. *Ibid.*
26. *Ibid.*
27. McIlwaine, interview, February 7, 1962.
28. *Farmville Herald*, July 18, 1955.
29. J. B. Wall, Sr., interview in Farmville, Virginia, April 5, 1962.
30. Fred Reid, interview in Farmville, Virginia, September 18, 1962.
31. Dr. N. P. Miller, interview in Farmville, Virginia, September 18, 1962.
32. J. G. Bruce, interview in Richmond, Virginia, February 20, 1962.

Chapter 8

1. *New York Herald Tribune*, July 20, 1955.
2. *Ibid.*
3. The Reverend James R. Kennedy, document in files.
4. Robert B. Crawford, interview in Farmville, Virginia, September 20, 1962.
5. *Richmond Times-Dispatch*, June 8, 1955.
6. The Reverend James R. Kennedy, interview in Front Royal, Virginia, August 12, 1960.
7. *Ibid.*
8. *Ibid.*
9. *Ibid.*
10. Lucy Daniels, "Blackout in Prince Edward," *Coronet* (August, 1960).
11. Foster Gresham, interview in Farmville, Virginia, February 7, 1962.
12. M. H. Bittinger, interview in Farmville, Virginia, February 6, 1962.
13. B. Calvin Bass, interview in Prince Edward County, June 11, 1962.
14. T. J. McIlwaine, interview in Farmville, Virginia, February 7, 1962.
15. *Farmville Herald*, June 10, 1955.

16. Minutes of the Prince Edward County Board of Supervisors, October 6, 1955.

17. John Lancaster, interview in Prince Edward County, August 19, 1961.

18. Minutes of the Board of Supervisors, November 3, 1955.

19. Minutes of the Board of Supervisors, December 7, 1955.

20. Lancaster, interview, August 19, 1961.

21. Minutes of the Board of Supervisors, October 4, 1956.

22. James Samuel Williams, Interview in Farmville, Virginia, June 3, 1960.

23. *Ibid.*

24. *Ibid.*

25. *Ibid.*

Chapter 9

1. *Minneapolis Morning Tribune* (Minnesota), January 4, 1956.

2. *Ibid.*

3. *Ibid.*

4. *Ibid.*

5. The Reverend L. Francis Griffin, interview in Farmville, Virginia, July 24, 1962.

6. *Ibid.,* interview in Farmville, Virginia, August 17, 1961.

7. *Ibid.*

8. Interview with the Reverend C. E. Griffin in Norfolk, Virginia, September 12, 1961.

9. The Reverend L. Francis Griffin, interview in Farmville, Virginia, July 9, 1962.

10. *Ibid.*

11. *Minneapolis Morning Tribune,* January 4, 1956.

12. Roger Madison, interview in Farmville, Virginia, July 25, 1962.

13. The Reverend L. Francis Griffin, interview, July 9, 1962.

14. *Ibid.,* interview, August 17, 1961.

15. *Ibid.*

16. *Minneapolis Morning Tribune,* January 4, 1956.

17. *Ibid.*

18. The Reverend L. Francis Griffin, interview, August 17, 1961.

19. The Reverend C. E. Griffin, September 12, 1961.

20. Madison, interview, July 25, 1962.

21. The Reverend L. Francis Griffin, interview, July 9, 1962.

22. James Rorty, "Desegregation in Prince Edward County, Virginia," *Commentary* (May, 1956).

23. The Reverend L. Francis Griffin, interview, August 17, 1961.

Chapter 10

1. Minutes of the Prince Edward County Board of Supervisors, July 30, 1955.

2. *Farmville Herald,* July 20, 1955.

3. Homer Bigart, *New York Herald Tribune,* July 24, 1955.

4. *Ibid.*

5. *Farmville Herald,* November 4, 1955.

6. C. Vann Woodward, "The New Reconstruction in the South," *Commentary* (June, 1956).

7. Benjamin Muse, *Virginia's Massive Resistance* (Indiana, 1961), pp. 20-22.

8. *Ibid.,* p. 18.

9. *Southern School News,* April, 1956.

10. *Farmville Herald,* April 17, 1956.

11. *Ibid.,* April 24, 1956.

12. Minutes of the Board of Supervisors, May 3, 1956.
13. *Farmville Herald*, May 8, 1956.
14. W. Lester Banks, interview in Richmond, Virginia, October 3, 1962.
15. *Sout ern School News*, September, 1956.
16. Affidavits submitted to a three-judge court sitting on the Prince Edward case, June 29, 1956.
17. Muse, *Massive Resistance*, p. 28.
18. *Southern School News*, December, 1956.
19. Judge Sterling Hutcheson, interview in Boydton, Virginia, July 25, 1962.
20. *Ibid.*, Opinion in the Prince Edward Case, January 23, 1957.
21. *Richmond Times-Dispatch*, January 26, 1957.
22. Muse, *Massive Resistance*, p. 60.
23. Judge Hutcheson, Opinion, January 23, 1957.

PART THREE   THE SCHOOLS

Chapter 11

1. Minutes of the Board of Supervisors of Prince Edward County, Virginia, June 2, 1959.
2. B. Calvin Bass, interview in Prince Edward County, Virginia, June 11, 1962.
3. John Riely, interview in Richmond, Virginia, April 1, 1963.
4. Bass, interview, June 11, 1962.
5. *Farmville Herald*, August 7, 1959.
6. Dr. C. D. G. Moss, interview in Farmville, Virginia, September 18, 1962.
7. *Ibid.*; the Reverend L. Francis Griffin, interview in Farmville, Virginia, June 22, 1960.
8. The Reverend L. Francis Griffin, interview in Farmville, Virginia, January 13, 1963.
9. Moss, interview, September 18, 1962.
10. *Ibid.*
11. *Ibid.*
12. J. B. Wall, Sr., interview in Farmville, Virginia, January 13, 1963.
13. Moss, interview, September 18, 1962.
14. *Farmville Herald*, August 7, 1959.
15. *Ibid.*, June 9, 1959.
16. *Ibid.*, September 4, 1959.
17. *Ibid.*, November 2, 1962.
18. *Ibid.*
19. Ben Bowers, interview at Virginia Beach, Virginia, April 18, 1963.
20. J. B. Wall, Sr., interview in Farmville, Virginia, August 20, 1961.
21. *Ibid.*, April 7, 1963.
22. Chet Huntley, "The Crippled Generation," narration on the National Broadcasting Company's television, August 3, 1962.
23. *Farmville Herald*, August 7, 1962.
24. Wall, interview, April 7, 1963.
25. *Ibid.*, August 20, 1961.
26. *Ibid.*, April 7, 1963.
27. *Ibid.*
28. Bowers, interview, April 18, 1963.
29. Roy Pearson, interview in Farmville, Virginia, April 29, 1963.
30. Paul Duke, *Wall Street Journal*, December 1, 1959.
31. *Farmville Herald*, August 18, 1959.
32. Robert Redd, interview in Farmville, Virginia, June 17, 1963.
33. Bowers, interview, April 18, 1963.

34. Duke, *Wall Street Journal*, December 1, 1959.
35. *Farmville Herald*, August 25, 1959.
36. *Ibid.*, September 15, 1959.
37. Duke, *Wall Street Journal*, December 1, 1959.
38. John I. Brooks, unpublished notes, June, 1960.
39. Bowers, April 18, 1963.
40. Benjamin Muse, *Virginia's Massive Resistance* (Indiana, 1961), p. 151.
41. *Richmond Times-Dispatch*, September 11, 1959.
42. *Ibid.*
43. Paul Hope, in the *Washington Star*, September 10, 1959.
44. W. Lester Banks, interview in Richmond, Virginia, April 1, 1963.
45. *Farmville Herald*, June 19, 1959.
46. Dr. N. P. Miller, interview in Farmville, Virginia, April 28, 1963.
47. The Reverend Dan Bowers, interview in Portsmouth, Virginia, February 23, 1963.
48. The Reverend L. Francis Griffin, interview in Farmville, Virginia, April 8, 1963.
49. *Farmville Herald*, September 10, 1959.
50. The Reverend L. Francis Griffin, interview in Farmville, Virginia, March 3, 1963.
51. *Farmville Herald*, June 4, 1959.
52. Wall, interview, April 7, 1963.
53. Dr. Roy B. Hargrove, Jr., interview in Farmville, Virginia, June 17, 1963.
54. *Farmville Herald*, December 22, 1959.
55. *New York Times*, April 17, 1961.
56. *Southern School News*, January, 1960.
57. Hargrove, interview, June 17, 1963.
58. Dr. C. D. G. Moss, letter to the author, May 13, 1964.
59. Hargrove, interview, June 17, 1963.
60. The Reverend L. Francis Griffin, interview, April 8, 1963.
61. Dr. C. D. G. Moss, interview in Farmville, Virginia, September 19, 1962.
62. *Southern School News*, January, 1960.
63. *Farmville Herald*, December 29, 1959.
64. *Southern School News*, February, 1960.

Chapter 12

1. Document in possession of author, dated April 26, 1960.
2. *Farmville Herald*, April 29, 1960.
3. Lester Andrews, interview in Farmville, Virginia, June 26, 1960.
4. *Ibid.*
5. *Ibid.*
6. Lester Andrews, interview in Farmville, Virginia, January 28, 1963.
7. M. H. Bittinger, interview in Farmville, Virginia, February 6, 1962.
8. Maurice Large, interview in Farmville, Virginia, June 23, 1960.
9. *Ibid.*, January 28, 1963.
10. *Ibid.*, June 23, 1960.
11. B. Calvin Bass, interview in Prince Edward County, Virginia, September 20, 1962.
12. Andrews, interview, June 26, 1960.
13. Document in possession of author.
14. *Ibid.*
15. Bass, interview, September 20, 1962.
16. Large, interview, June 23, 1960.
17. J. B. Wall, Sr., interview in Farmville, Virginia, June 22, 1960.
18. *Ibid.*

19. Andrews, interview, June 26, 1960.
20. *Ibid.*

Chapter 13

1. Ben Bowers, interview in Virginia Beach, Virginia, April 18, 1963.
2. *Farmville Herald*, September 5, 1961.
3. J. B. Wall, Sr., letter to the editor of the *Lynchburg News*, December 11, 1960.
4. *Lynchburg News*, December 1, 1960.
5. Wall, letter to the editor, December 11, 1960.
6. Editor's Note to Wall's letter to the editor, December 11, 1960.
7. Stuart Loory, in the *New York Herald Tribune*, August 22, 1961.
8. *Farmville Herald*, September 1, 1961.
9. Ben Bowers, interview in Virginia Beach, Virginia, April 18, 1963.
10. Document in possession of author.
11. *Southern School News*, November, 1961.
12. *Farmville Herald*, October 17, 1961.
13. *Southern School News*, April, 1962.
14. *Farmville Herald*, August 31, 1962.
15. *Southern School News*, February, 1960.
16. *Ibid.*, August, 1960.
17. *Farmville Herald*, January 24, 1961.
18. *Southern School News*, April, 1963.
19. *Farmville Herald*, July 10, 1960.
20. *Ibid.*, September 19, 1961.
21. *Southern School News*, May, 1961.
22. *Ibid.*
23. *Ibid.*
24. *Southern School News*, March 1960.
25. The Reverend L. Francis Griffin, interview in Farmville, Virginia, March 3, 1963.
26. Bowers, interview, April 18, 1963.
27. *Norfolk Virginian-Pilot*, September 24, 1960.
28. Document in possession of the author.
29. *Southern School News*, February, 1960.
30. *Farmville Herald*, September 6, 1960.
31. The Reverend Calvin Hill, interview in Prince Edward County, March 4, 1963.
32. W. Lester Banks, interview in Richmond, Virginia, April 1, 1963.
33. *Southern School News*, February, 1960.
34. *Ibid.*, June, 1961.
35. *Ibid.*, January, 1960.
36. *Richmond Times-Dispatch*, January 9, 1962.
37. Francis Mitchell, *Jet* magazine (May 18, 1961).
38. *Farmville Herald*, January 17, 1961.
39. *Southern School News*, January, 1961.
40. *Ibid.*
41. *Farmville Herald*, December 16, 1960.
42. Bonnie Angelo Levy, in *Newsday*, December 20, 1960.
43. The Reverend L. Francis Griffin, interview in Farmville, Virginia, April 8, 1963.
44. *Ibid.*, September 19, 1962.
45. Irv Goodman, "Public Schools Died Here," *The Saturday Evening Post* (April 29, 1961).

46. The Reverend L. Francis Griffin, interview, September 19, 1962.
47. *Farmville Herald*, August 7, 1962.
48. The Reverend L. Francis Griffin, interview, September 19, 1962.
49. *Ibid.*, interview in Farmville, Virginia, October 28, 1963.
50. The Reverend L. Francis Griffin, interview, September 19, 1962.

Chapter 14

1. *Farmville Herald*, November 2, 1962.
2. John Allan, interview in Farmville, Virginia, June 16, 1963.
3. Dr. Frank Lankford, interview in Farmville, Virginia, May, 1959.
4. Allan, interview, June 16, 1963.
5. Josephine Ripley, in the *Christian Science Monitor*, April 5, 14, and 18, 1962.
6. Allan, interview, June 16, 1963.
7. *Farmville Herald*, June 14, 1963.
8. Dr. C. D. G. Moss, interview in Farmville, Virginia, June 23, 1960.
9. *Ibid.*, January 12, 1963.
10. Philip Lightfoot Scruggs, interview in Lynchburg, Virginia, March 4, 1963.
11. *Ibid.*
12. Dr. Dabney Lancaster, interview in Richmond, Virginia, April 16, 1962.
13. The Reverend L. Francis Griffin, interview in Farmville, Virginia, July 9, 1962.
14. *Farmville Herald*, June 26, 1959.
15. Moss, interview, June 23, 1960.
16. Dr. C. D. G. Moss, interview in Farmville, Virginia, September 18, 1962.
17. *Ibid.*
18. Leonard G. Muse, interview in Roanoke, Virginia, June 1, 1963.
19. Dr. Francis G. Lankford, interview in Chapel Hill, North Carolina, November 7, 1964.
20. Document in the possession of the author.
21. Lankford, interview, November 7, 1964.
22. *Ibid.*
23. Allan, interview, June 16, 1963.
24. Scruggs, interview, March 4, 1963.
25. Irv Goodman, "Public Schools Died Here," *The Saturday Evening Post* (April 29, 1961).
26. Colgate W. Darden, interview in Norfolk, Virginia, March 25, 1963.
27. Moss, interview, January 12, 1963.
28. *Farmville Herald*, November 2, 1962.
29. *Ibid.*
30. *Ibid.*, November 9, 1962.
31. The Reverend L. Francis Griffin, interview, July 9, 1962.
32. Dr. C. D. G. Moss, interview in Farmville, Virginia, January 27, 1963.
33. Allan, interview, June 16, 1963.
34. *Farmville Herald*, July 30, 1963.
35. Willie Redd, interview in Farmville, Virginia, July 8, 1962.
36. *Richmond Afro-American*, July 28, 1951.
37. Redd, interview, July 8, 1962.
38. *Ibid.*
39. *Ibid.*
40. *Ibid.*
41. The Reverend L. Francis Griffin, interview in Farmville, Virginia, September 16, 1963.
42. Redd, interview, July 8, 1962.
43. *Ibid.*

Chapter 15

1. Dr. Lee Roth, "Schoolbells Ring for Freedom," unpublished essay, June, 1961.
2. The Reverend James Samuel Williams, interview in Farmville, Virginia, August 12, 1963.
3. *Ibid.*
4. The Reverend L. Francis Griffin, interview in Farmville, Virginia, September 16, 1963.
5. The Reverend James Samuel Williams, interview, August 12, 1963.
6. *Ibid.*
7. The Reverend L. Francis Griffin, interview, September 16, 1963.
8. Carlton Terry, *The Keith Junior High School Chronicle*, New Bedford, Massachusetts, May 28, 1963.
9. *Ibid.*, interview in Prince Edward County, Virginia, August 12, 1963.

Chapter 16

1. The Reverend L. Francis Griffin, interview in Farmville, Virginia, October 28, 1963.
2. *Richmond News Leader*, June 2, 1963.
3. *Richmond Times-Dispatch*, June 5, 1963.
4. *Richmond News Leader*, August 14, 1963.
5. The Reverend L. Francis Griffin, interview, October 28, 1963.
6. William Vanden Heuvel, interview in Washington, D.C., September 5, 1963.
7. Colgate W. Darden, Jr., interview in Norfolk, Virginia, October 17, 1963.
8. *Ibid.*
9. *Ibid.*
10. Vanden Heuvel, interview, September 5, 1963.
11. Darden, interview, October 17, 1963.
12. The Reverend L. Francis Griffin, interview, October 28, 1963.
13. *Ibid.*
14. Darden, interview, October 17, 1963.
15. Dr. Neil V. Sullivan, interview in Farmville, Virginia, October 28, 1963.
16. The Reverend L. Francis Griffin, interview, October 28, 1963.
17. Sullivan, interview, October 28, 1963.
18. *Farmville Herald*, May 27, 1960.
19. United States Census (1960), Prince Edward County, Virginia.
20. *Ibid.*
21. Associated Press news release, February, 1960.
22. Russell MacDonald, interview by Adam Clymer, in Prince Edward County, Virginia, November 8, 1962.
23. Dean Charles B. Vail, interview by Adam Clymer, in Prince Edward County, Virginia, November 7, 1962.
24. The Reverend Dan Bowers, interview in Portsmouth, Virginia, February 23, 1963.
25. S. Waverly Putney, Jr., interview in Farmville, Virginia, April 29, 1963.
26. *Ibid.*
27. The Reverend L. Francis Griffin, interview in Farmville, Virginia, September 19, 1962.
28. *Newsweek*, May 8, 1961.
29. Dr. Rachel Weddington, interview in Farmville, Virginia, August 11, 1963.
30. Mrs. N. P. Miller, interview in Farmville, Virginia, April 8, 1963.
31. Helen Baker, in the *Farmville Herald*, June 16, 1961.
32. Mrs. Mada McKnight, interview in Farmville, Virginia, April 8, 1963.

33. Document in possession of author.

34. Robert Lee Green, "The Educational Status of Children in a District Without Public Schools," Bureau of Educational Research Services, College of Education, Michigan State University (1964), p. 121.

35. *Farmville Herald*, August 28, 1962.

36. *Ibid.*, August 31, 1962.

37. *Lynchburg News*, September 30, 1962.

38. *Farmville Herald*, October 12, 1962.

39. Records in the office of the Superintendent of Schools.

40. Records of the Prince Edward School Foundation.

41. Report to the Prince Edward County School Board by Dr. George V. Zehmer.

42. *Farmville Herald*, March 24, 1961.

43. Green, "The Educational Status," pp. 255-57.

44. Helen Baker, in the *Farmville Herald*, June 16, 1961.

45. Barbara Ann Botts, interview in Farmville, Virginia, October 27, 1963.

46. *Ibid.*

47. *Ibid.*

48. Richard Parrish, interview in Prince Edward County, Virginia, August 12, 1963.

49. Dr. Neil V. Sullivan, "Making History in Prince Edward County," *The Saturday Review* (October 17, 1964), pp. 59-73.

Epilogue

1. *Southern School News*, April, 1963.

2. *Ibid.*, May, 1963.

3. Dr. N. P. Miller, interview in Farmville, Virginia, April 28, 1963.

4. Dorothy I. Height, interview in Washington, D.C., September 6, 1963.